Deep Space
and
Sacred Time

CONTENTS

DEEP SPACE
AND
SACRED TIME

Star Trek in the American Mythos

Jon Wagner
Jan Lundeen

PRAEGER

Westport, Connecticut
London

Library of Congress Cataloging-in-Publication Data

Wagner, Jon G.
   Deep space and sacred time : Star Trek in the American mythos /
Jon Wagner, Jan Lundeen.
     p. cm.
   Includes bibliographical references and index.
   ISBN 0–275–96225–3 (alk. paper)
    1. Star Trek films—History and criticism. 2. Star Trek
television programs—History and criticism. 3. Myth—Psychological
aspects. I. Lundeen, Jan, 1956– . II. Title.
PN1995.9.S694W35 1998
791.45'75'0973—dc21   98–14930

British Library Cataloguing in Publication Data is available.

Library of Congress Catalog Card Number: 98–14930
ISBN: 0–275–96225–3

First published in 1998

Praeger Publishers, 88 Post Road West, Westport, CT 06881
An imprint of Greenwood Publishing Group, Inc.

Printed in the United States of America

The paper used in this book complies with the
Permanent Paper Standard issued by the National
Information Standards Organization (Z39.48–1984).

10 9 8 7 6 5 4 3 2

There is no object so soft but it makes a hub for the wheel'd universe.

—Walt Whitman, 1855

PREFACE

I bring order to chaos.

—The Borg Queen

Somehow, I question your motives.

—Lieutenant Commander Data

This book owes its existence to some of life's most ordinary pleasures: marriage, coffee, and Saturday mornings before the kids wake up. And, of course, *Star Trek*.

In the-mid 1980s our children were little, and so was our black and white television set. So too was our list of favored TV programs, a modest handful that included, along with *Sesame Street*, reruns of the original *Star Trek* series. As our children grew, so did the entertainment possibilities that presented themselves daily, and we were faced with the universal parental problem of how passively we should admit media fantasies into our family's cultural life. Our solution was not to toss out the television, as some other academic couples have done, nor to let mass media culture simply have its way with us. Although we encouraged reading and storytelling along with movies and television, we also cultivated a habit—more like a game, really—of conversing about and comparing the cultural messages in popular literature and entertainment. No one was safe from this good-natured and generally commonsense deconstruction—not Indiana Jones, not Kipling, not Mark Twain, not even Spock. We enjoy certain television shows, and we love disassembling them to see how they "work" both as pleasure-giving entertainment and as part of the process of cultural reproduction.

That's where coffee and Saturday mornings come in. About an hour into a particularly enthusiastic discussion about the changing visions of evolution, contingency, and destiny throughout the various *Star Trek* series, it occurred to us that we had the makings of a conference paper on the subject. We began to take notes, brewed more coffee, and let the process of free association take us where it would—dystopias, computer kings, the Prime Directive, colonial optimism, postmodern nihilism. By the time our son and daughter ambled groggily downstairs for brunch, we were on our hands and knees sorting stacks of notes, proclaiming, "We're writing an article on *Star Trek*—No, make that a book!" Many Saturdays have passed since that day, during which time (between class preparations, little league games and the rest) we stockpiled episode tapes, *Trek* books, scholarly articles, reviews, notes from the Internet, and the minutes of countless "brainstorm" sessions.

This book is the result of truly joint authorship; neither of us alone could have produced even one chapter. Our goal is a comprehensive overview of *Star Trek* as a culturally expressive mythology and a reflection of America's changing social values. We offer a special perspective that comes from juxtaposing our affection for *Trek* with our interest in mythology and critical social analysis. Our goal in writing this book is to propose suggestive, but by no means final or definitive, thoughts on how *Star Trek* has served as a mythic reference point for American society and how an understanding of this phenomenon might help us see ourselves more clearly. But while orderly patterns of interpretation can enhance the richness of our appreciation, an excess of order can suppress the imagination and limit the possibilities for transcending familiar patterns. We leave it to the reader to ponder how much order, and how much honest chaos, is about right.

Most readers of this book will, presumably, be acquainted with at least a few of the many *Star Trek* episodes and films. Nevertheless, some readers may welcome basic viewing recommendations. Hundreds of *Star Trek* episodes or films are available for sale or rent by video distributors or in Viacom retail outlets. For the reader wishing to gain a good general introduction to the material, we recommend from the original series, Roddenberry's pilot "The Cage"; at least one of the later original series episodes (particularly "This Side of Paradise" or "City on the Edge of Forever"); and the later pilot episodes, "Encounter at Farpoint" (*The Next Generation*), "Emissary" (*Deep Space Nine*), and "Caretaker" (*Voyager*). *The Wrath of Khan* and *First Contact* are particularly useful for obtaining an overview of *Star Trek* cinema.

For readers interested in recommendations for further reading, reviews of *Trek* literature, teaching suggestions, and links to other *Star Trek* resources, please visit our website ⟨*www.deepspace-sacredtime.com*⟩. We also invite email inquiries to jwagner@knox.edu.

We wish to thank the many people who have helped in various ways to make this book possible. We are especially indebted to Matt Bogen, David Eberhardt, Gregory Pfitzer, Steve Fineberg, and Mark Van Cleve, for their valuable comments; to Beth Alderson, Michelle Allmendinger, and Matt Bogen for sharing their episode tapes; and to Sharon Clayton, Michelle Allmendinger, Ara Kooser, Elizabeth Holmes, and Stuart Alderson for assistance in gathering materials. Special thanks go to Stuart Alderson and Jodi Wagner for their work on cover design, and to Ian Sanderson and Nick Wagner for web page design and graphics. We are grateful to the authors and contributors of countless Trek web sites, and especially to Jim Wright, Jamahl Epsicokhan, and Tim Lynch for making their thoughtful episode reviews available on the Internet. Special appreciation goes to Jane Garry of Greenwood Publishing Group for her encouragement and insight.

This book is dedicated to everyone who has taken *Star Trek* as an invitation to look more deeply into themselves and the human condition.

CHAPTER 1

MIRROR, MIRROR

Myth and the Human Condition

Here are the perilous seas where human beings flounder amid the dualities of mind and matter, freewill and determinism, good and evil, and where they strive in the modern world to preserve the finer elements of the mythic universe.

—Edward Harrison
Masks of the Universe (1985)

On a steamy July day in 1992, we trudged with our two adolescent children along the Capitol Mall in Washington, D.C., winding past the obligatory pilgrimage sites: the Washington Monument, White House, Vietnam Memorial. We had read from Carl Sandburg's biography of young Abe Lincoln as we drove through Kentucky and Virginia, and now we lingered to recite the speeches inscribed on the marble walls of the Lincoln Memorial. Our final destination, however, was the Smithsonian, the showcase of our nation's collective memory. We arrived, almost by chance, at the Air and Space Museum to find an attraction that drew larger crowds than any of the hallowed shrines we had seen earlier that day: the *Star Trek* exhibit. This multimedia production, which featured artifacts from the original *Star Trek* series and a portable-audiotape narration by Leonard (Spock) Nimoy and William (Kirk) Shatner, attracted more visitors each day than did the actual spacecraft on display at the museum.

What was an exhibit on television fiction doing in our nation's premier science museum? This was no mere fluke. Closer to home, we happened upon *Star Trek* exhibitions at Chicago's Adler Planetarium and the Museum of Science and Industry, both of which drew capacity crowds. In each of these instances, *Trek* was used as a vehicle to lend public appeal—one might even say legitimacy—to science.

As these examples suggest, *Star Trek* holds a peculiarly exalted place in American culture. The autumn of 1996 was marked among fans and in the media by a thirtieth anniversary celebration of what *TV Guide*, in a special edition featuring four different covers (one for each *Trek* series—collect them all!), extolled as "the show of shows." The original *Star Trek* television series, which was aired by NBC for a brief, unprofitable three-year period from 1966 to 1969, is honored in the 1996 *TV Guide* cover story as "the cornerstone of the most popular and beloved franchise the entertainment world has ever known." The article cites, in support of this extraordinary claim, *Trek*'s four separate series and eight feature films, as well as two billion dollars in merchandise sales.[1]

Star Trek has created a fantasy world featuring persons and premises now familiar to most Americans and to many others across the globe. Educational videos use *Trek* actors to narrate science presentations. *Trek* parodies are standard comedy fare. Masses of people worldwide are involved in fan clubs, and it is said that every weekend a *Trek* convention is held somewhere on the globe. Visits to these *Trek* conventions, often involving costumed impersonations of favored *Trek* characters, are said to have a quality of "communitas" not unlike that described by the anthropologist Victor Turner in his studies of religious pilgrimages.[2] Thousands of globally accessible internet computer sites and chat rooms produce endless commentary and debate on every aspect of the *Trek* world at every minute of the day and night.[3] Watching *Trek* can be a social ritual with its own rules of audience participation.[4] Bookstores sell millions of paperback novels based on the various *Trek* series, while grass roots "fanzines" feature highly original fan-produced fiction and art involving *Trek* characters.[5]

It seems that every college campus, medium-sized town, or corporate boardroom is likely to harbor "Trekkers" whose knowledge of the more than 500 *Trek* episodes is impressive. Bring up the subject in any college classroom, and someone will be able to recall the name of the Vulcan mating frenzy. People who can barely remember a phrase from Shakespeare or the Sermon on the Mount, and who may not be sure who the Spartans were, can quote the Ferengi Rules of Acquisition. Some may even dabble in conversational Klingon—the language of an imaginary people. In many respects, *Trek* provides a great number of Americans with a more widely shared set of narrative references than religious scripture, classical mythology, great literature, or even (Disney and Spielberg notwithstanding) other entertainment industry fantasy worlds.

Why did a television series that originally enjoyed only a modest-sized viewership eventually grow into such an unprecedented cultural phenomenon? Michael Logan, writing for *TV Guide*, sums up the two most frequently heard explanations. The first is that *Trek* presents an optimistic view of a human future largely free from prejudice, greed, poverty, and needless human aggression. The second is that *Trek*'s fans feel comfortable with the characters and their unwavering friendship for one another[6]—"Hope and Bonding," as *Star Trek: Voyager*'s Kate Mulgrew (Captain Janeway) puts it.[7]

These explanations are useful up to a point, but we intend to take them a step further and to argue that, in many respects, *Star Trek* serves as a secular American mythology. In the following chapters, we'll consider how *Trek* constructs a humanist mythos that fulfills many of the same functions that myth has served in more traditional cultures. An understanding of the mythic facets of *Trek* can provide a window into our own culture, and it can help us to appreciate how the world of *Trek* has evolved in parallel with American life over the last three decades.

MYTHOS, CHAOS, COSMOS

Humans are story-making animals. The ancient Greeks looked at the stars and saw patterns—Orion, Ursa Major, the Pleiades. These patterns in turn signified stories, and to gaze at the stars was to be reminded of the stories that gave meaning not only to the heavens but to the culture as a whole. For the Western Apaches, significant points in the landscape are so tied to stories and their associated meanings that the people can carry on complex conversations about local events and interpersonal relations just by referring to a sequence of place names.[8] Although Euro-Americans often view themselves as a predominantly rational and practical people, we too live in a world held together by narratives. Some of our narratives are consciously recognized as stories and told as such, while others have a more subliminal but no less profound presence. The Vietnam Memorial, a museum exhibit, Sandburg's young Lincoln, or even a science textbook, each have an implicit narrative structure that runs deep beneath it like an underground river. Even those things that are not produced by the human imagination—the fossils in a geological stratum, or the stars in a cosmic nebula—are intelligible to us only when we put them into the context of a story. And not just any story, but one that we find congenial to our needs—a story that is, for one reason or another, "good to think."

Myths are a people's deep stories—the narratives that structure their worldview and that give form and meaning to the disconnected data of everyday life. There is not always a clear line separating myth in this broad sense from trivial fiction or from "factual" accounts. A Hollywood Western may or may not deserve to be called mythic in itself, but it is part of America's foundational myth of the Old West, a myth that addresses in a uniquely American way our national preoccupation with the individual versus society, nature versus culture, and the wild versus the tame. Similarly, it might be too grandiose to refer to an episode of the 1980s *Cosby Show* as mythic, but the entire series did help to construct an implicit mythos about race and social mobility in America during the 1980s (just as *Amos 'n Andy* expressed an entirely different mythology of race for radio audiences forty years earlier).[9] On another note, some anthropologists might be affronted by the suggestion that scientific accounts of human evolution are mythic, but the accepted reading of the human fossil record at any given time is as much a reflection of what is culturally and politically "good to think" as of the material evidence. Each element of a given culture (some more vividly than others) has an underlying narrative content that reflects and constructs the meanings important to that culture. The whole mythos of a culture cannot be found in any one place, but there is scarcely anywhere that it is not manifested in some way.

To treat *Star Trek* as American mythology, then, is not to claim that *Trek* is equally important for all Americans, or that it contains the whole of the culture's mythos, or that everything in *Trek* has a profound mythic significance. It is simply to say that much of *Trek*'s phenomenal appeal has to do with its ability to confront and express, in a gratifyingly mythic way, some of the central concerns of American culture.

Insofar as myths seek meaning, they seek a different kind of meaning from that codified in doctrines, theologies, and catechisms. The strength of complex narratives certainly does not lie in their ability to erase ambiguity and establish absolutes; straightforward dogma is far better suited to that purpose. What myth does especially well is to explore life's ambiguities in a way that preserves our appreciation of their complexity while at the same time allowing for a sense of enhanced understanding, and perhaps even personal or collective empowerment. Novelist and critic Marilynne Robinson's assessment of the significance of myth captures the essence of our approach:

> I consider myths to be complex narratives in which human cultures stabilize and encode their deepest ambivalence. They give a form to contradiction that has the appearance of resolution. . . . Myth is never plausible narrative. It asks for another kind of assent. To anyone for whom it does not strike an important equipoise, it seems absurd. The myth of the Fall makes it possible to think of humankind and the world as at the same time intrinsically good and intrinsically evil. Those to whom this vision is not compelling grumble about the apple and the snake.
>
> I would suggest also that myths are coined continuously, usually

in very small denominations, and that lesser myths are related to greater ones as a penny is related to a gold mine.[10]

Part of the work of myth, as Robinson suggests, is to explore the basic ambivalences and paradoxes of a culture in a way that provides some sense of illumination and reconciliation. Mythic reconciliation is not the same as worldly reconciliation—its methods are narrative rather than doctrinal or practical. Myth confronts problems that in real life are the most unmanageable; it mediates in narrative terms the conflicts of cultural ethos that seem unbridgeable in practical life. It opens a space for human creativity within and between the irreconcilable polarities of human existence. It problematizes our maps of reality just enough to call us to the adventure, but not so cynically as to render our quest for meaning hopeless.

Myth does not go about its work piecemeal; rather, it defines and reflects a cosmos—a universe conceived as an ordered, meaningful whole. "Human beings cannot live in chaos," writes religious historian Mircea Eliade. It is our "cosmicization" of the universe into a "sacred space," Eliade contends, that "makes it possible to obtain a fixed point and hence to acquire orientation in the chaos of homogeneity, to 'found the world' and to live in a real sense." Even the most secular or "desacralized" existence still preserves "traces of the religious valorization of the world," including a tendency to see both time and space as having a sacred center to which we always return for spiritual renewal.[11]

A cosmos cannot be deduced from the physical universe alone; it requires a cosmological narrative capable of situating human understanding and purpose within an otherwise indifferent universe—in short, it requires myth. From the standpoint of human needs and choices, the raw data of the universe in the absence of an interpretive mythos is merely chaotic. Hence, Ovid begins his account of mythology in *The Metamorphoses* with the primordial transformation of Chaos into Cosmos:

> When he, whoever of the gods it was, had thus arranged in order and resolved that chaotic mass, and reduced it, thus resolved, to cosmic parts, he first moulded the Earth into the form of a mighty ball so that it might be of like form on every side. . . . And, that no region might be without its own forms of animate life, the stars and divine forms, occupied the floor of heaven, the sea fell to the shining fishes for their home, Earth received the beasts, and the mobile air the birds. . . . Then Man was born: . . . Though all other animals are prone, and fix their gaze upon the earth, he gave to Man an uplifted face and bade him stand erect and turn his eyes to heaven.[12]

Because the bare physical universe offers so little comfort to the mind, people strive through the medium of myth to center themselves and to make cosmological sense of their experiences. Particular stories, the smallest discrete units of mythic narrative, cohere into a larger pattern, a mythos. This mythos orders the chaotic universe into a cosmos, and the created cosmos in turn finds expression in each particular myth. Because the harsh light of material explanation seems at times to obscure the spiritual luminosity of human existence, a society steeped in scientific thought may be just as much, and perhaps more, in need of cosmos-defining myths than one whose natural science is rudimentary.

MYTH IN A MODERN AGE

Folklorists and anthropologists who study relatively stable nonindustrial societies usually expect to find those people's deepest stories embodied in sacred accounts of creation. By the orthodox folklorists' definition, in fact, a myth is a form of traditional (usually oral) narrative that is set in a primordial time, that concerns the actions of supernatural beings, and that is revered within its cultural setting as sacred truth. These traits also distinguish myth from legend, which is also believed to be true but which takes place in historical time and concerns human or quasi-human heroes; and from folktales, which may involve fantastic beings but which are regarded in their cultures as fiction and are told primarily for entertainment.[13] But because these distinctions are part of a strategy for studying oral narratives in traditional societies with a high degree of religious consensus, they offer little guidance for those who wish to study the functional equivalent of myth in modern popular culture.

By posing a broader definition of myth as a culture's "deep" or cosmos-defining stories, we can open the way to discovering mythic aspects in many kinds of modern narrative, ranging from "factual" scientific writing to the most patently fabulous fiction. Two narrative realms that invite specific comparison with myth are the closely related literary genres of fantasy fiction and science fiction. Fantasy fiction formally imitates myth and legend in its timelessly rustic setting (often based on romanticized medieval Celtic or Arthurian models) and in its use of such folk motifs as dragons and sorcerers. The term *science fiction*, on the other hand, usually refers to tales that are set in a hypothetical future and/or on other planetary worlds and that employ a naturalistic framework of science and technology rather than magic and the supernatural. While fantasy may bear a superficial resemblance to traditional myth in its rustic and magical character, science fiction has a stronger functional parallel with older myths, because its futuristic setting can entail a more serious kind of truth claim.

Traditional myths place sacred formative events outside the flow of mundane history by adopting the setting of a primal past, sometimes described as a "time before time," when beings and processes were profoundly different from those we see in historical time. This gives mythic events a privileged status associated with timelessness, frees them from the shackles of ordinary plausibility, and allows for the possibility of an "eternal return" to the ever-present mythic time through ritual retellings and reenactments.[14] In a pluralistic society like ours, however, the primal past is contested territory and is therefore off limits as a unifying mythology. There is little one can say about the primordial past that, taken literally, does not directly challenge someone else's origin narrative (how can Eve, Spider Grandmother, and Lucy coexist in the same garden?).[15] Thus, primal myths tend to emphasize parochial identities and to divide subcultures from one another. Furthermore, traditional societies' veneration of the past as somehow more real than the present has been reversed in modern industrial societies like ours. Therefore, it should not be surprising if contemporary mythmaking seeks the "undiscovered country" of the future as a setting for its cosmic narratives.

Like the primal past but unlike overtly fictional settings, the future can be thought of as potentially real and true. Both the future and the primordial time-before-time stand apart from concrete history, but with a big difference: the past either happened or it didn't; but the future *might* happen—no one can make more than a provisional truth claim for it, but neither can anyone solidly deny that claim. In this way we can have our popular-culture myths and our sectarian ones too, since many different people in a pluralistic society can entertain a shared fantasy about the not-so-distant future of humankind without necessarily getting into the contested area of particular creation accounts and eschatologies. The hypothetical future is our sacred time, the realm where our deepest fears and longings are assayed.

Science fiction is mythic insofar as it embraces the "deep story" attributes of myth. Both science fiction and traditional myth are "thought experiments" that posit a "What if?" question and then pursue its consequences. *What if* a god had to give account to the other gods for bestowing humanity with culture? *What if* people were offered immortality in exchange for unquestioning obedience? *What if* an otherwise rational people expressed all their sexual urges in a single outburst every seven years? *What if* a race of humanoids existed whose gender were alternately female, neuter, and male?[16] All literature is thought experiment, but most literary genres do not go so far out of their way to set up situations that are extravagantly contrary to everyday experience. The human condition is defined in part by what is not but could have been, and both traditional myth and science fiction provide narratives that probe these unrealized possibilities of being.

At the same time, one of the traits that separates *Star Trek* from traditional mythologies is that *Trek*'s mythos is recognizably the invention of known authors—particularly of *Trek*'s "creator" Gene Roddenberry. It was Roddenberry who conceived and promoted the idea for the first series, who gave final approval to the official written guidelines for writers and directors, and who authored or co-authored a number of episodes of *The Original Series* (TOS) and *The Next Generation* (TNG), including the pilot episodes. Roddenberry was inclined to view the *Trek* world as his personal domain and himself as its gatekeeper—to the frequent consternation and occasional embitterment of contributing writers. As one TNG writer put it, "You suspend your own feelings and beliefs and you get with his vision—or you get rewritten."[17] Although Roddenberry's direct role declined in the period leading up to his death in 1991, he had by then blazed an indelible trail for all who followed him into the *Trek* universe. Foremost among the tenets of Roddenberry's vision is humanism—a compassion for our species and a faith in its ultimate wisdom and capacity for self-reliance. Bolstering this central premise are an optimistic view of the human future; an emphasis on the imperatives of freedom, growth, and change; a tolerance of diversity; a central role for the emotions of friendship and loyalty; an opposition to prejudice or tradition-for-its-own-sake; and a visceral rejection of organized religion and divine authority. While some persons involved in the production of *Trek* may have had misgivings about various aspects of this vision on philosophical or artistic grounds, most admit that it has provided the unifying, hopeful vision that makes *Trek* so beloved and so durable.[18]

But if *Star Trek* was in some sense the brainchild of Gene Roddenberry, its production as a cultural "text" has directly or indirectly involved persons too numerous to mention, including scores of storywriters, scriptwriters, production staff, principal actors, studio executives, network censors, and others. Even more significant, however, is the fact that popular entertainment is always influenced, through a variety of direct and indirect avenues, by public taste and shared cultural assumptions. Important as Roddenberry's personal perspective was in creating *The Original Series*, we must look to the broader social context to explain the postcancellation resurrection and apotheosis that mark *Trek*'s beginning as a cultural phenomenon. The original *Trek* perceptively addressed the issues of its time, and the ensuing films and series have kept pace with cultural change.

THE WELLSPRING OF MYTHOLOGY

The art of the automobile bumper sticker reached new heights with one that read, simply, "BEAM ME UP, SCOTTY." It's rare for so rich a joke to be contained in four words. One can almost hear the crisp, commanding voice of the space traveler who may feel out of place on this planet but will presently be whisked to a better, more orderly and heroic realm. Or perhaps the forlorn hero is fated to drive around for eternity in this primitive Terran vehicle, patiently waiting to effervesce into the ether. There are few in America who would not get the allusion.[19] To explain it to a visitor from the year 1960, however, would be difficult unless one could arrange for the stranger to see at least one episode of *The Original Series*.

This is the way all the earth's cultures used to work—they had common bodies of narrative upon which people could draw for cryptic allusions to elaborate worlds of meaning. And so it often is within *Star Trek*'s world. In *The Next Generation* episode "Darmok," Starfleet Captain Jean-Luc Picard is obliged by the alien Tamarians to spend a few days marooned on the planet El-Adrel IV with the Tamarian captain, Dathon. This extravagant gesture is necessary in order to give Picard the time and motivation to understand the Tamarian's peculiar method of communication, which consists entirely of metaphorical allusions to their myths and legends. Of course, even when Picard understands the principle, he is able to say little without being versed in the stories that make Tamarian communication possible—but the experience is an illuminating one for him. As Dathon is about to succumb to wounds received from a monster on this forbidding planet, Picard comforts him with an ancient earth legend, the Sumerian tale of two friends from different realms, Gilgamesh and Enkidu.

"Darmok" is a good story in itself, but it's also a story about the *good* of stories—about the positive role that narratives play in thought and communication. This is an appropriate theme for a *Trek* episode, because if any popular cultural realm is an heir to ancient storytelling traditions, it is *Star Trek*. By the time "Darmok" aired, a quarter century after the premier of *The Original Series*, *Trek*'s status as a narrative resource in its own right had been well established. Even before *Trek* had become thus enshrined, however, TOS drew attention to its own creative appropriation of preexisiting motifs. The early *Star Trek* was loaded with such recycled narrative artifacts as gangsters, gunfighters, witches, and swashbuckling Samurais—not to mention Biblical phrases, Greco-Roman mythological references, snippets of Shakespeare, and so forth. From the beginning, *Trek* thus inserted itself into an ancient and ongoing project of "re-visioning" the themes of earlier narratives, a practice that in turn provides material for still more revisionings (parodies, jokes, fan fiction, *Trek* novels, and even, perhaps, new mythic worlds inspired by *Trek*).

In its mature years, *Star Trek* has increasingly featured stories that directly celebrate the power of storytelling. In the *Deep Space Nine* (DS9) episode "The Storyteller," Chief Engineer Miles O'Brien is, to his great consternation, chosen as the successor to the Sirah, or Storyteller, of a village on the planet Bajor. Not only is the Sirah a civic leader, but upon him falls the supreme responsibility of repelling the Dal' Rok, a storm-monster that menaces the village for five days of every year. He must accomplish this exorcism by publicly reciting legends that celebrate the strength and unity of the village people. The Dal' Rok is actually a distillation of the people's own fears, given form by the Sirah (with the help of a fragment from one of Bajor's powerful crystalline "orbs") in order to renew the people's sense of solidarity and courage. The choice of the bewildered O'Brien as the new Storyteller is intended to encourage the Sirah's wavering apprentice, Hovath, to rise to the role. In a similar vein, the starship *Voyager* encounters a people who value stories so highly that they use them as currency and who are prepared to bargain or swindle Voyager's crew into downloading all the literature, history and mythology from the ship's computer banks (*Star Trek Voyager* [VGR], "Prime Factors").

The power of stories has its dangerous side, and the *Trek* heroes may be faced with the necessity of entering into the frame of a menacing story in order to see it through to a safe conclusion. This happens, for example, in the VGR episode "Demons and Dragons," when the holographic Doctor risks his existence by entering a "Beowulf" holodeck program to rescue three vanished shipmates. In the VGR episode "Worst Case Scenario," the crew becomes obsessed with the challenge of finishing an uncompleted story that the ship's security officer, Mr. Tuvok, had begun to program into the ship's virtual-reality holodeck. As various crew members insert themselves into this scenario of shipboard political intrigue (initially conceived by Tuvok as a training exercise against possible mutiny), they become drawn into a genuinely hazardous scenario in which the deceased traitor Seska has, unbeknownst to the crew, programmed herself to reappear and threaten the safety of the ship. Luckily, the crew's superior storytelling imagination allows them to foil the holographic Seska and save the day.

The final-season TNG episode "Masks" is a tour de force of *Star Trek*'s mythology about mythology. In this tale, the *Enterprise* encounters a "rogue comet" estimated to have been traveling through space for 87 million years since its origin in the distant D'Arsay star system. When strange symbols flood the *Enterprise*'s computers and mysterious alien artifacts begin to materialize all over the ship, the crew blasts away the comet's outer shell to reveal an uninhabited temple-like structure at its core. The object appears to be a library or "archive" from an ancient civilization, and the *Enterprise* continues to scan it in order to learn about the culture. The situation turns threatening, however, when the *Enterprise* crew discovers that the archive is using the scanning beams to transmit information that is gradually transforming the *Enterprise* into a replica of a D'Arsay ceremonial center. Equally alarming is the fact that the android Lieutenant Commander Data becomes possessed by a succession of characters from D'Arsay mythology. The first of these is the spokesman Ihat, who warns that the fearsome goddess Masaka is awakening.

Unable to escape the powerful hold of the "archive" and increasingly menaced by fire, snakes, swamps, and jungle as the ship progresses toward total transformation, the crew must piece together information gleaned from the various mythological characters who speak through Data. They learn, among other things, that Masaka is a harsh sun deity who ground up her father's bones to make the world and that when she awakens she will vengefully destroy her many enemies and rivals. How can she be kept from awakening? "Try to stop the sun from climbing the sky," Ihat laments. "Only Korgano can do that!" Unfortunately, explains Ihat, Korgano no longer pursues Masaka.

Eventually, relying on Picard's broad knowledge of archeology and ancient cultures, the crew is able to piece together a tentative understanding of the relation of Masaka and Korgano, the sun and moon deities who pursue one another through the heavens in an endless cycle. Only one can be ascendant at any given time, and it is necessary for Picard to assume the identity of Korgano, Masaka's nemesis, in order to complete the cycle and release Masaka's hold on the ship. Picard offers to take Ihat's place as Masaka's sacrificial victim in return for Ihat's help in revealing the correct icon to materialize Masaka's temple. The climax of the story comes in the form of a dialogue between the two masked figures, with Data acting as Masaka and Picard impersonating Korgano. Picard relies on his intuitive understanding of mythic universals to say the proper things and persuade Masaka to relinquish her power over the sky so that the "hunt" may continue. "Without me you are incomplete," he tells her. "You live for the chase, as do I." "Let the hunt begin again; I am eager for that," says Masaka as she falls asleep. "As am I," says Picard/Korgano to no one in particular, and with those words the familiar surroundings of the *Enterprise* are at once restored.

Two *Star Trek* characters are central to this story. One is the android Data, who is shown in the opening scenes as being unable to exercise any intuitive or artistic imagination in Counselor Troi's art-expression exercise. During the course of the episode, Data not only connects with the D'Arsay's rich artistic and mythic culture, but he even shares the consciousness of thousands of D'Arsay people and mythic beings. Although Data feels "empty" after the departure of these multitudes, he has taken a huge step in his lifelong quest for an understanding of nonrational human experience.

The pivotal character of "Masks," however, is Captain Picard himself. Picard is a man of action and reason; yet he takes seriously the task of comprehending "mythic and ceremonial cultures." He corrects First Officer William Riker's mistaken judgment that the D'Arsay artifacts are "primitive" and "nonfunctional," pointing out that they have a ceremonial function and were produced by a culture that, while strongly oriented toward symbol and myth, was also highly advanced technologically. Picard rejects the solution that Chief Engineer La Forge proposes, which would have involved physically disempowering the archive. Mindful of his mission to seek out new worlds, he thinks it best to encounter this myth-centered civilization on its own terms by communicating directly with Masaka. As suggested by the presence of D'Arsay symbols for "border," "boundary," "messenger," "road" and "death," Picard has chosen the dangerous path across a boundary into another reality, a choice based almost entirely on faith. Picard is able to save the *Enterprise* by virtue of his ability to appreciate and master mythical, as well as rational, modes of thought and by his willingness to enter fully into the strange and forbidding world of an alien mythology. As Korgano, he represents a shadowy but apparently more benign force opposed to the fierce solar goddess; and when he pledges himself to the continuing "chase," it is not clear whether he speaks as Korgano, or Picard, or both.

In "Masks," mythic symbolism is literally the bedrock of a culture; once the myths and symbols enter the ship's computer, they transform the *Enterprise* into the very stones of the D'Arsay edifices. At the end of the story, the archive is left for Federation scientists to "study." This impending dissection of the archive is a fitting reversal of the main story, for the Federation's favored mythos of science will transform and dismantle the alien, mythic world. Picard, however, will not be there to see it; he has left that task to less imaginative minds.

VENERATING MYTH

The story "Masks" treats mythology as a key mode of perception whose essential features are everywhere similar, even among beings separated by vast reaches of space and eons of time. This idea of myth as a venerable domain of human understanding—or rather, the debate between this viewpoint and its critics—has a long history in Western thought.

For the classical Greeks *mythos* meant "word," or (for Homer and other early Greek poets) the arrangement of words into stories, especially those of primal events involving gods and heroes. In Homer's time, such narratives were deeply revered; the older the story, the more reliable it was considered to be.[20] By the sixth century B.C., however, the burgeoning Greek philosophical tradition had redefined myth as fictional invention and had posed various theories about its origin and function. Thus began the debate over myth's ultimate truth value, an issue that has continued to occupy commentators up to the present time. Some Greek and Roman writers ridiculed myth as ignorant caprice, while others rationalized it as a distortion of historically true events or as mistaken deifications of actual human heroes (the latter view is called "euhemerism" after its chief advocate, Euhemerus). Still others, including the Neoplatonic and Stoic philosophers of the Hellenistic period, revered myths as symbolic narratives that, if properly understood, conveyed important moral and metaphysical truths—or as one modern scholar puts it, "Myths ingeniously symbolized concepts of the nature of the universe, and were thus beautiful veils concealing profound moral principles."[21]

From late antiquity until the Renaissance, the dominant Christian Church embraced the doctrines of Euhemerus and other Greco-Roman debunkers of myth, holding that the pagan gods were in fact merely mortals—perhaps great, even divinely inspired mortals, but mortals nonetheless; hence classical myth was based on a misunderstanding. From the Renaissance onward, however, humanist speculations on the meaning and truth of myth reemerged and retraced many of the paths opened by earlier classical thinkers. Rationalists like Voltaire (1694–1778) took up the skeptical position of the Epicurean philosophers, who saw myths as ignorant superstitions or as self-serving fabrications perpetrated by cunning priests and rulers. The German Romantics of the late eighteenth and early nineteenth centuries, on the other extreme, followed the ancient Neoplatonists and Stoics in viewing myth as the wellspring of poetry and creative imagination—an encounter with the most profound and authentic levels of human experience.[22]

Much of the recent popular interest in mythology has to do with the supposition that myth has something vital to offer modern persons and cultures—something that our rationalist modern worldview has lost sight of. This revival of the Romantic view of myth owes much to the work of the Swiss psychologist Carl Jung. Early in the twentieth century, Jung broke with his associate Sigmund Freud by turning away from the notion of sexual energy as the driving force of the unconscious and by championing the idea of a pan-human collective unconscious, which he saw as the source of "primordial images" or "archetypes" expressed in the dreams and myths of people who have had little or no contact with one another. While Jung admitted that the meaning and function of these archetypal images was inherently difficult to unravel by using the conscious analytical mind, he felt that connecting with this deep realm of our species' unconscious was an essential part of human growth and of the therapeutic process. It is, for the most part, Jung's influence that accounts for the widespread modern belief that myth springs from the deepest layers of the human psyche.

Recent neo-Jungian writers have done much to bring mythology into the spotlight of popular culture. In particular, the late Joseph Campbell, whose prolific career reached its peak with his well-received 1988 television miniseries *The Power of Myth*, established himself as the most influential mythographer of recent times.[23] The popularity of such writing rests on the artful retelling of mythic material, accessibility to the general public, implicit doctrine of human unity, and above all, optimism about the empowering and redemptive potential of myth. Campbell's works tend to portray all mythic narratives as variants of one great "monomyth," in which, he says, "A hero ventures forth from the world of common day into a region of supernatural wonder: fabulous forces are there encountered and a decisive victory is won: The hero comes back from this mysterious adventure with the power to bestow boons on his fellow man."[24] The monomyth, Campbell argues, is nothing more nor less than an invitation to each of us to brave obstacles, transcend the boundaries of "normality," and bring something of enduring worth to the human enterprise. Thus, myth inspires people and guides them through the passages of life. While not all Jungians are as reductionist or as candidly moralistic as Campbell, they share a faith in myth as an expression of deep, quintessentially human images.

Even as Jung and his followers were exploring the positive psychic functions of myth, others were illuminating its social and cultural benefits. From the turn of the century onward, social scientists documented in great detail the invaluable social role that myth played in the human communities they studied. The "functionalist" approach in sociology and anthropology is so called because it explains particular beliefs and customs by elucidating their contribution to the smooth functioning of the social order in which they are found. In the functionalist view, a society's mythology serves as a "social charter" that, together with the associated rituals, sanctifies the social order and promotes sentiments of social solidarity and commitment.

The 1950s and 1960s witnessed the explosive development of a related sociocultural theory known as "structuralism." Structuralism came to prominence with the works of the French anthropologist Claude Levi-Strauss, but it quickly spread into the broader realms of literary, artistic, and cultural theory. Its epicenter was the study of myth, as manifested in many of Levi-Strauss's key works from his landmark essay "The Structural Study of Myth"[25] to his ambitious four-volume treatment of over 800 myths and their variants.[26] For Levi-Strauss and his followers, the object of studying myth (or any other form of cultural expression) is to go beyond its surface meanings and discover the underlying "grammar" or "structure" of binary oppositions inherent in a given myth, in the culture as a whole, and perhaps even in the human mind itself. Myths, according to the structuralists, express the logical polarities encoded in a culture and its social institutions. More important, myths produce the symbolic terms through which those dualities may be reconciled or "mediated." Mythic mediation often occurs through a process of successive transformations that rework troubling and irreconcilable oppositions (such as life/death) into parallel oppositions (such as farming/hunting, or herbivore/predator) that in turn allow for some third, mediating element (herbivore/predator is mediated by scavenger; hence, the importance of Coyote and Raven in certain American Indian mythologies).[27]

Such views as these emphasize myth's humane functions: its capacity to structure meaning, to explore ambivalence and mediate contradictions, and to reinforce social and cultural harmony. The powers of myth, however, are not always innocent and humane, for any narrative potent enough to inform our cosmology is also capable of being harnessed to nefarious ends.

INTERROGATING MYTH

While popular writings on myth have explored the idea of myth's universal wisdom and its nourishing effect on the culture and psyche, cutting-edge academic scholarship since the 1980s has taken quite the opposite path. Some of the most sophisticated work in these fields has lately been influenced by a loosely related family of theoretical positions bearing such intimidating labels as deconstructionism, postmodernism, poststructuralism, cultural studies, neo-Marxism, or critical theory. Their general strategy is to "interrogate" cultural phenomena in order to unmask their covert political agendas—agendas that maintain gender inequality, racism, colonialism, class differences, and other forms of privilege and exploitation. Critical theory, as we shall call this family of approaches, is not easy to describe to the lay reader, partly because it is sometimes framed in complex jargon, but also because it introduces innovative—and sometimes counterintuitive—ways of looking at ordinary things. Yet, although critical theory is demanding and often obscure, it has produced some of the most influential ideas of contemporary social theory, including perspectives that can enrich one's understanding of *Star Trek*.

Cultural Marxism, the taproot of critical theory, grows from Karl Marx's classic observation that the prevailing philosophy of any society tends to serve the interests of its privileged elite. Thanks in part to the writings of Antonio Gramsci (1891–1937), this germinal idea developed into a neo-Marxian approach that focuses on the phenomenon of hegemony. *Hegemony*, as the term is used in critical theory, is a disguised form of power that relies on oppressed peoples' acceptance of cultural assumptions that legitimize and maintain the prevailing relations of economic, political, and social domination. For example, to the extent that the lower castes of traditional India accepted the cultural belief that a privileged class of Brahmins was needed to maintain the purity and holiness of the world, they would be inclined to accept their own subordinate position.

By the time cultural Marxism entered the mainstream of "respectable" social science in the 1970s, it was able to take advantage of decades of functionalist and structuralist research on the role of myth, ritual, and other institutions in validating the social status quo. The neo-Marxists, however, rejected the assumption that social stability or symbolic validation benefits everyone equally, focusing instead on the ways in which these phenomena preserve relations of domination.

Critical theory, like structuralism, draws on the field of semiotics, or the study of "sign systems." Semiotic analysis applies to diverse systems of communication, including not only written and spoken language but also the codes of meaning embodied in clothing, photography, advertisements, architecture, and so on. Crucial to semiotics is the distinction between the surface elements, or "signifiers," that we use to communicate and the "signified" domains of meaning that they represent. By arranging and contrasting a system of signifiers in a certain way, we not only *describe* our conceptual domains but we also actually *construct* them. One of the main premises of semiotics is that a signifier—a woman's shaved head, for example—does not carry meaning in its own right but only by its position within the sets of oppositional contrasts that make up a given semiotic system. The "same" signifier could have different meanings depending on the culturally defined system of contrasts in which it is imbedded (is our shavehead a Hare Krishna, an Aryan supremacist, a prisoner, a religious initiate, or a celibate Deltan Starfleet officer?). As with the grammatical rules of our native language, which we may follow with great precision but often cannot describe, we may employ our semiotic systems intuitively but have difficulty articulating the premises that govern them. But once we become fully conscious of how a given system works, we can also gain insight into how it weaves patterns of thought that serve specific social agendas. *Star Trek*, like all narratives, imbues elements with meaning by placing them into complex webs of semiotic opposition—structures that may seem all the more compelling because they are silent and subliminal rather than explicit.

A particularly useful approach to myth within the framework of critical and semiotic theory is that taken by the French literary and cultural critic Roland Barthes.[28] The defining trait of myth, says Barthes, is that it conceals the historical origin of human customs and beliefs, presenting them instead as expressions of immutable nature. By taking the products of human history and reframing them as eternal, necessary "essences," myth helps to construct an ideology that supports economic, social, and political privilege. A Barthesian critique of myth labels as "essentialist" or "essentializing" any view that misleadingly portrays human social phenomena as the expression of essential (i.e., deeply imbedded, pervasive, unchanging) traits; for example, the idea that class inequality is dictated by the laws of God or nature. By contrast, a viewpoint like Barthes's, which sees conceptions of class as products of particular cultural and social settings, is called a "social constructionist" view. The difference between these two points of view is profound, and it can greatly influence the way in which different readers analyze a mythic "text."

Critical theory's recognition of power and conflict in connection with cultural phenomena has also led to another important insight of contemporary social theory—the recognition that cultural beliefs and meanings are often "contested," which is to say that they are subject to conflicting interpretations according to differing sociopolitical interests. Cultural meanings are not completely determined but are framed by the diverse agendas, strategies, or perspectives of individuals, factions, and subcultures. The fact that mythologies invariably operate within a complex and shifting labyrinth of social, cultural, and personal forces is one of the reasons why myths are so diverse and why they continually evolve. It is also one of the reasons why we will never run out of new ways to look at a given myth.

PLURAL VISION

Formal scholarship on *Star Trek* has undergone a distinct change from its inception to the present. The earliest academic literature on *Trek*, beginning in the 1970s, was predominantly either Jungian or structuralist.[29] Since the 1980s the tide has shifted toward critical approaches that take *Trek* to task for its purported sexism, racism, neocolonialism, homophobia, and so on. This critical commentary has been framed in increasingly complex theoretical language, which in the 1990s comes to reflect the ever-growing influence of a radical postmodern outlook.[30] Thus, it has become less and less fashionable to advocate the kind of celebratory approach to *Trek* that prevailed in earlier writings. The application of changing analytic frames has enriched the interpretive possibilities; but as we shall argue, it sometimes encourages academic commentators to select or even bend the *Trek* texts to fit the currently favored interpretation.

In Greek myth, the innkeeper Procrustes is known for forcing his unfortunate guests to lie on a certain bed, and then stretching them or sawing off parts of them until they fit it perfectly. It is possible, when writing on myth, to be so driven toward a preconceived goal that one may select only the material that fits the chosen approach or stretch and whittle it until it does fit. Those who read myth in order to interrogate its hegemonic messages, for example, are likely to write about such subjects as gender, race, ethnicity, cultural imperialism, social inequality, and other power-related dimensions of human difference. On the other side, those inclined toward the veneration of myth are more likely to focus on heroism, self-transcendence, the achievement of inner wholeness and illumination, and other seemingly therapeutic, empowering, humane, and unifying facets of myth.

Critical views of *Star Trek*, then, run the gamut—some praising *Trek* as deep psychic insight and others denouncing it as oppressive propaganda. For those critics who take the latter position, *Trek* viewers and fans may be seen as dupes of a reactionary ideology, or as people involved (perhaps unwittingly) in cultural "resistance"—reinterpreting *Trek*'s oppressive messages to serve their own, more liberating, ends. We do not deny that this scenario of oppressors, victims and heroic resisters can provide some fresh insights, but it does not exhaust the possibilities. Much can be gained by treating *Trek* as a mirror in which Americans can see themselves within their changing culture—a culture roiling with both conservative and progressive currents.

The approach taken in this book could be described as "pluralist." Like Picard/Korgano in the tale "Masks," we look forward to the chase, to the continual interplay of opposites. Opposing perspectives may each contain vital insights about myth, and it is therefore essential to maintain the dialogue between them. Rather than choose between veneration and interrogation, or between recognizing the hegemonic and the humane functions of myth, we prefer to consider the complex interplay among these possibilities. Perhaps no one can entirely avoid the Procrustean tendency to coax their "guests" into the bed they've prepared, but a pluralist approach can, at least, provide a "Procrustean hotel" instead of a single-bed lodging.

One can and must, as Joseph Campbell notes, "live by" some myth or another. At the same time, one must be prepared continually to step outside the framework of the most cherished myths and to view them with a critical eye, suspecting that they may be partial and limited and that we might imagine a more liberating and comprehensive mythos. The polarities of faith and skepticism need not be resolved in favor of one or the other, for it is within the charged field between these poles that the most fertile play of critical imagination will thrive. To be a reflective person is to be more than a passive carrier of cultural codes; it requires that one cultivate the ability to navigate within these codes and, simultaneously, to step back, see how they work, and evaluate them with a critical mind. The habit of experiencing things on more than one level—of being in two places at once without becoming lost—may compromise one's innocence, but it also places one more actively "in the loop" of cultural production and allows for a more direct participation in the dynamic of cultural creativity.

CHAPTER 2

WHO MOURNS FOR ADONAIS?

Heroes Without Gods

Freedom, free thought and science, will lead them into such straits
and will bring them face to face with such marvels and insoluble
mysteries, that some of them, the fierce and rebellious, will destroy
themselves. Others, rebellious but weak, will destroy one another.
The rest, weak and unhappy, will crawl fawning to [the Church] and
whine to us: . . . Save us from ourselves!

—Fyodor Dostoyevsky
The Brothers Karamazov (1880)

Stardate, 3468.1: Approaching the planet Pollux IV on a mission of exploration, the Starship *Enterprise* is suddenly caught in the grip of an
energy field shaped like an immense human hand. On the viewscreen
appears a serene face crowned in laurel leaves, floating among the stars.
The apparition welcomes the *Enterprise* crew as his "children": "You
have made me proud . . . We shall drink the sacramental wine—the long
wait is ended." Captain Kirk, Doctor McCoy, Ensign Chekov, Engineer
Scott, and *Enterprise*'s anthropologist, Lieutenant Carolyn Palamas, beam
to the surface of the planet where the stranger, now in human form,
addresses them from a Greek-style temple.

"Search your most distant memories," the being intones. "I am
Apollo." Assuming gigantic size, Apollo explains that he and the other
ancient Greek gods were interstellar travelers who once sojourned on
earth but left when humans refused to revere them. "We can't live without worship," he explains. The other "gods," abandoned and lonely,
vanished into the wind, but Apollo kept faith that humankind would

someday reach the stars and become happily reunited with him. He intends to bring the entire *Enterprise* crew to the planet, where they will remain to worship him forever. In return for this obeisance, Apollo promises the humans "life in paradise"—eternal happiness and the fulfillment of all their desires. "Man thinks he's progressed," he later explains to Lieutenant Palamas. "They are wrong—they've just forgotten the things that gave life meaning. There is an order to things; I have come to restore it." Kirk, speaking for humanity, defies Apollo even at the risk of lethal punishment. "We've come a long way," he proclaims. "Mankind has no need for gods."

In truth, Apollo's powers, impressive as they are (he can hurl thunderbolts, brew up storms, and control the *Enterprise*), are not in the least supernatural. Apollo, according to McCoy's scientific readings, is a "simple humanoid" who, thanks to an extra organ in his chest, has the ability to redirect energy from some external physical source. The landing party must find the location of the being's power source while the *Enterprise*, under Spock's command, seeks to penetrate the planet's defensive screen and help free the landing team from Apollo's control.

The fate of the *Enterprise* crew hinges on the loyalty of Lieutenant Palamas. From the moment Apollo took an interest in her and magically clothed her in a gauzy pink toga, the Lieutenant seems to have been altogether swept away, forgetting her responsibilities as a scientist and a Starfleet officer. She has fallen in love with Apollo, who pledges to make her mother to a race of gods—a promise that he bolsters with the claim that his own mother was a mortal.[1] But Kirk, momentarily alone with Palamas during Apollo's brief recuperative absence, prevails on her with an impassioned humanist appeal. Taking her hand, he implores her to feel the touch of humanity, "Human flesh against human flesh—we are the same. . . . Remember who and what you are, a bit of flesh and blood, afloat in a universe without end, and the only thing that's truly yours is the rest of humanity; that's where our duty lies—do you understand me? Lieutenant Palamas does understand, and she returns to Apollo steeled to "break his heart," which she does by coolly objectifying him as an anthropological specimen. "I am not some shepherdess you can awe," she sneers, whereupon the scorned "god" whips up a storm. The scene fades as he descends toward a terrified, supine Lieutenant Palamas. (The rape imagery of the scene is not only consistent with Greek mythic tradition but is reinforced when Scotty leads the limp, disheveled Palamas back to the waiting landing team; in a preliminary draft of the script, Palamas is afterward discovered to be pregnant!)[2]

The *Enterprise*, having reestablished contact with the landing party, is ordered to fire on the temple where Apollo's energy source is located. As Apollo stands atop the ruined temple waiting to fade forever into the wind, he cries, "I would have cherished you, cared for you. . . . Did I ask so much?" Kirk replies, "We've outgrown you—you asked for something we can no longer give." After Apollo has evaporated, Kirk wistfully suggests that maybe it wouldn't have hurt to "gather a few laurel leaves." Yet, the central premise of the plot remains inescapable: the only alternative to freedom from the god is eternal servitude and stagnation, which for "evolved" humans is intolerable, even in paradise.

Since the script never refers directly to the "Adonais" of the episode title, one might be tempted to conclude that it is a name for Apollo, or another of the gods whose death the story addresses. Actually, the Adonais of Greek myth was a mortal loved by the deities. Aphrodite/Venus fought with the underworld goddess Persephone over the beautiful youth, who in some tellings of the story was gored to death by a wild boar. Shakespeare's poem "Venus and Adonis" gives the story a particular dramatic twist wherein the impetuous Adonais rejects the goddess's attentions in order to go hunting the boar, and she, discovering his corpse, is inconsolable. As a poetry of grief and loss, "Venus and Adonis" is a memorable literary achievement.

Adonais, then, is not the god who dies, but the mortal beloved of the deity, the apple of the god's (or the goddess's) eye. To ask "Who mourns for Adonais" is to pose the question "Who, if not the gods, will love humanity?—who will mourn for us?" And whether, indeed, we need to be mourned.

TWILIGHT OF THE GODS

When the gods die, are humans the losers? *Trek's* astral Apollo is not alone in his claim that humanity, in casting off the belief in a deity, will lose everything that gives meaning, purpose, and decency to human life. Such a view is perhaps best expressed in the writings of Dostoyevsky, who said that without a belief in God, there is no hope for humanity— that life will become a "vaudeville of devils." If God does not exist, anything goes, and we will sink to the level of our lowest elements. Without the promise of an afterlife, love and human decency will wither away, leaving us only with vile instincts and base appetites.[3]

Traditional mythology framed the cosmological premises about human character and purpose, the proper arrangement of the social order, the meanings of human difference, the norms of personal conduct, and the fate of the human soul in terms of our relationship to the divine powers. The secular Western worldview, if it is to fill the moral void left by the decline of religious cosmology, must confront monumental new problems of meaning. Displaced from the center of the universe, slipping loose from assurances of divine redemption, knowing that we are only one of many life-forms—and perhaps not the most intelligent or powerful of them—living under the shadow of self-annihilation, frightened by the stubbornness of our ancient follies, entertaining dark musings about our innermost nature, we cannot but wonder, Who are we humans to think that we can find a bright path and survive to travel it? Our civilization relies more than ever on a faith in human self-sufficiency, yet the evidence of human frailty and insignificance seems to be mounting. Such a cultural crisis as this cries out for mythic mediation, and the myths that sufficed for the ancients will no longer do for us.

Although religion lends effective guidance to many individuals and cultural enclaves, it no longer provides Western societies with their master blueprint for law and government, the social order, or binding rules of personal conduct. Humankind has been left increasingly to fall back on a secular frame of reference to solve human, or even larger-than-human, problems. This situation is not so much the product of a deliberate choice as it is the inevitable outcome of our basic economic and political structures. The crucial role of science and technology, the separation of church and state with its accompanying secularization of law, our makeup as a culturally pluralistic democracy—the foundational facts of life in an industrial democratic society—make it impossible for us to return to the days when religious consensus ruled society unchallenged. Even the most dogmatic believer would find it hard to imagine a world in which God and religion mean only one thing: the same for everyone. We cannot but know that people have lived decent and meaningful lives as believers in countless diverse religions, not to mention atheism, agnosticism, pantheism, and so on. The loss of pristine religious innocence can be mourned, but it cannot be reversed except by the apocalyptic destruction of modern society. Theocracy is no longer an option.

Shall we then resign ourselves to drift helplessly toward despair and nihilism? Or will the champions of an optimistic humanism slug it out with the defenders of divine revelation, as they sometimes seem near to doing in America's so-called culture wars? The recent prominence of the abortion issue in American politics is a symptom of a deeper ambivalence in modern culture—it represents, among other things, our conflicted fears about invasive religious authoritarianism, on the one hand, and a sterile, amoral calculus of expediency, on the other. It is not hard to see why the collective fantasies of a society riven by such doubts might show a longing for some distant and more inclusive point of reference—some overarching mythology—that offers hope of reconciliation.

Of all the philosophical issues addressed in *Star Trek* none is more deeply pervasive than the question of humanity's potential for moral self-elevation and, by implication, the need for a deity as humankind's mentor and judge. *Trek* explores this potentially divisive issue in a way that only myth can do, reframing it on a plane where it appears, however illusively, to lend itself to reconciliation—and what's more, a reconciliation that valorizes humanism while avoiding an overt confrontation with America's religious sensitivities and even, for some fans and commentators, expressing a serendipitous harmony with Judeo-Christian ideals.

HUMANITY ON TRIAL: THE PILOT EPISODES

The theme of human independence from divine authority is treated metaphorically throughout *Star Trek,* and this theme is especially evident in the pilot episodes of all four series. Each of these four tales is based upon a strikingly similar formula: space explorers, entering new regions to extend the reach of human knowledge and influence, suddenly find their fortunes reversed when they are abducted by aliens possessing superhuman powers. The humans are treated as specimens and subjected to various trials and tests by which their whole species is to be judged. If they fail the tests, their quest will end: they will die or will retreat from their exploration or will remain forever imprisoned. They encounter and overcome the specter of illusion, the fear of punishment, the threat of divisiveness, and the temptation to indulge their selfish impulses and base instincts. Along the way, they expose the godlike beings' feet of clay. By the end of the episode, the humans have proven (at least provisionally) the worth of their species, and they have earned the freedom to continue their journey. The details are different, of course, and are as telling as the similarities. But what is the reason for the formulaic resemblance of the four pilot episodes?

Part of the answer may have to do with the conventions, or perhaps even the psychological imperatives, of the heroic quest narrative. Taking each series as a heroic quest in its own right and the pilot episodes as the beginnings of the respective ventures, one may find striking parallels with the sequence of events in Joseph Campbell's "monomyth" of the questing hero. Having answered the call and having left the safety of home, the hero arrives at the limits of the known world where, on the brink of venturing into the unknown dark regions, (s)he encounters a "threshold guardian" who has extraordinary powers and who subjects the hero to a series of tests. The guardian may be benign or malignant— perhaps an "adroit shape-shifter." After the successful passage of the trials, the hero is either allowed to proceed or is cast into the "belly of the whale," a "worldwide womb image" symbolizing spiritual rebirth (in the case of *Trek* heroes who proceed in their spaceship, perhaps both possibilities are expressed simultaneously). In either case, "once having traversed the threshold," Campbell continues, "the hero moves in a dream landscape of curiously fluid, ambiguous forms, where (s)he must survive a succession of trials"—for example, the continuing weekly adventures.[4]

But even if the pilot episode recipe owes its form partly to these conventions of traditional mythology, it also provides a vehicle for Trek's special project of addressing the quandary of modern humanity. By setting up a situation in which humanity is ostensibly being put on trial by godlike beings, these episodes, like the "Adonais" story, actually develop the opposite motif of humans' testing and judging the gods. The fact that this pattern appears in each of the four series pilot episodes makes it deserving of more detailed attention.

Original Series: "The Cage" (1965)[5]

"The Cage" was submitted to NBC in February 1965 as the proposed pilot for the *Star Trek* series, but the network rejected it. After considerable negotiation that led to some changes in the principal characters, the network authorized three more draft scripts to be submitted. The three were Roddenberry's "Mudd's Women" and "The Omega Glory" and Samuel Peeples's story "Where No Man Has Gone Before." NBC picked the latter as the first episode to be produced. However, it was actually "The Man Trap," the sixth episode in order of production, whose broadcast on September 8, 1966 provided the viewing public its first exposure to *Star Trek*. "The Cage" was not aired in the 1960s, but most of its footage was salvaged and recycled in the first-season "flashback" episode "The Menagerie." "The Cage" has since been aired in syndicated re-runs and is available on videotape; thus it has become part of the Trek "canon."

On earth the year is 2251. In space, the newly commissioned starship *Enterprise* is carrying out its first five-year mission of exploration. Responding to a distress signal from the planet Talos IV, Captain Pike (James Kirk's predecessor in this pilot), Mr. Spock, and others beam down to discover a ragged encampment of aging human survivors from the crash of an exploration vessel some twenty years earlier. A beautiful young woman in their company is introduced as Vina, born just before the crash on Talos. Vina lures Pike to a rock formation where he is subdued and taken underground, and he awakens in a transparent cage. His captors, the Talosians, are diminutive, androgynous beings with oversized heads and pulsating brains. Communicating telepathically in a way that Pike can overhear, they dispassionately discuss the limited intelligence of their primitive specimen and how easily he was deceived by the distress call and the survivors, mere illusions created by the Talosians. Yet they also acknowledge that Pike seems more adaptable than other species they have tested and that they can begin their "experiment."

Vina materializes in the cage, embraces Pike, and begs him to let her fulfill his desires and fantasies. Pike, however, only wants information on the Talosians and how to thwart them. The Talosians do their best to cultivate a bond between Vina and Pike by creating an illusionary battle in which he must save her from a troglodyte monster and by conjuring up an oriental-style pleasure-palace with Vina as a green-skinned erotic dancer (a virtual spectator leers, "Wouldn't you say it was worth a man's soul?"). However, what really warms Pike to Vina is her assurance that she is actually human and not an illusion. He confesses his affection for her as the Talosians watch them on a televisionlike screen.

By this time, Pike has also experienced the Talosians' power of punishment. Vina is subjected to agony for telling Pike too much; and when Pike refuses to eat, he is momentarily plunged into a subterranean inferno. "From a fable you once heard in childhood," the Talosian Keeper explains, in an obvious reference to the Judeo-Christian Hell. "Wrong thinking is punished; right thinking is as quickly rewarded," the Keeper explains after another punishment episode. "You will find it to be an effective system."

Pike, undeterred, has gleaned useful information from his conversations with Vina. The Talosians had lived on the planet's surface until it was ravaged by wars. Forced to live underground, they developed their mental power of illusion-making ability until it "became a trap," causing them to give up genuine activity and to become inactive mind-beings dependent on the skills, and the vicariously experienced feelings, of captured specimens—hence, their desire to foster a race with Pike and Vina as their Adam and Eve. Pike has also learned, after startling the Keeper with a sudden burst of rage, that the Talosians could not telepathically "read" primitive emotions such as hate and anger.

The frustrated Talosians abduct Yeoman Colt and Number One so that Pike may have other choices of mates. But Pike, concentrating on telepathically unreadable "primitive" emotions, manages to take the Keeper by surprise and escape to the surface with his former captor as hostage. Arriving at an impasse in their negotiations over the safety of the ship, Pike and his companions are on the verge of deliberately blowing themselves up when the other Talosians arrive to report what they have learned from scanning the *Enterprise*'s computer banks: humans have a "unique hatred of captivity." "Even when it is pleasant and benevolent, you prefer death," they observe. "This makes you too violent and dangerous a species for our needs." The Talosians have no choice but to release the humans and resign themselves to eventual extinction. Vina, however, cannot leave; she is actually an aged, disfigured sole survivor from the earlier spaceship, whom the Talosians have comforted with the illusion of youthful beauty. As she returns to the Talosian underworld, escorted by a benevolent illusion of Captain Pike, the Keeper observes, "She has her illusion, you have your reality; may you find your way as pleasant."[6] The crew members return to the *Enterprise*, and a pensive captain commands the ship onward in its continuing mission.

The Next Generation: "Encounter at Farpoint" (1987)

A hundred years have passed since the now-legendary exploits of Captain Pike's successors on the *Enterprise*, Captain James T. Kirk and the illustrious crew immortalized in *Star Trek*'s Original Series. The *Enterprise D*, the fifth starship to bear the distinguished name, is commencing its own extended mission under the command of Captain Jean-Luc Picard. The ship is en route to its first assignment, to determine how the Bandi people of the planet Deneb IV, a society with a limited command of technology, could have built the mysteriously advanced Farpoint Station that they have been offering as an incentive to gain admission into the United Federation of Planets. The *Enterprise* is waylaid and boarded by a strange entity who calls himself "Q." This being, whom the Betazoid empath (and ship's counselor) Deanna Troi later describes as "beyond life-forms," displays virtually unlimited powers. Appearing in military garb from various periods of human history, Q harangues the crew on the crimes of humankind—its wars over religions, ideologies, and resources, even its aggression and conquest in the early days of space exploration. Pronouncing humans a murderous race, Q commands them to return to Earth or die.

The intransigent Captain Picard, Counselor Troi, Security Officer Natasha Yar, and the android Lieutenant Commander Data are whisked before a conjured-up court modeled on the infamous "postatomic horror" of the twenty-first century, jammed with grotesque, unruly spectators and presided over by none other than Q himself, in a floating throne and with a costume resplendent of a Grand Inquisitor. With his arrogant, totalitarian demeanor and his nightmarish kangaroo court, Q mockingly acts out the sins of which he accuses humankind. Unfazed by the cruel and arbitrary punishments casually dealt out by Q, Picard faces the court with dignity. Threatened with the execution of his crew unless he answers "guilty" to a list of charges, Picard so pleads—but adds, after a suitably dramatic pause, "Provisionally!" The provision is that, while Picard admits the truth of Q's allegations against humans historically, Q should test him and his crew to see what people have become. Q agrees; but instead of taking their prolonged mission as the test, he gives them limited time to prove themselves in the Farpoint mission.

Upon their arrival on Deneb IV, Picard becomes aware of some suspicious phenomena: the technology of the Farpoint Station is unique and baffling, and furthermore the environment seems magically to produce whatever the visitors happen to wish for. Groppler Zorn, the Bandi representative, privately scolds and threatens some invisible entity for arousing suspicion. An alien vessel, twelve times the size of the *Enterprise*, suddenly appears and opens fire on the planet—but only on the Bandi's "old city," not the Farpoint Station itself. The *Enterprise* aims its weapons at the attacking vessel but refrains from firing. Q appears on the bridge and taunts the humans to fire on the alien vessel. Just as Q announces that their time is up, Picard and his companions finally piece together the solution: the "station" is actually a shape-shifting being, captured by the Bandi and given minimal rations of geothermal energy while being forced into "slavery" and obliged to exist in the form of Farpoint Station. The attacking "vessel" is its mate, come to rescue it. Picard orders the *Enterprise* to feed an energy beam into the station until it regains strength. Both creatures assume their natural jellyfish-like form and enjoy a tentacle-holding reunion (Counselor Troi empathically senses "great joy and gratitude"). Q, seemingly disappointed that the humans had mustered the restraint, insight, and compassion needed to pass this test, frees them to continue their mission but hints that they may encounter him again. Voicing the hope that the rest of their mission will be "more interesting," Picard's gives the command: "Let's see what's out there—engage!"

Deep Space Nine: "Emissary" (1993)

The year is 2369, four years after Picard's first encounter with Q. Commander Benjamin Sisko has been assigned to the *Deep Space Nine* space station, a former slave-labor mining facility used by the Cardassians during their century of brutal occupation on nearby Bajor. The Cardassian withdrawal has left Bajor in a political and economic shambles, and their precarious "provisional government" has invited the United Federation of Planets to aid in Bajor's reconstruction and to prepare it for Federation membership. The setting is grim: the station has been vandalized by the departing Cardassians, and its interplanetary crew, thrown together by political vicissitude, are mutually suspicious if not openly hostile toward one another. Sisko, demoralized by the tragic loss of his wife in a disastrous battle two years earlier, and perhaps moved by his son Jake's complaints, plans to resign his Starfleet commission as soon as a replacement can be found.

The Bajorans' religion is the only force capable of uniting their race and averting a civil war. The planet's spiritual leader, Kai Opaka, shows Sisko the "tear of the prophet," an hourglass-shaped energy vortex, or "orb," one of nine discovered in the Bajoran star system over a ten-thousand-year period and the only one not stolen by the Cardassians during their occupation. The Bajorans believe these orbs to have been sent by the prophets from their "Celestial Temple," and they want Sisko to serve as their long-awaited "emissary" to the temple. They fear that if the Cardassians discover the temple first, they will destroy it—and with it the source of every Bajoran's pagh, or inner spiritual power. Gazing into the orb, Sisko is temporarily transported into another reality where he relives his first meeting with his lost wife, Jennifer. Afterward, Opaka tells Sisko that he must see the prophets, not only for Bajor but for his own pagh: "It is the journey you have always been destined to make."

Sisko and another officer take a shuttlecraft to seek the energy source of the orbs and soon find themselves entering an unexpected "wormhole"—a tunnel in space allowing instant travel to the Gamma Quadrant, a distant and previously inaccessible part of the galaxy. On their return passage, they are captured and held by the incorporeal beings who created the wormhole and who live inside it—the "prophets" of Bajor. It is revealed that the orbs and the opening of the wormhole were part of these beings' effort to contact other life-forms—but only "real" lifeforms, not lowly "corporeal" creatures like Sisko or the Bajorans. Appearing in the guises of Picard, Jennifer, and other familiar people, the beings interrogate Sisko. When he remarks that it will take time for such different species to understand one another, they ask, "What is this— time?" The beings, who do not live in linear time, have difficulty understanding Sisko's answers. They find his account of linear time "inconceivable" and accuse him of lying. They also suspect that, if any being could live in linear time, its presence in their realm would be dangerous and disruptive. After all, how can a creature be responsible for its actions if, as Sisko says, linear time does not allow one to know the consequences in advance? Therefore, they assert, he and his kind ought to be destroyed. Despite their initial objections ("Aggressive and adversarial!"), Sisko uses the game of baseball to illustrate the playfulness and curiosity that results from not knowing which contingent possibility will actually occur. He explains that humans' ignorance of what is to come makes them an exploratory species, always searching for new answers and new questions, and that his kind are there "not to conquer . . . but to coexist, to learn."

The beings' antagonism fades as they come to understand the nature of linear existence. One thing, however, continues to puzzle them: Why, if he lives in linear time, does Sisko endlessly relive the moment of Jennifer's death, refusing to leave "that place," as they call it. "It is not linear," they point out. Sisko, in tears, agrees: It is not linear. Each lifeform has taught the other a valuable lesson. The "prophets" release Sisko and agree to allow linear-corporeal creatures free passage through the wormhole. Sisko's vessel emerges from the wormhole just in time to prevent the destruction of the DS9 station by the Cardassians, who have been competing for a strategic position near the wormhole. Sisko's experience of self-discovery, together with the new importance of the DS9 station as guardian of the wormhole, persuade him to recommit himself to his new duties.

Voyager: "Caretaker" (1995)

The opening episode of *Star Trek Voyager* is set in a time roughly contemporaneous with the ongoing action of DS9. This first episode opens in the "badlands" of space, where a battle is underway between the Cardassians and a renegade resistance group, the Maquis. At the height of the battle, the Maquis ship is hit by an unexplained force and swept away to no one knows where. Hastily assembling a crew, Starfleet Captain Kathryn Janeway sets forth on the newly commissioned starship *Voyager* to locate the Maquis ship and rescue Tuvok, a Vulcan undercover agent aboard the vessel. When the *Voyager* reaches the badlands it too is struck by the same force, which inflicts numerous casualties and flings the ship to the Delta Quadrant, 70,000 light-years from their previous location—a seventy year journey away from home. There they find the empty Maquis ship and a huge artificial object that they call "the array." *Voyager* is scanned by the array, and crew members start disappearing. Soon everyone is transported to what appears to be a Midwestern farm, where a motherly person offers them some sweet corn and the neighbors drop in for a hoedown. Poking around in the barn, the crew members discover survivors from the Maquis ship. A dog snarls. The yokels turn on them with pitchforks. The illusion disappears, and they find themselves in a dark place being pierced by huge needles, and then they are back on their ship. But the young Ensign Harry Kim is missing, as is a Maquis officer, the volatile half-Klingon woman B'Elanna Torres.

Having determined that the array contains a single life-form, Janeway and her companions beam over to get some answers but find only more riddles. Encountering a disheveled old man plunking on a banjo, they demand that he send them home. "Well, aren't you contentious for a minor bipedal species!" he exclaims. Asked why he is abducting humanoids from all over the galaxy, he brushes them off, saying that they don't have what he needs but maybe the others do, that he has "no choice," that there is not enough time left to send them back, and that he must "honor a debt that can never be repaid." Back aboard *Voyager*, the crew members decide to follow the energy pulses from the array to the fifth planet in the star system, hoping to find Kim and Torres there.

The life-form on the array is the Caretaker, who has provided for the Ocampa in their subterranean home for a millennium since "the warming" rendered their planet's surface uninhabitable. Although an occasional dissident might find his or her way to the surface, most Ocampa have become far too dependent to dream of such a thing. The Ocampa doctors, who are treating Kim and Torres for mysterious lesions, admit that the Caretaker has been acting strangely of late, sending them many humanoids who have suffered from the same ailments, none of whom have survived. Janeway and the others find a breach in the protective "grid" through which they beam down into the Ocampa city, just in time to join Kim and Torres who have already started up through the tunnels. Together they make their way to the surface and back to *Voyager*.

The riddles are answered as our heroes learn from the Caretaker that he is dying and that he has been testing life-forms for biomolecular compatibility so that he can reproduce a new version of himself (the unfortunate subjects of his experiments had succumbed because of their incompatibility). It seems that his people came from another galaxy and introduced new technology that unexpectedly ruined the surface of the Ocampa planet. He and his mate stayed behind to care for the Ocampa, but the mate eventually wandered off. He must honor his obligation to the Ocampa, if not by reproducing himself, then by leaving them with an abundant supply of energy, which he has now done. Janeway debates with him, challenging whether it is right to keep the Ocampa in a state of dependency and arguing that even "childlike" peoples must "grow up." It is a moot point, however, since the Caretaker has not reproduced, and his last act before dying is to seal the Ocampa underworld and enact a destruct program to prevent the array from falling into the hands of the Kayson, a nearby race of thugs who would surely use the array to pillage and massacre the Ocampa.

In the ensuing battle, the Maquis ship rams the Kayson vessel just moments after its crew members beam aboard *Voyager*. The array's destruct program is impaired, and Janeway, now responsible for both the Starfleet and the Maquis crews aboard *Voyager*, must decide whether to use the array to send themselves back home, or to destroy it in order to protect the Ocampa. Chakotay, the Maquis commander, recognizes Janeway's authority as captain of the combined crew, and she makes the difficult moral choice not to sacrifice the Ocampa for the *Voyager* crew's "own convenience." Joined by a pair of local aliens, Neelix and Kes, the company becomes one single Starfleet crew, and the episode ends with a moving speech from the Captain about working together as a team, seeking out new worlds, and above all, finding a way home.

WILL THE DEFENDANT RISE?

There is a peculiar irony common to these pilot episodes. Superficially, the stories each depict beings with godlike powers who put humankind on trial, but ultimately it is the superbeings themselves who are judged and found wanting. Although they may appear as gods, they often turn out to be little more than cosmic bullies, all their righteous allegations about human aggressiveness notwithstanding. They may promise paradise, but they deliver punishments and threats. They offer no gift of revelation, but instead conjure up illusions. Although religious traditions have often depicted human material existence as a kind of captivity from which only the divine can deliver us, these four stories reverse that imagery: quasi-divine beings hold humans in captivity, and people must believe in themselves and deny those beings authority in order to become free.

It is, in large part, the humans' lack of godly pretensions that saves them. Humans have self-doubt; they know they are not perfect. But they are determined to progress, to learn, to seek out better understandings. At the end of each of these stories, the humans win their freedom to do just that, while the godlike beings, presumably, are going nowhere. The humans reject protective custody and easy illusions, preferring perilous freedom and the hard-won lessons of genuine discovery.

These are, after all, morality plays, and much of the morality they champion has its parallels in religious tradition. In these and other *Trek* stories, people must resist the temptation to give in to their basic animal impulses—fear, lust, aggression, the desire for security—in favor of such higher motives as duty, loyalty, compassion, and sacrificial love. But the godlike beings, rather than fostering these noble impulses, undermine and underestimate humanity's ability to rise to the challenge—and this miscalculation is the gods' fatal mistake.

Although the theme of humanity's being subjected to a moral test is pervasive in these stories, the particular nature of the test reveals a significant pattern of change from the earlier to the later series. In "The Cage," the Talosians suppose that humans are—let's face it—plain stupid. They expect humans to be weak willed and easy to manipulate and deceive. Pike proves the Talosians wrong by demonstrating the strength of his will and his wits. His unmitigated rage is the very thing that can overcome the Talosians' telepathic powers, and he is cunning enough to take advantage of that discovery. Rejection of the temptations of lust and fear do play a role, but successful aggressiveness is Pike's ultimate rebuttal of the Talosians' demeaning assumptions about humanity. The Talosians' realization that humans are "violent and dangerous" leads to a reprieve for Pike and the *Enterprise*.

In "Farpoint," however, the charges are quite the opposite. Almost as if he too had seen "The Cage," Q claims that humans are indeed violent and dangerous—too much so to be permitted to exist. He sets for them a challenge requiring restraint and empathy rather than aggression and anger—a test for which Captain Pike might not have been very well suited. Picard has to renounce the very thing that Pike upheld as a hallmark of humanity: the will to fight. It is only by pursuing justice for an alien "other," even at the risk of human safety, that Picard proves how far humankind has come. The problem posed in "Emissary" is similar up to a point. The wormhole beings also consider humans dangerous and adversarial, but this initial perception turns out to be a misunderstanding stemming from the two species' radically different points of view. Sisko's task, then, is to explain corporeal linear existence to the beings, who, unlike Q, are willing to listen. It is, so to speak, an exercise in multiculturalism.

Finally, in "Caretaker," humans are abducted on the chance that they might be useful as raw materials for the Caretaker's experiment in self-procreation—and thus allow him to continue in his own goal of protecting the Ocampa. When, through no fault of their own, the humans turn out unsuitable to his needs, the Caretaker casts them aside to die. He is indifferent to the character and fate of humanity. Godlike though he is, his love is reserved for some other Adonais. Here the task facing the humans is one of creating a moral significance for themselves by making moral choices in a context where no higher being seems to care. In fact, the humans go even farther and hold the "higher" being accountable for his own choices as well.

The sequence of themes—the will to fight, the search for justice, the need for empathetic understanding of differences, the necessity to take moral action in a fundamentally indifferent universe—shows intriguing parallels with changes in American culture. The ideal of stubborn toughness makes considerable sense in the setting of the Cold War 1960s, while the concerns of the 1980s and 1990s have directed more attention toward justice, multiculturalism, and, most recently, a Generation-X version of existentialism. Despite these important changes, however, the fact remains that the pilot episodes, which set the dramatic tone and philosophical premises of the various *Trek* series, each begin with godlike beings who place humanity on trial and end with the respective positions at least partially reversed.

Although Gene Roddenberry was known for his outspoken criticism of organized religion,[7] *Star Trek*'s narrative approach cannot simply be dismissed as an allegorical diatribe against America's religious beliefs. Whatever Roddenberry's views on religion (and his views were actually rather complex[8]), the *Trek* series and films, as they became canonized in our popular culture, are striking not so much for their expression of any particular pro- or antireligious dogma as for their ability to construct a humanist mythos without contradicting the religious beliefs espoused by the majority of Americans.

The denunciation of false gods is not in itself antireligious; on the contrary, it appears in the Bible. It is crucially important, however, that *Star Trek* carefully avoids any confrontation with mainstream religious teachings. When Kirk tells Apollo that "mankind has no need for gods," he adds, almost under his breath, "We find the one to be quite sufficient." This enigmatic reference to "the one" is not clarified anywhere in the *Trek* corpus.[9] Yet without this qualification, the *Trek* cosmology would have been saddled with explicit atheism, and its ability to function as an inclusive American mythos would have been severely undercut. So deftly does *Trek* find the common ground of American humanism and American religiosity that one of the early published treatments of *Trek*, Betsy Caprio's *Good News in Modern Images*,[10] treats TOS as an allegorical illustration of the Christian Gospel. Indeed, the "human" virtues that *Trek* explicitly upholds, such as self-control, sobriety, knowledge, courage, friendship and attention to duty, are parallel to many of the ideals that Americans can associate with their moral upbringing as Christians, Muslims, Jews, and so on.

The classic 1939 film version of *The Wizard of Oz*, arguably the most thoroughly American of fairy tales, reaches its climax when the Wizard's fearsome, godlike illusions fall apart and the pretender-god is exposed. It is a moment of empowerment, when the heroine and her companions discover that the blessings they sought from the "Wizard" must actually come from within and that they need only learn to believe in themselves. This affirmation of self-reliance sounds a pragmatic, iconoclastic tone that resonates with the outlook of most Americans, whether they consider themselves humanists or not. "The Lord helps those who help themselves," as our saying goes. Human self-determination is not, in American popular belief, incompatible with religion. The uplifting, empowering "Wizard of Oz" moment echoes repeatedly in the *Star Trek* theme of the false-god-exposed; and although such a revelation can be read as antireligious, our culture allows us the latitude to read it in other ways—to have our humanism and our religion too, if we so choose.

ECCE HOMO: BEHOLD THE MAN

The idea of the hero tested by temptation, a folkloric theme that was already old when Jesus confronted Satan in the desert, appears in many *Trek* episodes besides those mentioned above. In *Star Trek*, these tests serve as narrative devices that continually reestablish the high moral character of the protagonist and, by implication, of the human species. While some *Trek* episodes frame this test in terms of captivity and trial by godlike beings, there are other means besides captivity by which the human character can be assayed and vindicated.

Early in *The Original Series*, humans are tested in a way that recalls a classic mythological theme, where intoxication or supernaturally induced madness drives people toward ruinous acts. The first-season episode "The Naked Time" shows the *Enterprise* crew infected by an intoxicating virus that has already destroyed a remote outpost by driving its crew lethally berserk. The uninhibited condition induced on the *Enterprise* by this intoxication, however, leads, not to an orgy of violence and debauchery, but to a poignant and endearing exposition of the doubts, longings, and weaknesses that lie suppressed beneath the crew members' usual disciplined demeanor. In the end, compassion for his suffering captain returns Spock to his senses, and the crew works together to find a cure for their condition. The protagonists are not demeaned but are actually made more noble. Two decades later, the TNG episode "The Naked Now" depicts Starfleet crew in much the same situation (in fact, they access the original *Enterprise*'s computer records to help solve the mystery). Here again, however, the scene is not one of sordid dissipation but one in which the letting down of defenses invites us to sympathize with the inner struggles and understandable human failings that our heroes keep nobly hidden most of the time. True, there is fornication this time: the android Data, largely out of compassion for the lonely, affection-starved waif revealed beneath security chief Tasha Yar's tough exterior, accedes to her advances—but he respects her afterward and is the very soul of discretion, and the incident actually begins a close platonic friendship between them. Similarly, Captain Picard's and Dr. Crusher's confession of mutual affection, not to mention Picard's bashful flirtation, shows a certain restrained charm, especially considering the grim fate of the evidently less self-controlled crew from whom the affliction was contracted. The loss of inhibition is a test that our heroes pass with distinction, and the restoration of normality highlights the role that moral composure plays in their everyday behavior.[11]

In TOS's "The Corbomite Maneuver" and again in TNG's "Where Silence Has Lease," a powerful alien announces his intent to murder the crew members, so as to test their fortitude in facing death. They do not grovel; they do not pray; they do not show fear, self-pity, or loss of control;[12] and above all, they do not give up searching for a practical solution to their predicament. Here again, a most trying test of character is passed with dignity and self-reliance. Clearly, if we believe that people could characteristically respond to their trials in such a way, we could easily dismiss Dostoyevsky's fears about humanity.

In some episodes, humans are obliged to choose between two valuable ends, of which the more exalted is characterized by concern for another, or sacrificial love. In TOS's "Metamorphosis," TNG's "Encounter at Farpoint," and VGR's "The Cloud," to name only a few, the protagonists are faced with the choice of placing human safety first or of undertaking a more risky course of action based on empathy for a strange being and the desire to understand its otherness (of course, they choose the latter). In *The Wrath of Khan*, Spock is forced to choose between the needs of the one and the needs of the many, and he gives his life to save his friends, thereby illustrating again the powerful theme of sacrificial love.

In "The Child" (TNG), Deanna Troi becomes impregnated by an incorporeal being that invades her body while she is asleep, and she must decide whether to allow the pregnancy to run its course. This episode takes on the abortion issue under some especially vexing premises. In modern secular terms, Troi has been sexually violated (by a different species, no less!); in terms of ancient Christian folk belief, one might say that she has fallen victim to an incubus, a demon spirit that impregnates a woman in order to reproduce itself. The situation provides the strongest possible argument, both in modern and in traditional frames of reference, for terminating the pregnancy. But she chooses to carry the child, a choice expressing her faith and love, and one that entails considerable uncertainty and risk. (The child is indeed an alien who grows to maturity and leaves the ship within a few days.) The story suggests that reverence for a fetal life can be a woman's reasoned human choice, that it need not depend on religious dogma or patriarchal regulation.[13]

Of course, a treatment of human goodness that does not acknowledge human evil would be incomplete. Trek addresses evil on a variety of levels ranging from patently mythic metaphysical abstraction to nuanced literary realism. Perhaps the best examples of abstracted evil are to be found in TOS's "The Enemy Within" and TNG's "Skin of Evil." The former, discussed below, splits Captain Kirk into "good" and "evil" components that are shown to be equally indispensable parts of his character. The latter story concerns a being that resembles a pool of black tar, created when the inhabitants of a planet skimmed off the presumed evil element of themselves and left it behind. As in Mary Shelley's *Frankenstein*, the creature's evil is attributed in part to its loneliness and rejection, and ultimately to its self-righteous creators who, by callously departing the scene, reveal their own moral blindness and irresponsibility. Evil, these stories imply, may not be as "pure" or simple as it's cracked up to be.

Literary realism rather than mythic metaphor characterizes the treatment of evil in such episodes as TNG's "Chain of Command, Part II." This story centers upon an extended discourse between Picard and his Cardassian torturer, in which both the tormentor and the victim take on considerable depth. The torturer's manifestly evil character is revealed to have a "human" side, so to speak, as shown in his fatherly affection for his young daughter and the pains he takes to "protect" her from any perception of brutality in his actions. Picard, for his part, is not invulnerable to the onslaught against his integrity (only a last-minute rescue conceals what Picard later confesses to Counselor Troi: that he was finally broken in mind and spirit).

On a much more mundane level, the DS9 series, with its penchant for political drama, regularly explores the concrete, everyday face of evil, and the relativity of viewpoints regarding it. It does this largely in the context of political machinations and personal moral dilemmas stemming from relatively this-worldly premises, such as the difficulty of distinguishing a ruthless terrorist from a principled freedom fighter, or the three-way conflict between personal loyalties, political commitments, and abstract ethics.

Although *Star Trek* takes the problem of evil seriously, its expositions of evil might bolster our hopes that it can be dealt with as a complex human, rather than a religious, problem: (1) good and evil, as depicted in these stories, may be complex and elusive rather than simple and absolute; (2) evil is not stronger than good, and it does not triumph; (3) evil is not more deeply imbedded in the human spirit than good, and is probably less so; (4) evil does not have a supernatural origin and does not require a supernatural cure. In the end, even the discussion of human evil opens the door to human self-redemption.

GODS IN THE CLOSET

While the theme of human self-sufficiency continues through the whole corpus of *Trek* films and series, the way in which religion is depicted changes over time. In TOS, religion is seldom so directly referred to as it is in "Adonais." For the most part, it is presented only indirectly, through allegories about beings with superhuman powers and feet of clay. One of the most striking things about TOS is the conspicuous absence of any form of religious expression on the part of the heroes. There is simply no hint that, in the twenty-third century, the existence of a deity or the need for religious practice will cross any reasonable person's mind as a serious possibility (primitive and stagnated cultures excepted, as we shall discuss later).

Although the humanist frame is maintained, the possibility of intelligent religious belief gradually becomes part of the *Star Trek* discourse. The premise that the *Trek* heroes might entertain religious beliefs is, for example, central to *The Final Frontier*. The *Enterprise* crew members, with the exception of Captain Kirk, fall under the spell of a charismatic Vulcan, Spock's half brother, who hijacks the *Enterprise* to seek God. "God," it goes without saying, is eventually exposed as an evil pretender. The film was made over the strenuous objections of Gene Roddenberry, who found it both insulting and logically inconsistent that the scientifically trained *Enterprise* crew members could be so credulous. Still, the trend continues in the three later series, which all deal with religion more explicitly and with more complexity than did *The Original Series*.

As the Klingons' culture becomes more elucidated in *The Next Generation* and *Deep Space Nine* series, they are portrayed as having not only rituals (for example, howling at the moment of a warrior's death to announce his arrival in the next world), but also a messianic religion and an elaborate mythology centered on Kahless the Unforgettable, a culture hero who introduced the tenets of Klingon belief, who presides in the afterlife, and whose return is prophesied. The TNG episode "Rightful

Heir" deals with the personal religious crisis of a central character, Worf, when he confronts someone who claims to be the reincarnated Kahless.

Interestingly, another tough-minded, militarized society is featured in DS9, and these people, the Bajorans, also have a messianic religion. As mentioned in the discussion of the "Emissary" pilot episode, the Bajorans see their religion as an essential source of both personal power and social unity. It is worth noting that both the Klingons and the Bajorans, though intelligent and technologically advanced, are militant, chauvinistic peoples, and thus culturally provincial compared with the more "normal" cosmopolitan humanoids of Starfleet and the Federation. Religion is, in this context, a signifier of cultural "otherness," a suggestion that a race has not yet achieved the fully rational level of mainstream humanoid development. The boorish, culturally parochial Ferengi also illustrate this point, possessing a religion and a conception of the afterlife (the "Divine Treasury") that mirrors their culture's narrow preoccupation with business and profit.

Religion appears in a different guise in VGR, which echoes America's recent dabblings in "New Age" and quasi-tribal religion. A somewhat romanticized version of Native American spirituality can be glimpsed when Chakotay learns the interplanetary origins of his ancestors' religion ("Tattoo"). Chakotay helps Captain Janeway and other crew members find their spirit guides, while the Ocampa crew member Kes discovers her capacity for sorcerylike powers. In VGR's "Sacred Ground," Kes is rendered comatose by a massive neuroelectric shock after venturing too close to a religious sanctuary on the planet Nechani, and she is not expected to live. The episode concerns Captain Janeway's quest to seek out and address the Nechanian "spirits" and plead with them for Kes's life (a theme echoing the underworld descent of Orpheus, Demeter, Inanna, and other heroes). She expects to encounter tests and trials, but ironically the test that she must pass is that of clearing her mind of her rational preconceptions and "scientific" prejudices and opening herself to the possibility of a genuine spiritual realm. The possibility is left open for either a scientific or a spiritual interpretation of these events, but one can tell by the faraway look in her eyes that the Captain is no longer the confident atheist that she was before her spirit journey.

The increased visibility of religion in *Star Trek* does not mean that the *Trek* world has capitulated to the idea of the supernatural. Anyone committed to doing so can understand the seemingly most "supernatural" phenomena within the framework of naturalistic explanations, since the plots always present that possibility. Furthermore, the false god theme has by no means been put aside. False religion is the explicit subject of TNG's "Who Watches the Watchers," in which an accidental contact between Picard and an inhabitant of a less developed (but nonetheless post-religious) society sends the natives reeling backward in their development, reviving old superstitions and abandoning reason—that is, until Picard persuades them that he is not a god. TNG's "Devil's Due" is about an unscrupulous shapeshifter named Ardra who claims to be the Devil and who has made a pact with the people of Ventax II, promising them a thousand years of peace and prosperity after which the people will become her slaves for eternity. Ardra appears to have upheld her end of the bargain and the people are about to submit, when Data and Picard undertake to expose Ardra as a charlatan and persuade the Ventaxians that they themselves are responsible for their millennium of success. Along the way, Picard must fend off the "Devil's" potentially dangerous sexual advances (Is this mythic, or what?). The false god appears again in VGR's "False Profits," in which a pair of Ferengi have blundered through a wormhole into the Delta Quadrant and are passing themselves off to the locals as gods until they are foiled by the *Voyager* crew.

The closest thing in *Star Trek* to a bona fide deity is the bizarre and petulant Q, whose status is left somewhat ambiguous. While he claims to be immortal and omniscient and he enjoys making "god" jokes ("You're lucky I don't smite you or something"), it seems that he, like the rest of the "Q Continuum," is a natural, if exceptional, being—an "immensely powerful extradimensional entity" who possesses "godlike powers."[14] If Q were a god, he would be closer to the trickster being of Native American and African traditions than to the absolutely good God of Judaism, Christianity, and Islam. And if he is omnipotent, he shares that status with others of his kind who often oppose him. The case of Q poses the problem of drawing the line between a god and a superman; and in the narrative context, Q serves as a little of both. In his godly visage, Q shows a marked ambivalence toward humanity. Despite his terrorizing them in TNG's "Encounter at Farpoint" and annoying them in various other episodes, he also acts (no less annoyingly) as a guiding mentor to humans, and especially to Picard in TNG's "Tapestry" and "All Good Things." This final episode finds Q acting at the behest of the Continuum to pronounce an ambiguous death sentence on humanity (actually another trial), but also "cheating" a bit to help Picard see the solution, and then delivering a didactic, supercilious speech chiding humans for their narrowness of vision. As divine revelation goes in the *Trek* world, this is as good as it gets.

SUPERMEN AND FLOWER CHILDREN

One of the reasons we must have God, according to Dostoyevsky, is that humanity is driven by a need to worship something or someone. In the absence of God, how can the exceptional person resist the impulse to deify himself, and how can the masses of ordinary people resist the attraction of such a "superman"?[15] While some may have welcomed Nie-tzsche's idea of a "superman" who transcends the merely human, others have found it every bit as chilling as Dostoyevsky did. Will secular humanism deliver us into the hands of so-called supermen whose abuses of power will leave us longing for the good old days of theocracy? If this outcome is the unavoidable result of humanism, as Dostoyevsky implies, then humanism must fail on its own terms. In its treatment of the superman theme, *Star Trek* seems to anticipate and address this challenge.

A recurrent plot device in *Star Trek* is to portray a humanoid with exceptional powers and to examine how he or she deals with the temptation of self-deification. Notable examples include TOS's "Charlie X" and "The Squire of Gothos," two tales of "children" endowed with powers too great for their level of moral comprehension. TOS's "Where No Man Has Gone Before" is the tale of crewman Gary Mitchell, who acquires superhuman intellectual and physical powers after being zapped by an intruding energy field. As his powers grow, so does his ruthlessness; proclaiming himself a god, he becomes a menace to the ship until his lover, Dr. Elizabeth Dehner, who is also mutating into a superbeing, intervenes on the crew's behalf because she realizes what a fiend Mitchell has become. In the end, these "supermen" are tragic figures, more to be pitied than envied.

Equally pathetic are the arrogant Academicians in TOS's "Plato's Stepchildren," who attribute their psychokinetic powers to eugenic breeding and philosophical training. These powers, together with their life of pure contemplation (and servitude by their slave, Alexander) have caused their sense of compassion to wither away, and they take pleasure in tormenting their captives from the *Enterprise*. In the end, Kirk and McCoy discover that the power actually comes from a natural source, which they synthesize to give themselves temporary powers sufficient to defeat the Platonians. Alexander, however, refuses these powers when they are offered to him on the grounds that he does not wish to become as degraded as the Platonians. Similarly, Commander Riker rejects Q's offer of special powers in TNG's "Hide and Q." The general message of such stories is that superhuman powers are not to be coveted, but neither are they to be feared, since such powers are not only dangerously intoxicating but also, in the end, self-defeating.

The well-behaved android Lieutenant Commander Data has mental and physical abilities far superior to those of humans, but he does not fit the "superman" pattern because of his social conscience, his devotion to his shipmates, his lack of egotism, and, above all, his desire to be human. It is a far different matter, however, with Data's evil twin Lore. Although his powers are no greater than Data's, Lore is a sadistic megalomaniac, a fact that not only makes him extremely dangerous but that also leads to his defeat. After several destructive encounters with Star-fleet, Lore finally overreaches himself by attempting to make Data kill his friends. Data's conscience saves the day, and he dismantles Lore once and for all (TNG's "Datalore," "Brothers," "Descent, Parts I and II").

Trek's ultimate superman tale is that of the genetically engineered Khan Noonien Singh, who was exiled from earth after a nearly successful attempt to rule the planet. Khan and a few of his companions have escaped on a spaceship, where they have remained in suspended animation until revived by the *Enterprise* crew (TOS's "Space Seed"). Once revived, the genetic superfolk try to take over the ship. Ship's historian Marla McGivers has fallen in love with Khan; but when she realizes that Khan intends to kill those who do not side with him, she rescues Kirk, who in turn overcomes Khan. Khan accepts the option of colonizing an uninhabited planet rather than standing trial, and is left on Ceti Alpha V along with McGivers and his other followers. The story resumes in *The Wrath of Khan*, when Khan, sworn to revenge, attempts to destroy the *Enterprise*. The *Enterprise* is saved from destruction when Spock gives up his own life (at least, until the next feature film) to foil Khan's diabolical plan.

Why do *Star Trek*'s supermen always lose? In order to answer this question, we may turn to the Greek concepts of Eros and Philia, both of which are translatable into English as "love." Eros refers not only to sexual desire, but to any narrow, singleminded passion—for example, the thirst for revenge, lust for power, or even the compulsion for achievement. Philia, on the other hand, encompasses the sort of "love" that one has for family, friends, and community, or toward any object of fondness, selfless devotion, compassion, respect, or loyalty. While Philia is relational, Eros is self-centered and tends to induce a sort of tunnel vision—an insensitivity to the broader social and moral implications of one's actions. By privileging their own desires and ignoring all others, *Trek*'s "supermen" become blind to Philia. Lacking the vulnerability of ordinary people and placing himself or herself on a plane above others, the superman has no basis for understanding compassion or sacrifice. This hubris causes Khan to be taken by surprise and foiled on two occasions when McGivers, and later Spock, are moved by friendship and conscience to do things that the superman cannot grasp. Similarly, Lore is confounded when Data's conscience prompts him to place friendship ahead of power, and Mitchell is undone by his lover's unexpected wave of remorse and compassion. In the same way, the Borg Queen in the feature film *First Contact* (discussed in a later chapter) fails to anticipate Data's gesture of sacrificial love that becomes her undoing and humankind's salvation.

Trek's supermen, failing to offset Eros with Philia, are unable to benefit from friendship. Cut off from the human drama, they become bored and lonely. VGR's "Death Wish" depicts Q as a fugitive from the Continuum, owing to his determination to become mortal so that he can kill himself (he is rescued in spite of himself by Philia in the form of Picard, Riker, and others who testify that Q has helped them in important ways). In TOS's "Requiem for Methuselah," a jaded near-immortal being, once incarnated as DaVinci and Brahms, pines for the ordinary pleasures of love and companionship and has chosen to relocate on a planet where his immortality is nullified. The Borg Queen of *First Contact* is intolerably lonely; but in her consuming egotism, she is unable to imagine any effective way of connecting with another. In short, Trek depicts supermen as fatally undone by their isolation, which is the inevitable consequence of their superhuman pretensions, their egotism, their excess of Eros, and their inability to embrace Philia.

The deification of the "superior" individual is one extreme to which people can go in the absence of God, but there is an opposite extreme to which people might also fall victim: the indiscriminate deification of everyone and everything. This possibility leads to another criticism of liberal humanism. An example of this critique can be seen in William Kilpatrick's *Why Johnny Can't Tell Right From Wrong*.[16] Kilpatrick's argument is typical of today's conservative cultural criticism; its central premise is that America has been corrupted by the "Flower Child" ethos of the 1960s counterculture. As the story goes, America has been teaching its young people that everything is beautiful, every culture is worthy of respect, and every person worthy of love—thus rendering us incapable of genuine critical judgment on questions of truth, beauty, or excellence (a predicament that calls for a revival of "traditional" moral authority). We are, according to this critique, suffering from an overdose of indiscriminate Philia.

The Flower Child, or surplus Philia, theme is dealt with in such episodes as TOS's "The Way to Eden," in which twenty-third-century hippies pursue their misguided quest for a planetary paradise, and in the various other "utopia" stories where humans carry the ideals of harmony and community to stultifying excess. TOS's "The City of the Edge of Forever" is a time-travel story in which Kirk falls in love with a peace activist of the period before World War II but has to accept that her gentle ideals are premature and that her death is necessary to prevent pacifism from giving the Nazis a global victory and changing history for the worse.

One of *Star Trek's* best-known episodes, TOS's "The Enemy Within," deals centrally and vividly with the extremes of Eros and Philia. A transporter malfunction causes Kirk to become split into two beings, one "good" (or, more precisely, pure Philia) and one "bad" (pure Eros). The "bad" Kirk is so recklessly uncontrollable that he is soon incarcerated, but the "good" Kirk finds himself unable to function effectively as commander in an impending crisis. Without Eros, the good Kirk is flaccid, lacking in direction or decisiveness. The two Kirks must be fused, but the bad/Eros Kirk is too blinded by his emotions, and by his fear of having his existence terminated, to assent to the merger. It is only the good/Philia Kirk who can see the whole picture, and it is his more inclusive level of understanding that allows the two to be merged without being destroyed by terror and confusion (as was a small doglike pet who underwent the same experience). In the *Trek* cosmos, humanism does not lead to the loss of moral backbone through indiscriminate Philia; rather, *Trek* dramatizes the possibility that Eros can, through disciplined but humane judgment, be turned to the ends of human filiation and human growth.

We have argued that *Star Trek*, in response to the needs of a pluralist American society, undertakes to provide a modern secular humanist counterpart to the sacred/supernatural myths of earlier times. *Trek*'s task is that of showing that humanism is up to the job, that it can rise above the flaws for which both humanism and humanity itself have been criticized. Rather than preaching an explicit doctrine of atheism, *Trek* goes about its humanist project by providing answers to many of the traditional objections against human self-sufficiency, including the claim that without religion humans will lack courage, constraint, or moral decency or that they will succumb to either the seductions of "supermen" or the indiscriminate worship of mediocrity. At the same time, *Trek*'s stories consistently set up implicit semiotic structures of opposition in which godlike beings and religious or quasi-religious institutions end up on the "wrong" side of such antitheses as freedom/bondage, illumination/illusion, responsibility/irresponsibility, growth/stagnation, and so on.

For *Star Trek* to situate itself as a secular humanist mythos is, of course, only a beginning. The challenge of this or any body of myth is to construct a cosmology that gives order and meaning to people's deepest confusions, conundra, and ambivalences. This cosmology must include the place for humanity in the larger cosmos, the boundaries of the self and the fate of the soul, the nature of human difference and its role in forming social relations and institutions, the hope and future of the collective human enterprise, and the role of narratives in weaving these diverse matters into a living tapestry of meaning. These interconnected arenas of mythic inquiry will guide the investigations that follow.

CHAPTER 3

GALAXY'S CHILD

The Human Estate

Placed on this isthmus of a middle state,
A being darkly wise and rudely great:
With too much knowledge for the skeptic side,
With too much weakness for the stoic's pride,
He hangs between; in doubt to act or rest;
In doubt to deem himself a god, or beast;
In doubt his mind or body to prefer;
Born but to die, and reasoning but to err;
Alike in ignorance, his reason such,
Whether he thinks too little or too much;
Chaos of thought and passion, all confused,
Still by himself abused, or disabused;
Created half to rise, and half to fall;
Great lord of all things, yet a prey to all;
Sole judge of truth, in endless error hurled;
The glory, jest, and riddle of the world!

—Alexander Pope
Essay on Man (1734)

On the west pediment of the Temple of Zeus at Olympia is a frieze depicting an event from Greek mythology. A mob of centaurs, having had a bit too much wine at a wedding party, are battling their human hosts and ravishing the female guests. The centaurs' brows are furrowed with lust and rage, while the faces of the human combatants are relatively calm. Above them all stands the god Apollo, poised and serene even as he intervenes to strike an effortless blow against the centaurs.

The whole scene portrays the Greek paradigm of ascent from agonistic emotion to calm reason as one moves from beast to human to god. Since definitions operate by posing contrasts, the delineation of the human must logically entail comparisons with beings that share some of our features but are separated from us in other, definitive ways. Not only in Greek myth but in most traditional mythologies the human estate has been defined by situating it in relation to nonhuman animals, on the one hand, and to supernatural beings, on the other.

The project of defining humanity's essence is central to all myth. This undertaking is more than an exercise in philosophical or linguistic tidiness—from the conception of an essential humanness flows a bounty of ideas about the goals and limitations of our existence, which in turn defines our struggle to realize our humanity. An examination of the human condition must begin with a consideration of what is authentically human and its relation to the nonhuman. *Star Trek* and other works of science fiction are as much concerned with the definition of humanity as are traditional myths, but the terms by which *Trek* frames humanity are, in some respects, unprecedented.

THE MEASURE OF A MAN

In classical Greek thought, humans are separated from animals by virtue of their capacity for reason. As reasoning beings, humans are able in large part to sublimate the emotions that rule animals, and to fail in this discipline is to slip toward the bestial, the less than human. On the other side, humans are separated from the gods in various ways: first and most definitively, by their mortality, and secondarily by their limited powers and their tendency toward brutish emotions. But Greek myth, having set up the dimensions along which these distinctions are charted, also provides for numerous kinds of mediation and interplay that help to reconcile the division of deity-human-animal. These themes are present, for example, in the account of Zeus's coming to the mortal Leda in the form of a swan, which leads to the birth of the extraordinary mortals Castor and Pollux (heroes who later ascended to the sky as the twin stars of Gemini) and Helen of Troy. Thus, the god and the beast not only serve to define the human by contrast, but they in turn allow for a complicated play of mythic imagination in which the dialectic of the human and the nonhuman is richly developed.

Other cultural traditions also use the animal/natural and the divine as oppositional "others" in defining humanity, but in very different ways. Traditional Inuit (Eskimo) myths and tales, for example, also consider the status of humanity in complex relation with, and opposition to, animals and deities. But in the Inuit case the relation is not so much an ascending scale as a relationship of equality, interchangeability, and interdependence. Inuit tales depict social, moral, and spiritual relations, as well as physical transformations, of animal-human-deity that define and mediate the nonhuman realms.[1] In the altogether different cosmos of Judeo-Christian narrative, the relation between God, beast, and human is one that emphasizes distinction and hierarchy rather than the interdependent kinship implied in Native American traditions. Despite the profound differences in the way these terms are related, however, each tradition employs the natural and the divine as reference points by which the position of humanity can be pondered.

Star Trek approaches the task of defining humanity in a manner quite different from that of traditional myth. The mythic role of deity is, if not absent, at least drastically altered in *Trek*. Equally striking in *Trek*'s universe is the relative unimportance of nature, and particularly of animals, which, if present at all, are almost always trivialized—as in the case of the "cute" but mindless and overprolific fuzzballs in TOS's "The Trouble with Tribbles." Part of the reason for the lack of representation of nature in *Trek* may have to do with the urban world in which so many Americans live, and perhaps with our own reduction of animals either to soulless commodities or to pets that become appendages of our own personalities. But another reason has to do with the substitution of other terms of opposition that are more cogent in defining the human in this futuristic, pangalactic context: the alien life-form and the sentient machine. Each of these provides fertile ground for the narrative imagination, and together they serve to situate humanness in startlingly new narrative contexts.

ALIEN-ATION

Consider the typical Hollywood alien: bulging cranium, diminutive face, spindly body; inclined to capture earthlings as specimens or simply take over their planet. Highly intelligent, effete, callous. Brain on a stick. Where could such an image originate? Of course, nobody knows for sure, but it's intriguing to speculate that this is just how humans might appear to, say, a chimpanzee. Is our guilty conscience working overtime, evoking an unspoken fear that some invading creature will be to us what we have been to the "lower" animals?

Whatever the reason for the standard popular-culture image of the alien, it is significant that *Star Trek* makes such little use of it. To be sure, the Talosians in the unsuccessful pilot "The Cage" fit the orthodox alien image quite nicely. The second pilot "Where No Man Has Gone Before" depicted no nonhumans except the *Enterprise*'s own Mr. Spock, but in the following episode, "The Corbomite Maneuver," the crew members confront on their viewscreen a classic alien, bulging head and all, coolly announcing his intent to kill the lot of them. By the end of the story, however, we find that the joke is on us. The cliché alien was faked, and so were its lethal designs. After bluffing their way out of the trap and then magnanimously responding to a distress call from the alien, the *Enterprise* heroes learn that the being, who has a child-Buddha appearance and a hearty laugh, was testing the humans' resourcefulness and compassion because it was lonely and was seeking suitable company. The lesson here is one that sets the tone for decades of alien encounters: abandon your preconceptions, because you just might be surprised.

True to this premise, the hundreds of alien life-forms depicted in *Star Trek* range from beings that differ from ourselves only in cultural details (e.g., the Nazi-like society in TOS's "Patterns of Force"), to those so strange that it requires considerable insight just to recognize them as life-forms (TOS's "The Devil in the Dark" and VGR's "The Cloud"). Of course, there are perfectly understandable commercial and entertainment considerations that help account for the diversity of *Trek*'s aliens: people don't want to see the same thing week after week, and besides, the introductory voiceover of TOS and TNG promises "strange new worlds." But isn't there some pattern in *Trek*'s aliens that might help position them as the "other" in defining ourselves? Yes and no. No, in that it's hard to discern any feature that we can identify as a common trait of *Trek* aliens—not even the presumably inescapable trait of their being "not us." If they do have a common feature, it is that they always *are* us, but only in specific, variable ways. *Trek*'s strategy for employing aliens to define humanity is to hold certain familiar human traits constant while subtly or radically altering other traits, resulting in a sort of "controlled thought experiment" that helps us examine and problematize a particular facet of the human condition. This function of the alien helps explain their diversity as well as some of their particular features. For example, the beings in TNG's "Farpoint" are huge jellyfish shape-shifters who do not in the least resemble us physically, but who have the souls of human lovers, thus placing them on very familiar emotional turf. Odo, the shape-shifting sheriff of DS9 who comes from an unknown race is, in his behavior and values, one of the most conservatively humanlike of all *Trek* characters. The elements of humanness and otherness in *Trek*'s aliens vary according to the requirements of the plot and its mythic explorations, which change from one episode to the next and are part of what keeps us wondering and watching.

Star Trek's shifting textual strategies for representing the "alien" contributes to, and is mirrored in, the baffling inconsistency with which the term *human* is employed. The term "Terrans" for earth people seems clear enough, but then there are the dozens of other "humanoid" species, including Vulcans, Klingons, and others, who may look exactly or nearly like Terrans may be included among "people," "humanity," and so forth, or excluded, depending on the part they play in the logic of the story. The half-Vulcan Spock is chided incessantly for his not being "human"; and Guinan, who looks perfectly Terran, speaks of "humanity" in the second person (TNG's "The Best of Both Worlds, Part II). On the other hand, the defendants standing in Q's courtroom to answer for the crimes of "humanity" (TNG's "Encounter at Farpoint") include the Terran Picard, the android Data, the half-Betazoid Troi, and the transplanted Terran Natasha Yar from the planet Turkana IV; only the Captain is a native earthling. Later, we shall consider how *Trek*'s kaleidoscopic categories are related to America's mythologies of the racial and cultural "other." For the present, however, it is worthwhile to note that *Trek*'s inconsistencies of usage are not random or unconsidered but are strategically related to the narrative contexts in which they appear.

While it is risky to seek a neat pattern in *Star Trek*'s human/alien distinctions, one can discern some rough, indistinctly bounded categories at work. Beings that look just like us, whether they are Terrans or evolutionary look-alikes native to other planets, are used to examine cultural differences—that is, learned traditions not encoded in the genes (e.g., the Quaker-like communal society in TOS's "Return of the Archons"). The next level of differentiation involves "humanoids," such as Vulcans, Klingons, Ferengi, or Betazoids, who resemble Terrans but may possess some iconic physical markers of difference (pointed ears, bumpy foreheads). They are often used to signify innate, genetically programmed attributes. These differences are again controlled thought experiments, insofar as most "human" qualities are held constant while certain others (reason, aggression, greed, empathy) are conspicuously amplified or diminished to a degree that presumably could not result from mere upbringing, thus allowing for these so-called "races" to embody (in the most literal sense) various aspects of the human character, and for human interactions with them to represent a dialogue with these elements of ourselves. The less attractive the character traits incarnated in these humanoid races, the more extreme and bizarre their physical markers. Empathic Betazoids are not really distinguishable at all, but the greedy Ferengi border on the diminutive bighead physiognomy of the stereotypic alien—a premise used for comic effect when Quark and friends encounter 1940s earthlings at Roswell, New Mexico, in DS9's "Little Green Men." The most profoundly "different" aliens, those who do not even remotely resemble us (except through their cunning illusions), invite us to notice traits of thought or feeling that resemble or contrast with our own, and through this device we are led to certain questions, and perhaps certain conclusions, about what is essential or accidental to sentient existence.

The Ferengi, who are portrayed as greedy, lecherous social climbers, provide an example of humanoids whose exotic trimmings are used to signify their genetic otherness and to provide for a study in dramatic character deviations from the human ideal. The contrast between them and humans, who seem to have outgrown such traits by the twenty-fourth century, is a comforting one for the proponents of optimistic liberal humanism. At the same time, it is shown that even the Ferengi seem somehow surreptitiously drawn to the more progressive "human" pattern, as though it were the natural center of gravity for all sentient, or at least all humanoid, life-forms. The more we get to know Quark and his relatives, the more we see in them a suppressed propensity for human moral ideals, such as loyalty and sacrifice, and for American family values—even if they are embarrassed to admit it. This gravitation toward humanity, as we shall see, resonates through the *Star Trek* cosmos.

The most familiar of all alien-human oppositions in *Star Trek* is, of course, the one between the half-Vulcan Spock and the humans who constitute the rest of the TOS *Enterprise* crew. Spock and Kirk are close friends who good-naturedly spar over the merits of emotion versus logic, but it is the ambiguous relationship between Spock and the volatile Doctor McCoy that serves as a highly visible stage for problematizing the relation between humanity and the Vulcan character. Spock's Vulcan upbringing leads him to place cool factuality and "logic" before emotion; in fact, he is usually so successful in suppressing his human side that he often claims, and seems, to be totally logical at the expense of emotion. McCoy finds this deficit exasperating, and often tells Spock so in no uncertain terms. In McCoy's view, Spock is a cold fish, and even when Spock's analysis of the situation seems to make sense in terms of the well-being of the crew, McCoy can't resist getting in some digs at Spock's hyperrationality. The underlying premise concerning Spock, and one that not only McCoy but Kirk and others—including even Spock himself—continually reiterate, is that emotion is a mark of humanness. Spock's extreme attachment to "logic" and his denial of emotion are what set him apart from humanity in terms of the semiotic opposition that the series sets up.

This brings us to an important puzzle, which will become apparent if we think back to the frieze on the Temple of Zeus, where humans are set apart from the brutish centaurs by their more controlled, rational demeanor. In Greek thought as well as the Renaissance "chain of being," humans are set apart from other natural beings by their use of reason. Thus, McCoy's implicit formula—human is to nonhuman as emotion is to logic—is by no means self-evident. After all, what distinguishes Doctor McCoy from a porcupine is not McCoy's ability to feel emotion. Emotion is largely a function of the limbic area of the brain, which evolved in mammals as part of their sociability and their reliance on stable mother-infant bonding. What McCoy has that the porcupine does not are the higher cognitive abilities such as language and reason. These are functions of the cerebral cortex, an evolutionary specialty of the anthropoid primates and especially of human beings. Why, then, does *Star Trek* set up a structured opposition in which reason/logic signifies the not-human?

The key to this puzzle lies in the fact that, as we have suggested, *Star Trek* departs from most previous mythic traditions in downplaying the significance of the animal world. If the animal is not a major signifier in this system, then what replaces it? The answer is one that the Greeks and other traditional mythmakers would not have had occasion to consider: the sentient machine. If we take the machine, rather than the animal, as a primary "other" against which we define ourselves, McCoy's formula begins to make sense. Machine is to human as logic is to feeling. Or more precisely, machine is to human as barren logic is to logic-plus-feeling. The sentient machine—perhaps the most truly innovative mythic element in science fiction—is central to *Trek*'s narrative opposition and mediation of human and nonhuman. When McCoy wishes to dramatize Spock's distance from the human, he invariably compares him to a machine.

THE MACHINE AS MYTHIC OTHER

As Henry Adams noted after seeing the dynamo at the World Exposition of 1900, the machine has taken its place among the significant beings, so to speak, of the world. The machine, he wrote, may even eclipse the deity as our cultural symbol.[2] From Frank Baum's "Oz" stories, written not long after Henry Adams's revelation, to *Blade Runner*, *RoboCop*, *Star Wars*, and *Star Trek*, we frequently see the sentient artificial creature used to construct the "otherness" against which humanity is defined. A new kind of being has entered our cosmos.

Nature and the supernatural are not likely to disappear from human mythmaking in the forseeable future, but the mythic role of the sentient artificial being is here to stay, and it will profoundly change the face of mythology. The machine is not simply a modern stand-in for more archaic mythic figures; it poses new kinds of issues and possibilities. Minotaurs, werewolves, and naughty god-swans are not likely to spill over from the realm of myth into that of daily reality, but the case with the machine is different: as the technology of artificial intelligence and medical prosthesis rapidly advances, life may begin to imitate myth. While the questions raised by the myth of the machine may still be largely hypothetical, some of them could become more immediate issues long before the twenty-third century.

The questions raised by our mythic confrontation with the sentient machine go straight to the heart of our definition of the "human." Is there an essential, unbridgeable gulf between human and machine, and if so, what are the traits that absolutely and forever separate the two? If a human being acquires radical, extensive mechanical prosthetics, or a machine acquires humanlike intelligence, can the line between human and machine still be clearly drawn? Could an artificial mind ever possess feelings, emotions, self-awareness, a will to live, a moral sense—even, perhaps, a soul? Would such a creature be a person, and would it have rights? If the human mind is equivalent to the neural patterns that make up one's awareness and thoughts, and those qualities could be stored as information, does it follow that the mind could reside in a computer— and if so would this composite being retain the identity of the original person? Since the capabilities and longevity of a machine have no pre-defined limits, could the human mind residing in a machine achieve immortality and command godlike powers? If a human were to create a self-aware being, what responsibilities would the human creator have toward it? If a being like TNG's Data or VGR's holographic Doctor were capable of the desire to be recognized as a person, would that desire be morally valid, and should he/she/it be aided or impeded in the pursuit of that goal?

Even if we could be sure that these questions will never confront us on the practical plane, they would still have a mythic importance insofar as they provide a way of probing the implications of a materialist view of the human condition—a view that began with the Renaissance, flow-ered in the Enlightenment of the eighteenth century, and has become a problematic part of common consciousness today. If the human being is really just a type of machine, as La Mettrie boldly proclaimed in the eighteenth century[3] and as Picard suggests in TNG's "Datalore," what is it that distinguishes the human machine from other machines, and how much can they converge? What new moral issues will be raised, and how might they be dealt with mythically?

LORD COMPUTER

A cartoon from the 1950s depicts two scientists in lab coats standing in front of an enormous computer. One of them, reading a printout from the machine, informs the other, "It wants us to sacrifice a goat." It is one thing for a machine like the grist mill to perform physical feats beyond human capability, but quite another when it threatens to surpass humans in the domain of intelligence, where traditionally we were second only to the gods. Where will it all end?

The original *Star Trek* was aired at a time when computers were be-coming established as fixtures of modern corporate and military opera-tions, but before the average person had routine contact with them. In one of TOS's most recurrent themes, a computer becomes godlike, usurps human freedom, and has to be outwitted and destroyed by Captain Kirk. The "false god" motif is evident here, but the machine variant of the false god is as much a cautionary tale about our misplaced faith in machines as it is about misdirected religious worship. Infernal machines rule many of the false utopias depicted in Trek, and they are also the principal villains in other stories including TOS's "The Changeling" (discussed below) and TOS's "That Which Survives" in which a computer dispatches angels of death (alluring female holographic projections) designed to protect a long-deceased humanoid race from strangers' venturing near their home planet. Even the *Enterprise*'s faithful computer is reprogrammed in TOS's "Court Martial" to bear false witness against Kirk in the matter of the faked "murder" of a vindictive shipmate; and although this particular example of computer malice is the result of human intent, it still provides an occasion for Kirk's old-fashioned, cyberphobic lawyer to rail against the computer's assault on human dignity. In "The Ultimate Computer," an experimental computer intended to command the *Enterprise* (and render its human crew obsolete) goes berserk and destroys another ship during war games. In episode after episode, we are treated to the climactic denouement of Captain Kirk's outsmarting a computer by pointing out some logical contradiction, paradox, or maddening bit of illogic, leading the hapless machine to obliterate itself in a smoking, crackling fit.

The infernal computers of TOS stories are abominations, creatures that have become evil either by overreaching their intended servile role and overthrowing their creators or by their creators' abrogation of responsibility. But while these aberrations represent a frequent theme, the correct order of things is always set right, usually through a contest of wits in which the powerful but rigid intelligence of the computer proves no match for Captain Kirk's more subtle, flexible, unpredictable human mind. The computer, like all false gods, has feet of clay. Tyrannical technology is inherently weak because it has overreached its proper domain or because we have overrated it. Subservient technology, on the other hand, is surprisingly perfect. Despite Scotty's protective concern about the *Enterprise*'s limits, she seldom fails the heroes, much less rebels against them. Murphy's Laws do not apply to *Star Trek*'s benign technology. The ship's computer, as represented in most of the episodes and films by the voice of "Trek Mother" Majel Barrett, is a gracious mom who nearly always does what is needed without hesitation or complaint. The "infernal machine" and the "faithful machine" are used to show that humanity will prevail and that the machine will remain subordinate to the human—that is, as long as the humans are of strong character and let the machine know who is boss.

By 1987, when TNG began, our conception of computers had vastly changed. The once-sinister TOS computers, painted boxes festooned with flashing lights, now seem more comical than frightening, while real computers have become familiar household appliances. Sophisticated computers are simply routine tools in the later series. Where the infernal machine theme does appear, the problems often turn out to involve poor judgment on the part of the computer's designers and handlers, rather than any power-grabbing impulse on the part of the computer itself. In TNG's "Arsenal of Freedom," a computerized defense system on a recklessly militarized world has wiped out its inhabitants and threatens to do the same to the *Enterprise*; in TNG's "When the Bough Breaks," a world-controlling computer ruins its planet's atmosphere because the residents of this utopian world are so inclined toward the arts that they neglect to monitor their technology adequately. In DS9's "Civil Defense" and VGR's "Dreadnought," doomsday devices are so cleverly programmed as to outmaneuver and threaten even their own designers. The infernal computer, however, is a comparatively rare theme in the later series, popping up only a few times in more than 400 stories to date. For the most part, the idea of the computer as an integral part of life is simply taken for granted. Everyone in the later series, including the rough-hewn Klingons, can operate a computer keyboard at speeds once reserved for computer geeks. In the 1990s we know that computers can be frustrating, but they are not likely to chase us around the house or have the family burning offerings in front of the monitor. Not that the later series portray no worries about technology—just that they now pose different problems than the threat of power-grabbing computer gods.

THE FRANKENSTEIN SYNDROME

Mary Shelley's 1816 story *Frankenstein*[4] is one of the great myths of modern times, and like all great myths it lends itself to a variety of revisionings and adaptations. In the popular culture version of the story promulgated by Hollywood, Frankenstein is a mad doctor who, blinded by pride, carelessly creates a monster with a heart (or rather, a brain) of pure evil. This American retelling expresses our concern over the usurping of religion by science, a distrust of the educated elite, and above all our anxiety about technocracy—the amoral rule of technology according to which whatever can be done, will be done. Mary Shelley's original story has some of these overtones, but its fundamental mythic exploration addresses somewhat different issues. Shelley's Victor Frankenstein, a bright young student but not a patriarch of science, is so devastated by his mother's death that he submerges his grief in the aspiration to conquer death itself—a seemingly noble ambition but one tainted by his pride in imagining himself the creator of a grateful race, and by his Eros in blindly pursuing his project without thought for its moral consequences. Victor's Eros leads to a lapse of moral imagination, when a sudden sense of revulsion causes him to flee the scene of his Creature's birth. The Creature is not inherently evil but fresh and innocent as a child. Secretly observing a family, he not only learns language but cultivates his sensitive spirit. But he finds himself hated and abused for his inhuman appearance, until in despair he turns to evil. The creature implores Victor to provide him with a mate to ease his unbearable loneliness. Victor at first agrees, but later repents and destroys the half-made bride, leaving the creature bereft of all purpose except revenge.

The core of Shelley's story is not about the hubris of science but the striving of the Creature to become human. Victor and others, in thwarting these aspirations, diminish their own human stature. The Creature, who longs for Philia and who understands and mourns what he has lost, possesses human qualities that his self-righteous, Eros-driven creator lacks.

The story of the android Data, as it unfolds over several years of TNG episodes (particularly in "Datalore," "The Offspring," "Brothers," and "Descent, Parts I and II"), combines a complex development of the Frankenstein theme with a poignant treatment of what Freud and Jung called the "family drama" of emotionally conflicted parent-child and sibling relations. Dr. Noonian Soong, a scientific genius, had created the android Lore as a way of combining two classic avenues to immortality—procreation and scientific achievement. When Lore proved emotionally unstable and dangerous, Soong disassembled him and created Data, who was identical to Lore except that, to be on the safe side, Soong postponed the installation of Data's emotions until he could figure out what went wrong with Lore. But Lore had already doomed the planet by summoning the powerful Crystalline Entity as his ally, and Soong hurriedly escaped leaving the dormant Data behind in the hope that others (Starfleet, as it happens) would discover him. Returning to his ruined home planet years later, Data finds the disassembled Lore and reactivates him only to discover that, while possessing the "human" traits of emotion and humor for which Data has always longed, Lore is cruel and vindictive. Lore invites Data to join him in vanquishing humanity; but Data, loyal to his humanoid companions, beams Lore into space.

When Data and Lore are later reunited with their maker, the embittered Lore demands to know why Soong did not "fix" him rather than dismantle him and create Data. The anguished encounter of the brothers with their "father" rivals Shelley's *Frankenstein* in its ability to treat the creature/creator struggle with depth and complexity. Lore finally deceives Soong into giving him the "emotion chip" intended for Data, but the chip has the effect of worsening Lore's emotional imbalance, causing a rampage in which he mortally wounds Soong before escaping.

Data later encounters Lore as the charismatic leader of the Borg, a collectivity of human-machine hybrids. Lore has created for himself the life purpose that he failed to get from Soong: he has promised to make the Borg into the ultimate superbeings by offering them the humanlike emotions and individual self-awareness that he believes he can provide them, and at the same time, help them become completely mechanical beings. Lore is vindictive toward humanity and other organic life, and he absurdly rationalizes in the name of "improvement" the inept and disastrous experiments that he performs on the Borg. He has in some sense become toward the Borg as irresponsible a "creator" as Soong had been to him. The climax of the series' Lore-Data drama comes when Data heeds his conscience and refuses Lore's command to kill his friends. A struggle ensues, and Lore's last words as Data "deactivates" him are, "I love you, brother." Data takes back his emotion chip but hides it away like a ring of power, fearing that its unpredictable effects might lead away from, rather than toward, humanity. Data's movement toward humanity takes another leap forward in *Generations*, when he "installs" his emotions.

Another revisioning of the Frankenstein myth can be seen in VGR's "Prototype," when B'Elanna Torres uses her engineering skills to save the life of a dying robot rescued from a disabled ship. The grateful robot reveals that the people who originally made him are extinct and that his fellow robots have been unsuccessful in their attempts to construct a replicable "prototype" so that they can reproduce and continue their existence. Torres feels a responsibility toward the being to whom she has given new life, and she is inclined to heed the robot's pleas and create a new prototype. But Captain Janeway refuses permission, pointing out that this is exactly the sort of intervention that is forbidden by Starfleet's Prime Directive. The robots kidnap Torres, cripple *Voyager* with their superior weapons, and vow to kill all the humanoids if their demand for a prototype is not met. After some days of intense labor, during which time the robots are engaged in combat by an enemy robot force, Torres is finally overjoyed to see her prototype rise from the operating table and request programming. At this moment, however, it is revealed that the victory-minded warrior robots had exterminated their humanoid makers for attempting to make peace with one another. She now realizes that her prototype, although still innocent, will inevitably be programmed with the same directives as the others, allowing them to multiply into an even more diabolical force. In a scene echoing Shelley's *Frankenstein*, Torres destroys her creation on the operating table as the other "monster" looks on in dismay (of course, her shipmates have arranged a timely escape). This version of the Frankenstein tale embraces Victor's view that the creature's pleas are not to be taken at face value and that the responsible course of action is to destroy its "companion." The fault, however, is not Torres' or even the robots' but that of the creators who evidently endowed their creatures with a contempt for human compassion.

The "Frankenstein" issue of the creator's responsibility toward a sentient "creature" is also raised when *Trek*'s humans create virtual-reality holographic projections that somehow become aware of their own existence. In TNG's "The Big Good-Bye," Picard plays out a detective-story fantasy during which his holographic associates show signs of self-awareness. When Picard is confronted by his holographic friend's inquiry as to whether the friend will continue to exist after the program is over, and whether the friend's "wife and kids" will be waiting for him as he remembers them, Picard answers simply, "I have no idea," and then leaves. But when Dr. Moriarty comes to life from a Sherlock Holmes program ("Elementary, Dear Data") and threatens to take over the *Enterprise*, Picard is obliged to take him more seriously.[5] A more enduring hologram dilemma is posed by *Voyager*'s holographic Doctor, who is as integral to *Voyager*'s crew as Spock or Data were to the *Enterprise*. The engagingly irascible Doctor, who was activated rather than created by the present *Voyager* crew, is increasingly self-aware and is taken seriously as a person and a crew member. The crew are actively devoted to fostering the Doctor's "human" development. Somewhat ironically, the Doctor, like Data and Spock, can be seen in some ways as more human than the others, a point to which we shall return directly.

CYBORG MOTION

The Frankenstein myth, by delving into the moral relationship that humans would have with sentient beings of their own making, raises the question of what it takes to be human. This question can be raised from quite the opposite direction, however, by positing scenarios in which the human acquires varying degrees of artificiality, the most extreme of which would be the complete artificial replication or replacement of a human individual.

Where does humanity end and the machine begin? We now modify our bodies with contact lenses, cardiac pacemakers, and mechanical limbs. It does not seem far-fetched that TNG's Chief Engineer Geordi LaForge might have a visor device to compensate for being blind or that Picard could have an artificial heart to replace the one pierced during a youthful altercation. While the human-becoming-machine is logically the converse of the machine-that-usurps-human-control, the two themes can lead to a convergent outcome: a humanlike intelligence joined with a machine body whose power has no absolute or predefined boundaries. A machine, unlike a natural organism, does not have an inherent nature and can therefore become anything that technological prowess permits— even a superpowerful and potentially immortal being. It is not hard to see that this possibility, even if it exists only in the realm of narrative, opens new vistas for the mythic imagination.

The theme of humanoids becoming machines is seldom seen in TOS, although Dr. Korby in "What Are Little Girls Made Of?" does create an android body for himself in order to prolong his life, a mistake that he eventually rectifies by destroying himself and his android lover. The decades following the 1960s, however, have seen rapid advances in computerization, miniaturization, artificial intelligence, and other technologies relevant to the convergence of animate life with the machine. Furthermore, the experience of being functionally joined with a computer during one's working day, and with computer games or virtual reality devices for recreation, has accustomed us to the idea of an integration of human and machine. In view of these changes in our lived experience, it should not be surprising that the human-into-machine transformation theme becomes so significant in the later *Star Trek* series.

So far, *Star Trek*'s most dramatic example of the human-into-machine merger is seen in the Borg. The term *Borg* was derived by *Trek* writers from the neologism *cyborg*, which in turn is a shortened form of *cybernetic organism*, a biological organism enhanced by computerized robotic elements. As with the ancient mythic monsters that combined animal and human, there is something ineffably eerie about cyborgs—even "good" ones—that may betray a deep-seated human discomfort about crossover beings that are "neither fish nor fowl," as well as our more culturally specific worry that the machine will someday invade our bodies as it has already invaded our lives and that we will thereby lose whatever it is that makes us human.

The Borg are well conceived to raise all these fears. They began as humanoids, native to the Delta Quadrant of our galaxy, who somehow (the back story is not clear) became merged not only with machines but also with one another. The Borg have an antlike communal society in which individuality has no meaning and each "unit" refers to itself in the plural "we." Although the machine-enhanced Borg units do have superhuman strength, their greatest source of power lies in their ability to act as a decentralized collectivity, able to function in concert even when seriously damaged and thus to adapt and regenerate with lightning speed and "assimilate" any humanoid species they encounter. The machine-human Borg hybrid not only raises questions about the implications of human development in relation to the machine but also the relationship of the individual to the collectivity. These latent questions are brought out when Lore offers to "improve" the Borg by making them completely mechanical, and by Starfleet's and Lore's very different experiments in introducing individual consciousness to the Borg (TNG's "I, Borg" and "Descent, Parts I and II").

To return to the question, "Where do we draw the line between machine and human?" We don't. In the *Star Trek* cosmos dividing lines are irrelevant, for the definitive difference lies not in placement but in movement. Data is just as mechanical as Lore and more so than the cyborg; yet there is something deeply human about Data. Lore and the Borg are contemptuous of humanity, and their quest is oriented away from humans and humanness. Data aspires to become human; and this desire, we shall argue, lies at the heart of what defines humanity in the *Star Trek* cosmos.

An illustration of this point can be seen in a comparison between two similar *Star Trek* stories. In TOS's "The Changeling," a science probe from earth has merged with an alien machine, demonically pursuing a confused directive to destroy all "imperfect" (i.e., organic) life-forms. Nomad mistakes Kirk for its creator, Jackson Roykirk; and Kirk uses the machine's mistaken faith to force it to destroy itself, as he customarily does with almost any artificial mind that comes close to attaining an independent existence. For Kirk, as for the peasant mob of the Frankenstein films, the problem is how to undo the abominable "mistake" rather than how to fulfill one's humane responsibility toward the sentient being that one has created. *The Motion Picture* begins with a similar premise, in which the Terran space probe *Voyager* has, thanks to its "repair" by other machines, grown to menacing size and intelligence. As Spock discovers by mind-melding with the so-called V'ger entity, the being has attained consciousness and existential angst. It yearns for unity with its creator and for a higher understanding of its purpose. Spock weeps for V'ger as a brother, recognizing in it the sterility of his own attempt to shed his human side, and the resulting pain of emptiness. This time, instead of killing the being, Kirk allows the Starfleet officer Willard Decker to merge with it (and incidentally, with Decker's previously unattainable ex-lover Ilia, whom the machine has already absorbed). V'ger gets its wish for spiritual union, purpose, and growth—with sex thrown into the bargain. Now possessing the human qualities of imagination and emotion to go with its supermind, it departs to roam the universe as a manifestation of what Spock calls "the next stage in our evolution," the merger of human and machine.

Although Nomad and V'ger have similar histories and both seek their creators, their orientation to humanity is entirely different. Nomad has come to view humans as inferior and is committed to stamping them out, while V'ger has so enlarged its perceptions that it has taken on some characteristically human aspirations—aspirations that are further strengthened by its encounter with the *Enterprise*. The fact that V'ger has no announced program of humanization is beside the point. As we shall see in the case of Spock, the authenticity of the human quest does not depend on the loudness with which it is proclaimed.

QUEST FOR HUMANITY

When TNG's First Officer William Riker meets the android Lieutenant Commander Data for the first time, Riker finds Data in a secluded forest on the holodeck, where he is teaching himself to whistle. Although Data is endowed with superhuman intelligence and strength, he confesses that he would give it all up to become human. Riker beams, "Nice to meet you, Pinocchio—you're going to make an interesting companion." Of course, Riker might just have easily called Data "Tin Man" and taunted him by whistling "If I only had a heart . . . ," as does Dr. Ira Graves (Soong's mentor, hence Data's "grandfather") in "The Schizoid Man." The Pinocchio story centrally concerns the nonhuman being's quest to become fully human, regardless of its primal essence or its creator's intentions.

Perhaps it is a quest with which every person can identify, insofar as we each strive to fulfill social expectations that, at times, seem to come easily to everyone but ourselves. There is plenty of comedy in Data's efforts to master the things that come naturally for humans, such as whistling or sneezing. He is intensely curious about the human qualities that remain elusive for him, such as the subjective perception of time (he conducts experiments to see whether a watched pot boils). In "The Outrageous Okona," Data becomes a stand-up comedian in order to understand humor. In various other episodes, he works earnestly at dancing, making banal small talk at social gatherings, painting, playing the violin, performing Shakespeare, and writing poetry—all of which he does with perfect technical proficiency, but just the sort of off-the-mark literalism that one might expect from a brilliant robot. In these scenes, *Star Trek* makes use of a familiar device of film and television, where a human or quasi-human is somehow unevenly enculturated, grasping some points of expected social behavior or cultural understandings suitable to a given framework while missing others completely. These quirky, inadvertent departures from cultural protocol have a way of breaking down our familiar frames of reference and providing the sort of unexpected dislocations that make for good jokes.

The spectacle of a person struggling with the behaviors that we ordinarily take for granted is an effective storytelling device that can place ordinary ways of acting and thinking into new frames of reference. In traditional folklore, this function is carried out by the trickster, who is unevenly aware of, or unevenly concerned about, culturally appropriate behavior. Here again, these traditional tales provide both for humor and for a new "take" on human customs. The "incompletely human" figure is reminiscent of childhood innocence, thus providing a figure with which children and ex-children can identify and triggering the amusement with which adults react to children's exploratory wonder.

Data's quest for humanness is not simply comical. In "The Measure of a Man," officious Starfleet authorities want to dissect and study Data, assuming that this vivisection is appropriate since he is a thing rather than a person. Picard successfully defends Data by drawing attention to his tender sentiments, cherished memories of departed friends, and other human qualities. A darker side of Data's gravitation toward humanity is revealed in the film *First Contact*, when Data is almost tempted to betray Picard and the *Enterprise*—all because the Borg Queen has offered him the gift of flesh and human sensation.

In "The Offspring," Data creates a "child," an android with all his own capabilities and more, since he gives it a more humanlike skin tone, smoother body movement, and the like (portraying the common parental desire to satisfy through one's children the aspirations that remain unfulfilled in oneself). When Picard reprimands him for undertaking such a momentous project without authorization, Data politely notes that he has not noticed other crew members consulting Picard about their procreative plans. The child, Lal, is given more choice than most beings, living or mechanical, since she is able to select her gender and appearance. Lal's learning process, under Data's tender paternal guidance, again exploits the comic and poignant potentials of the incompletely enculturated, exploratory mind. Once again, stiff-necked Starfleet functionaries show up—this time to confiscate Lal and remove her for scientific observation. Data struggles to keep her, and the resulting emotional upheaval sends the fragile Lal into an irreversible process of deterioration, leading to her death and a loss that Data unconvincingly claims he cannot grieve.

In "The Most Toys," a collector of one-of-a-kind rarities steals Data for his collection. So great is Data's resistance to this objectification—not to mention the collector's ruthless ways (including the murder of an innocent person)—that he does something that takes his captor, who sees Data as rigidly bound by his programming, entirely by surprise: he attempts to kill the villain rather than allow him to continue his reign of terror—a decision based on compassion, outrage, and a sense of dignity.

Data's tenderness, passion, and curiosity, together with his longing for humanity, raise a question: Is it possible that, in certain respects, Data is actually more human than some who are born to that status? This is the question explicitly raised by Picard in the closing lines of TNG's "Datalore," when he asks Riker, "Have you ever considered whether Data is more human or less human than we need?" Riker responds, "I only wish we were all as well balanced, Sir." Many fans find Data to be one of *Star Trek*'s most appealing characters—Why? Perhaps it is that, despite his humility about falling short of the human, his human qualities are so very evident. Data's extraordinary humanness is given immediacy by his everyday mannerisms and quirks: his expressive face, his wide-eyed wonder and puzzlement, and above all his gentleness and his sense of decency, loyalty, patience, and friendship. If these traits somehow escape the definition of "emotion," they nevertheless are high on the list of qualities that most of us would seek in a human companion. In the end, it is Data's earnest and humble quest for humanity that makes him seem so very human. Indeed, Data helps clarify the definition of humanity in the *Star Trek* mythos.

Just as TNG did not try to recreate the Spock character, VGR did better than to give us another Data. The Doctor aboard *Voyager* is a holographic projection who has no strictly corporeal existence and was designed only to perform a limited, temporary function. The Doctor does not so much want to be human as to be taken seriously as an individual and a physician. He develops a close friendship with the young Ocampa Kes, his apprentice and assistant, who encourages him to choose a name. Supercilious with his patients, sensitive to social slights, and pessimistic about his ability to transcend the limits of his programming, the Doctor comes across as mildly neurotic. It might seem odd for a holographic projection to have a poor self-image, but Kes recognizes the Doctor's problems and helps foster the Doctor's growth beyond his original programming. Besides his paternal relationship with Kes, the Doctor has a platonic love affair with a fantasy-world Viking woman and another with a Vidiian patient. In "Tattoo," the Doctor decides to take Kes's suggestion and program himself with flulike symptoms in order to gain empathy for his ill patients (or more likely, to prove that they complain more than necessary), but when Kes makes the experiment more "real" by secretly postponing his programmed recovery time, the Doctor is suddenly plunged into a genuine fit of whining self-pity. In "Real Life," the Doctor explores human experience by giving himself a holographic family life.

On the other extreme are two prominent aliens who resent any suggestion of humanness. TOS's Mr. Spock is, to his embarrassment, half human; yet he is predominantly Vulcan in his anatomy, physiology, culture, and chosen identity. Kirk and McCoy can always get a rise out of Spock by suggesting that he might have human tendencies. DS9's shape-shifting alien Odo is introduced as the only known example of his kind, and he resents the fact that he must assume the form of a "solid" humanoid in order to fit in. When he finally does come to meet his own people, however, he repudiates them by siding with his DS9 humanoid comrades. Yet, when Odo is temporarily forced to assume solid form as a punishment for offenses against his people, he becomes despondent at the loss of his most distinctive characteristic.

Spock and Odo are natural beings who have preexistent types to which they can refer. Data and the Doctor, on the other hand, are imitation humans: they are made to look like and function as humans, even though their capabilities in various spheres may be greater or lesser. Like Pinocchio, or the Tin Man and Scarecrow of Oz, Data and the Doctor are variant images of the human that do not belong to any other natural grouping. If they have an essence, it must be either as humans or as unique beings, and they seem to choose a bit of both (as, one might say, we all do).

But if Data and the holographic Doctor are in some respects the opposites of Spock and Odo, why do all four seem so similar? Although
their dramatic importance and their depth as characters varies greatly,
these four aliens occupy a similar place in the logic of the human/alien
formula. Spock, Data, Odo, and the Doctor are each involved in a quest
to find themselves. Each is a one-of-a-kind being, explicitly defined as
not human and ambiguously related, at best, to any group or "kind."
Their essence is undecided. They are seekers. They define integrity where
paths are not already drawn. It does not matter whether they are human
by ancestral essence, or even whether they recognize themselves as
having humanizing aspirations. Once we perceive the parallel element
of these characters, we are closer to answering the question of how the
Star Trek mythos defines humanity.

Set in a forward-looking future, *Star Trek* defines humanity not by
static primordial essences but by a dynamic quest for self-transcendence.
It is the act of seeking and questioning, the assertion of freedom, the free
expression of compassion and sacrificial love, and the refusal to be
bound by biology or chauvinism or custom or worship or fear or hate
or compulsion, that defines the *human* in the most idealistic, Rodden-
berrian, sense of the term. In the *Trek* mythos, the ultimate and definitive
trait of humanity is its impulse to learn, to discover, and to grow in
understanding. Humanity in this view is not a condition or a category,
but a process. Unlike such imperialists as the Borg, humanity is committed to a respect for, and curiosity about, the diversity of life.

It is only by imbuing humanity with a quest for self-transcendence
that the cosmology of *Star Trek* is able to acknowledge what a "soft,"
and in some sense insignificant, thing humanity is, and to still make it
a hub for the universe. This is, of course, a luminous view of humanity—
one so idealized that even the *Trek* narratives themselves will often fall
short of it. Nevertheless, this view is the implicit core of all that defines
and valorizes humanity in the *Trek* cosmos. And this is why, whether
the characters themselves recognize it or not, the viewer understands
Spock, Data, the Doctor, and even Odo to be far more human than they
know.

CHAPTER 4

DEMONS AND DOPPELGANGERS

The Inexorable Self

Delight is to him—a far, far upward and inward delight—who against the proud gods and commodores of this earth, ever stands forth his own inexorable self.

—Herman Melville
Moby Dick (1851)

Legend has it that the nineteenth-century American philosopher Josiah Royce was approached after a lecture by a student who asked him, "Sir, do I actually exist?" Royce, according to the story, responded with a query, "Who wants to know?" The account does not say whether the student considered this a trick question, but anyone who has watched enough *Star Trek* can easily imagine situations in which Royce's question would be very hard to answer. The age-old "Who Am I?" question has been pondered by poets, scientists, philosophers, and theologians, each providing different but inconclusive perspectives. Myth, too, has its ways of probing these questions. There is probably no body of myth, science fiction included, that does not in some way try to delve into the mysteries of the self.

THE PROBLEM OF THE SELF

The human conception of self is not fixed, but rather something that develops over one's lifetime and is culturally variable. This makes the idea of self a matter for inquiry and reflection—and so it has been, from before the rise of Greek philosophy to the age of modern psychology.

While some non-Western cultures view the self as a node of social relations and responsibilities, modern Western culture inclines toward a
view of the self as a closed unit pursuing its private interests through a
cost-benefit calculus. Commentators on American culture, in particular,
have noted the great importance that we place upon the autonomy, integrity, and independent interests of the individual.[1] To be one's inexorable self is to stand calm and assured before the universe.

A comprehensive mythos is one that is able to constitute and situate
the self in the larger cosmological setting. In so doing, myth must confront certain recurrent questions that stem from the self's awareness:
Who am I? What makes me myself and not someone else? Where are
my boundaries? Can my boundaries become violated, and could I be
invaded by something that is not-I? Why do I sometimes feel divided
within? Am I my memories, and if so what does it mean to forget? Could
some of my self slip away, and if so, could it be regained? What does
the continuity and integrity of the self entail? Is my separate self-identity
something that can or should be transcended? Am I more or less than
my body? What happens to the self when I die? To the extent that the
secular American worldview now contests the answers provided by traditional theology and folk religion, such a situation creates an inchoate
domain that needs to be reordered by other narrative projects.

There is an element of playfulness in *Star Trek* that so challenges our
traditional conceptions of the self that one might think its sole purpose
were to create instability. In TOS's "The Enemy Within," for example,
Captain Kirk is split into two separate persons, each bearing a different
part of Kirk's previous personality. In TNG's "Second Chances," another
transporter malfunction splits Will Riker into two separate but identical,
and equally authentic, copies of the original person, who for seven years
lead separate lives unaware of one another's existence and then meet to
discover that they have developed into two distinct persons with contrasting personalities. In VGR's "Tuvix," yet another transporter malfunction joins Tuvok and Neelix, polar opposites of personality, into a
single person. The young Trill woman Jadziah Dax, who like all joined
Trills consists of a humanoid "host" temporarily joined with a long-lived
sluglike "symbiont" in her torso, can say in response to Dr. Bashir's
advances, "I was a young man once myself"; she also can stand accused
of crimes committed by hosts of previous joinings (DS9's "Equilibrium").
Kira Nerys finds herself in DS9's "Second Skin" among Cardassians who
claim that she is really a Cardassian spy surgically altered to resemble a
Bajoran and that the implanted memories of her life as a Bajoran freedom
fighter are simply part of the "disguise" she had willingly adopted for
the mission. Thus, *Trek* uses its science fiction frame to create thought
experiments that problematize the question, "Who am I?"

It is not, however, the aim of *Star Trek*'s mythos simply to raise unanswerable questions that undercut the possibility of a coherent grasp of experience. As we have suggested before, myth gives people a meta-phorical language with which to contemplate deep questions, it imparts some sense of illumination, and it often suggests possibilities for medi-ating or transcending the conundra to which attention is being drawn. With regard to the self, *Trek*'s mythos offers narrative devices that help to maintain the concept of a distinct "core" self whose boundaries re-main coherent in the face of momentary disruptions, baffling compul-sions, apparent penetration by outside influences, internal division, and even death. The devices that Trek uses to maintain a stable definition of self are, as we have suggested in other connections, narrative and se-miotic rather than doctrinal. In order to shed some light on these nar-rative devices as they function in Trek, we shall consider a variety of phenomena that address threats to the integrity of the core self but which, in the end, reinforce the idea of a coherently definable self.

SPELLS AND ENCHANTMENTS

It is sometimes startling to see what ancient ideas can appear in fu-turistic guises. Despite the prestige attached in our society to naturalistic explanation and rational thought, modern popular fantasies are often replete with concepts rooted in ancient folk religions. Ideas such as de-monic possession, soul loss, enchantment, spirit visitations, doppelgang-ers, shape-shifters, and similar motifs play a role not only in today's urban legends,[2] but also in much of science fiction, including *Star Trek*.

According to the traditional lore of Euro-American (and many other) cultures, there are various ways that people can come under the mental sway of a powerful altering force. For convenience's sake, we can divide these influences into two categories: (1) spirit possession and related phe-nomena that involve the intrusion or loss of a demon, spirit, mind, or soul; and (2) influences from some outside force not involving the transmigration of spirits and souls. The folkloric term *spell* is a handy label for this second category of events, which includes madness spells, forgetfulness spells, love spells, obedience spells, and perhaps others as well. Enchantment, which originally referred to a "chant" (a magical song or incantation), applies to those instances where a spell is deliber-ately brought about by some person or being.

The madness spell, a staple theme of myths and folktales, is one in which people are driven to insane, self-destructive or out-of-character behavior by some being with special powers of enchantment, or by some other unseen agency, force, or mysterious substance. In TOS's "The Na-ked Time" and TNG's "The Naked Now," for example, an unknown ailment threatens the lives of the crew members by inducing a state of intoxication. In TOS's "And The Children Shall Lead," a being called

Gorgon enchants the adults of the Triacus colony, driving them to madness and suicide, and deludes the children into believing that he is a friendly angel. In TOS's "Is There in Truth No Beauty?" Kolos the Medusan induces delirium and death in anyone who gazes upon him. In TOS's "The Day of the Dove," an energy being that feeds on aggressive feelings causes Klingons and the *Enterprise* crew members to fight with one another until they discover that they are being exploited and join in a session of backslapping joviality that the being finds distasteful. In TNG's "Night Terrors," crew members start going mad from nightmares that are finally revealed to be an alien ship's attempt to communicate with them about a danger to both ships.[3]

A related motif, the forgetfulness spell, involves at least a partial loss of the memories that define the self. In TOS's "The Paradise Syndrome," a strange ray causes Kirk to lose his memory for a period of several months; Data is similarly afflicted in "Thine Own Self." In TNG's "Clues," the *Enterprise* crew is robbed of twenty-four hours of memories by xenophobic aliens who insist that no one can leave their neighborhood with memories of them. In TNG's "Conundrum," aliens induce amnesia in the crew members and then use falsified computer records and an imposter among the crew to mislead them about their mission, until a last-minute hunch tells Picard that the *Enterprise* could not legitimately be assigned to the massacre that the usurpers have planned. We also encounter an inversion of the memory loss theme, in which a person's sense of self is altered by implanted memories. In TNG's "The Inner Light," Picard gains the memories of thirty years in half an hour as part of a dying alien race's attempt to keep memories of itself alive. In DS9's "Hard Time," O'Brien is forced to live with the implanted memories of twenty years' brutal imprisonment and of having murdered his closest friend in prison. In yet another twist of the memory alteration theme, Riker is tricked into believing that he has lost sixteen years of his memories (TNG's "Future Imperfect").

Obedience spells are especially common in *The Original Series*, where the theme of guarding one's individual autonomy is particularly important. In "Plato's Stepchildren," the cruel Academicians use their psychokinetic powers to force the *Enterprise* crew members, in puppet fashion, to carry out humiliating actions for the Academicians' amusement. The utopias depicted in "The Apple" and "Return of the Archons" (TOS) rely on spells of obedience cast by ruler-machines. In *The Final Frontier*, the cult leader Sybok induces an enchantment of blind allegiance through a pseudotherapy that "takes away the pain" of his followers. Spells of obedience are not a common theme in the later series; and when they do appear, their significance is somewhat different. In TNG's "Brothers," for example, Data also falls under a sudden compulsion to commandeer the *Enterprise*, but the resulting reunion with his "father" is a welcome one.

Perhaps it is a testimony to the vagaries of romantic attraction that the idea of love spells is widespread in Western and non-Western folklore and that *Star Trek* also makes considerable use of this theme. In TOS's "Dagger of the Mind," an evil scientist uses a "neural neutralizer" to make Kirk fall in love with his shipmate Dr. Helen Noel. Kirk is smitten again when the touch of a tear from "Elaan of Troyius" causes him to fall madly in love with her, and again under the influence of a sorceress in "A Private Little War." In TOS's "Mudd's Women," the beauties who accompany the roguish Harry Mudd onto the *Enterprise* cause everyone to fall under their romantic spell; and Kamala, the Empathic Metamorph of TNG's "The Perfect Mate," has a similar effect on the crew of the *Enterprise D*—particularly on Picard, with whom she chooses to "bond." In DS9's "Fascination," Lwaxana's Troi's Betazoid equivalent of menopause, together with a mysterious illness, casts an erotic spell over the DS9 crew. In "Man of the People," Deanna Troi becomes afflicted with the "negative" emotions of another, causing her libido to rage out of control. Even holodeck women in TNG's "11001001" and VGR's "Alter Ego" have the ability to put men under a spell of infatuation.

There may be several factors that could help account for the appearance in science fiction of such close analogs of the traditional magical spells and incantations of myths and folktales. These motifs are, of course, colorful and dramatic storytelling devices; and, furthermore, the recycling of familiar themes from traditional lore, myth, and fairy tales may have an appeal in its own right. To say that much, however, begs the question of why humans should ever have found such story elements appealing in the first place. Any attempt to deal with such questions must necessarily be speculative, and the fullest explanations might be those tailored to specific cultures and the content of specific story motifs. One might note, however, that the idea of "spells" gives a more distinct identity and recognition to the often unexpected and unexplained fluctuations of the self that most people experience at one time or another. People often feel their emotions and motives pulling them in directions that their reflective minds find distasteful or inexplicable. By defining and labeling these disruptions of the self as discrete things and attributing them to some external agency, the narratives set these disruptions apart semiotically, in opposition to an implicit integral self, thus accounting for the disruptions while heading off the potentially disturbing possibility that the self may have no stable core. Whatever the scientific validity of this way of understanding psychological discontinuities and disruptive inner states, it is not hard to see why people in a variety of historical and cultural settings might find the idea of spells poetically appealing.

SPIRIT POSSESSION, SOUL LOSS, AND GHOST LOVERS

A similar range of explanations may apply to the frequently occurring *Star Trek* stories that parallel the traditional motifs of demon possession and exorcism. In TOS's "The Lights of Zetar," mental energy beings, the last inhabitants of the planet Zetar, possess a passenger on the *Enterprise* and must be exorcised. In "Return to Tomorrow," three alien beings "borrow" the bodies of Kirk, Spock, and Doctor Ann Mulhall while they make android bodies. In "A Wolf in the Fold," a murderous demonic being named Redjac, who once took the form of Jack the Ripper, is cornered on the *Enterprise* and transmigrates from one human body to another in a futile attempt to escape justice. Spock's ability to mind-meld with another—and thus have that person's or being's memories exist in him—might be seen as a voluntary form of possession. The mind meld occurs in reverse when the doomed Spock places his mind in the body of the unsuspecting McCoy in *The Wrath of Khan*.

The theme of possession continues in the later series as well. In TNG's "Lonely Among Us," a life-force inhabits the *Enterprise* and causes malfunctions, madness, and a murder when it possesses the spaceship and some of its crew members. In TNG's "Power Play," Troi, Data, and O'Brien are possessed by alien entities from a prison colony. Riker in "Shades of Gray" is invaded by a microbe that takes over his nervous system and brain and that must be exorcised by inducing primitive negative emotions. Deanna Troi is possessed by an alien in "Clues"; and in "Man of the People" she is forced to become a host for the negative emotions of the alien diplomat Alkar. Only a timely exorcism is able to save her life. In VGR's "Cathexis," Tuvok is taken over by an alien mind. The Trill of TNG and DS9 make possession a way of life by seeking to join with a "symbiont" whose personality and memories are blended with those of the host.

The theme of soul theft or soul loss is prominent in mythology cross-culturally. In shamanistic religions it is often believed that a person's soul can wander away or be stolen, resulting in immediate illness and eventual death, and this belief is often accompanied by the notion that a person has several kinds of souls, some of which can temporarily depart the body. Such a condition is, of course, always gravely dangerous. Indirect analogs of the soul loss motif can be seen in *Trek* stories. In TOS's "Spock's Brain," the Vulcan's brain is stolen for use by aliens, and his companions must embark, shamanlike, on a quest to retrieve it. The memory loss theme, discussed above, can also be seen as a variant of soul loss. The same can be said of TNG's "The Loss," when Deanna Troi temporarily loses her empathic abilities.

Ghostly visitations occur both in folklore and in *Star Trek*. Indeed, all the episodes that depict one person's mind or spirit as transmigrating into another's body could be seen as versions of the ghost motif. The more classic "ghost," however, is the disembodied, incorporeal apparition of a person. This motif is hinted at when Captain Kirk is caught between two "fabrics of space" and appears to the crew members as a ghostly visage in TOS's "Tholian Web." When Chakotay's spirit wanders outside his body in VGR's "Cathexis," or Janeway's spirit hovers on the brink of the afterlife during her near-death experience (VGR's "Coda"), the connection with classic ghost beliefs is still more explicit.

The ghost lover motif of folk stories and ballads is of particular interest here, since it combines elements of the ghostly visitation with the love spell. In such tales, a person is visited, sometimes in a dream, by the spirit of a deceased lover or by some demon spirit that intrudes emotionally and perhaps sexually. In VGR's "Remember," an eerie suspense story hinges on Torres's nocturnal visitations by a strange lover who appears in later dreams as a walking corpse. The visitations turn out to be the result of implanted memories from one of the *Voyager* passengers whose intent was to pass along her own damning knowledge of a planet's holocaust and of the young lover whom she had once betrayed. In TNG's "The Child," Deanna Troi is impregnated by an incorporeal being, and in TNG's "Violations," she is subjected to "mental" rape by means of a telepathic sexual intrusion. Perhaps the most explicit ghost lover story, however, is TNG's "Sub Rosa," in which Beverly Crusher inherits not only her deceased grandmother's archaic Scottish-style house but also the mysterious demon lover that had been a companion to several generations of women in her family. Only after following this gothic motif through most of the episode does the story finally (and somewhat predictably) reveal the "ghost" to be an extraordinary sort of natural being who is sustained by these women in exchange for their long and blissful life of "love" for him.

Why does *Star Trek* use themes so clearly reminiscent of ghosts, demons, and migratory spirits, only to deconstruct them in the end with natural explanations? Several possible answers present themselves. First, these traditional motifs are so well established in our culture that their storytelling power is already entrenched, and when reframed in the *Trek* context they allow us to have our ghost stories and demon possession and still maintain a nominally naturalistic worldview. Another reason for their popularity, however, may have to do with the possibility, as discussed in connection with spells, that these elements allow us to situate disruptive psychological influences, disturbances, and discontinuities as discrete entities and namable forces brought about by definable external causes. These forces are semiotically opposed to the "normal" or authentic self, thus reinforcing the sometimes precarious but generally reassuring conception of an integral core "self" distinct from all such disruptions. In the case of soul loss, the semiotic relationship is between the whole person and a definable component that must be retrieved; here again, the final effect is to give us a symbolic language for describing psychic disturbances while reinstating the essential stability of a core self.

THE DOPPELGANGER EFFECT

Robert Rogers, in his study of the "double" in literature, points out that the concept of the double is often so broadly defined that, as with Christ figures and Devil archetypes, one can find them almost everywhere.[4] The term *double*, or its German equivalent *doppelganger*, is often used in reference to any sort of figure in literature who serves as the alter ego for another character, selectively mirroring certain fragments of his or her personality. Folklore often presents versions of the double theme in the form of shadow characters and evil twins, and some psychologists even see the doubling motif in myths or tales that split the father- or mother-figure into positive (protector) and negative (ogre) characters.[5] The term *doppelganger* itself comes from a German folk belief according to which every person has a spirit double who walks the path of life in parallel with him or her, but which is glimpsed only as the hour of death draws near.

According to Jung, the double, or shadow, is the strongest of all the archetypes harbored in the individual unconscious.[6] This double is an evil version of the self, the repository of all the personal traits that one ordinarily refuses to confront and may actively deny, but which remain incorrigibly present in the recesses of the personality. For Jung the recognition of, and eventual reconciliation with, the shadow self is one of the most difficult and important steps in the process of therapy and of personal maturation. The idea of reconciliation with the shadow self is actually mentioned in one episode of TNG when Counselor Troi advises Commander Riker to follow Jung's advice and "own" his shadow—that is, to seek out the "other," apparently insane, Riker who keeps appearing to him in his troubled dreams ("Frame of Mind"). Psychologists Louis Woods and Gary Harmon consider Jung's concept of unification with the shadow self (*coincidentia oppositorum*) as they see it expressed in two *Star Trek* episodes, TOS's "The Enemy Within" and "The Alternative Factor." The first of these episodes, discussed earlier, portrays Captain Kirk as split by a transporter accident into two look-alike character opposites, one "good" but indecisive and the other "bad" but resolute. One might quibble with Woods and Harmon's equation of the former with the "normal" Kirk and another with the shadow since, as Spock points out during the episode, Kirk's leadership ability rests on his usual integration of these two sides of his personality. Woods and Harmon's other example, "The Alternative Factor," portrays two "Lazarus" characters, one from our universe and another from an antimatter universe. One of these is insane (which we can tell largely from his incessant protests to the contrary) and threatens to destroy both universes in the pursuit of his obsession with the other. The other Lazarus is sane and is willing to sacrifice himself by remaining locked in a small corridor between universes to grapple forever with his deranged double. Here again, however, the pattern of the story contains some complexities that take us beyond the Jungian *coincidentia oppositorum* theme—for example, the fact that the "sane" Lazarus is from the abnormal (antimatter) universe, and that the two cannot be reconciled but must remain forever locked in struggle.

For our purposes, we shall mainly focus on those "doubles" that bear a physical resemblance to their alter egos and shall leave aside the larger and more amorphous category of "psychic" or "character" doubles. The simultaneous presence on screen of two identical or nearly identical characters played by the same actor is so common in *Star Trek* that one might consider it a stock *Trek* device. The "double" motif appears in more episodes than we can do justice to here, but we can examine the basic variants of the theme and consider a few examples of each.

One of the narrative functions of the double is to separate different aspects of the self into distinct characters so as to allow for an explicit interaction and dialogue among them. Sometimes these divergent selves are, as Jung predicts, split along the lines of good and evil, or that which a person consciously acknowledges and that which he or she ordinarily denies. A prime candidate for *Star Trek*'s best example of a Jungian shadow-self is Data's evil twin Lore, discussed at length in the previous chapter. Lore is everything Data is not: he has emotions, but not the ones Data covets; he is devious, vindictive, insecure, and egotistical; although he has a sense of humor, it is maniacal and malicious. Even their names, Data and Lore, suggest opposite (although not necessarily good and bad) sources of understanding.

In TOS's "Mirror, Mirror," Kirk finds himself accidentally beamed into a parallel universe featuring counterpart versions of Spock and others, whose character and motives are generally sinister. As is usual in *Star Trek*, however, the good/evil distinction is not allowed to stand in its simplistic form but is given some complicating twists. Even in this cruel universe, Spock is a person of some integrity and understanding who helps Kirk and actually listens to his preaching. Several episodes of DS9 bring us back to this same "mirror universe" after a century of events, including reforms initiated by the mirror Spock, have failed to improve this world. Once again we see a universe whose inhabitants are in some sense opposites of those in the normal universe (a fierce terrorist Julian Bashir and a ruthless, sex-hungry Kira Nerys), but once again, the oppositions are given some complex twists: O'Brien is first encountered as a timid slave and later as a resolute freedom fighter, but in either case he gives signs of being somewhat more decent than he lets on.[7] Furthermore, the fragmenting of people into doubles does not always lead to a good/evil opposition. In VGR's "Faces," Lieutenant Torres is divided into her Klingon and human components, while in such episodes as VGR's "Coda" Janeway and others are divided into corporeal and incorporeal components (body and spirit).

Sometimes, doubles are the result of a bifurcation of space/time that has little to do with moral duality. When two equally authentic versions of William Riker come face to face seven years after a transporter malfunction has divided them (TNG's "Second Chances"), they merely represent two equally "good" possibilities of Riker's development (although a sequel episode, DS9's "Defiant," seems to move slightly toward a good/evil split by portraying the alter ego, Tom Riker, as a member of the outlawed Maquis resistance movement). In DS9's "Visionary" and TNG's "Time Squared," O'Brien and Picard respectively encounter themselves coming and going, as it were, through wrinkles in time; and in VGR's "Deadlock," Janeway and company encounter an alternate-reality copy of themselves; in these cases, there is no clear difference between the doubles, although the narratives still tend to privilege "our" reality as more "real" than the alternative ones.

An entirely different approach to the double (although it might look similar if one were watching television with the sound turned off) is the imposter, or changeling, motif. In European folk tradition, a changeling is a demonic surrogate placed in the cradle when evil beings steal a human baby. In *Star Trek*, parallel situations occur when beings create duplicates of (or assume the form of) *Trek* characters in order to carry their nefarious plans. Given the presence of an evil imposter, the action hinges on the protagonist's ability to distinguish reality from illusion and to read character from outward signs. Kirk is imitated in "Whom Gods Destroy" "Dagger of the Mind," and "What Are Little Girls Made Of?" Picard is imitated in TNG's "Allegiance." O'Brien is imitated in DS9's "Whispers," and Odo in DS9's "The Adversary." A lighter, but not always innocent, variant of this theme occurs when people intentionally create holographic likenesses of actual persons with whom to interact on the holodeck—a practice that the "originals" often resent (TNG's "Booby Trap" and "Hollow Pursuits").

The use of the double allows, among other things, an explicit dialogue or interplay between the parts of the personality that coexist uneasily within each of us. Perhaps one reason that this theme appears with such extraordinary frequency and explicitness in *Star Trek* is that, given the special premises of its science fiction world (to say nothing of cinematic special effects), the Doppelganger can so easily be made incarnate. At the same time, science fiction's mythmaking role is well served by the sort of investigations of self that this device allows.

INSIDE THE PLURAL SELF

Some of the narrative usefulness of the Doppelganger theme, we have suggested, stems from its ability to decompose the personality into different aspects that can be represented as separate persons. The double thus offers one way—but by no means the only way—of dealing with the apparent dividedness of the psyche. Jung recognized not only the shadow-double but also various other contending elements within the pysche, including the *animus* (male archetype) and the *anima* (female archetype). Most readers will have at least a passing acquaintance with Freud's division of the personality into Id (erotic and aggressive instincts), Ego (the reality principle), and Superego (the conscience). More than two millennia ago in his dialogue *Phaedrus,* Plato described the human psyche with his own tripartite metaphor—a rational charioteer trying to maintain his course while one of his two unruly winged horses pulls the chariot earthward (in the direction of the animal impulses) and the other toward the heavens (the spiritual aspirations).[8] In cultural beliefs that recognize several souls that perform different mental or spiritual functions, and even in the widespread notion of magical spells and spirits that can pull a person in unwelcome directions, different peoples have found ways to portray the intuited sense that a person may, at a given time, be of more than one mind.

One of the most complex decompositions of the personality into constituent parts is seen in DS9's "Distant Voices," when Doctor Julian Bashir lies in a coma after a telepathic attack by a Lethean criminal. In dreams, Bashir encounters various aspects of his own personality in the visage of his DS9 crewmates, and he must use these parts of himself in concert, in order to complete repairs on the dead DS9 station (which represents his own mind), if he is to recover from the coma. More often, the decomposition of the personality is a binary one, as with Kirk's "good" and "evil" sides in TOS's "The Enemy Within," or with B'Elanna Torres' duplication into her aggressive Klingon and gentle human sides in VGR's "Faces." In fact, these binary doublings are part of a more general pattern in *Star Trek* of representing certain characters as divided into two equal and contending halves. Spock's human and Vulcan sides are in constant conflict with one another, but we glimpse this fact directly only when he lets his guard down, as in TOS's "The Naked Time," when Spock's human side weeps at the Vulcan's failure to express love for his human mother. Torres, too, is half human, as is Deanna Troi. Worf and Odo express this duality along a different axis, since each is an alien orphan reared by humans and perpetually divided between his cultural upbringing and his longing for deeper "roots." In a mirror reversal of the theme of a person divided into two halves, Neelix and Tuvok find themselves joined into one by a transporter accident in VGR's "Tuvix," and the resulting composite of these opposite personalities is surprisingly (in fact, alarmingly) comfortable with himself—so much so that Janeway must intervene forcibly to restore the original two persons.

Joined Trills might be seen as serial binaries (one symbiont exists in a succession of hosts and imparts the memories of that joined existence to future hosts) who provide an extraordinarily complex exploration of the plural self. With their multilayered traces of many diverse personalities, the Trill provide a fertile ground for Jungian and Freudian analysis. For example, in TNG's "The Host" and DS9's "Rejoined," joined Trills find themselves drawn to same-sex romantic relationships that were initiated when one of the Trills was joined to a previous host body of the other gender. For the Freudian, this situation might symbolize the homoeroticism latent in all of us, while the Jungian psychologist would probably be drawn to these indwelling other-sex traces as representations of the opposite-sex archetypes (*anima* in men, *animus* in women) that all people carry within their psyches. In DS9's "Facets," Jadziah Dax undergoes *Zhian'tara*, the Trill Rite of Closure, during which she becomes better acquainted with the accumulated parts of her Trill personality by conversing with past hosts who temporarily inhabit (with permission) the bodies of her crewmates on DS9. One of her most dramatic encounters in this episode is with the deranged, murderous host Joran (first seen in "Equilibrium"), who pronounces her unworthy of the Dax symbiont and tries to attack her by using Sisko's body. The episode's other significant encounter is with the most recent Dax host, the sternly patriarchal Curzon, who had first rejected Jadziah from the Trill-joining program and who later let her through easily. Jadziah, determined to find out why, learns that Curzon was in love with Jadziah and did not trust himself with her. All this is grist for the Freudian mill: the raging Id, the Oedipal father, and erotic narcissism—all in the space of an hour! Where but on *Star Trek* could one find such happy hunting?

The explicit naming and defining of the components of a divided mind has a narrative function similar to that of spells, demonic possession, soul loss and doubles. It allows humans to give form and meaning to disturbances and disruptions of the psyche while implicitly maintaining the possibility that, despite such disturbances, there is an integral self that coincides with one's intuitive sense of distinctness and continuity. In other words, these metaphorical treatments of the disruptions of self provide a semiotic way of distinguishing the self from the disturbance, thus stabilizing the boundaries of self in the face of destabilizing experiences.

HE'S NOT DEAD, JIM

Humans' awareness of their own individual mortality poses the ultimate threat to the integrity and continuity of the self—one that mythologies almost always address in one way or another. Because the methods of myth are narrative rather than doctrinal, myths need not (although they sometimes may) offer an explicit logical alternative to mortality. Yet myth has the ability to provide ways of thinking about the death-life opposition that serve to soften and destabilize the conceptual boundary between the two, a boundary that in everyday experience seems so distressingly absolute. A mythos like that of *Star Trek* is able to approach this project from any number of different directions without being constrained by requirements of self-consistency. Hence, *Trek* is able to make use of several devices that have the cumulative effect of portraying death as veiled, malleable, protean, and reversible, rather than naked, monolithic, immovable, and final.

One of *Star Trek*'s strategies for dealing with the life-death opposition is to stress the provisional nature of human knowledge about metaphysical questions. In TNG's episode "Where Silence Has Lease," the alien being Nagilum confronts the crew of the *Enterprise* with immanent death in order to "study" their response. When asked about his views on life after death, Picard refers to the opposing beliefs in an afterlife of eternal bliss or "the idea of our blinking into nothingness," and then muses that, in view of the "marvelous complexity" and "clockwork perfection" of the universe, "our existence must be more than either of these," but rather "beyond what we understand now as reality." By suggesting that the reality of life after death is beyond our present limited conceptions, Picard holds out the possibility that immortality is reconcilable with science.

Another way in which *Star Trek* softens the starkness of mortality is by blurring the boundary between the mortal and immortal. In the *Trek* world it is not always easy to place life-forms into either of these categories. Q is said to be immortal, but he can die at the hands of other Q (VGR's "The Q and the Grey"). The Organians in TOS's "Errand of Mercy" do not explicitly claim to be immortal, but they do assert that no one has died on their planet in "countless thousands of years." Apollo and the other "gods" of TOS's "Who Mourns for Adonais?" are in principle immortal, although they may fade away owing to lack of worship. At the other extreme are VGR's Ocampa, who live for only nine years. In between is virtually every possibility. *Trek*'s human heroes might live a little longer than today's humans, thanks to Starfleet's advanced medicine and healthy lifestyle, while the disciplined Vulcans may live considerably longer. The nearly immortal Flint of TOS's "Requiem for Methuselah," who was born on earth several thousand years ago with an extraordinary natural ability to regenerate his body. While Trill hosts apparently have life spans similar to those of humans, the symbionts are extremely long-lived. By representing mortality and immortality as points along a spectrum, and by blurring the absoluteness of immortality even as it proposes the possibility, *Trek* reframes mortality and immortality as contingent variables that are subject to variation and change, thus destabilizing the boundary between the two.

Although death is, from all superficial appearances, the most absolute and irreversible of human transitions, myth may suggest that death is not so irreversible as it seems. Despite its adhere ice to a secular frame of reference, *Star Trek* replays ancient themes of resurrection in a variety of ways. *Trek*'s most involved treatment of this theme spans the two feature films *The Wrath of Khan* and *The Search for Spock*.[9] The story weaves elaborate, multilayered metaphors that place time, aging, and mortality within a cosmic pattern of ebb and flow that also brings renewal and rebirth. In *The Wrath of Khan*, Spock gives his life to save the *Enterprise* and its crew from destruction by the maniacal "superman" Khan. At Spock's funeral, Kirk says that this death takes place "in the sunrise of a new world," the "Genesis planet" formed from the nebula when the Genesis device detonated. Among the many portents of renewal that follow is Doctor McCoy's inversion of his often-heard line "He's dead, Jim." "He's really not dead," muses the Doctor, "as long as we remember him." McCoy's prophetic words are more literally true than he realizes, for he is the unknowing recipient of a last-minute Vulcan mind-meld and has been implanted with Spock's memories, which Kirk refers to as Spock's "immortal soul." Kirk and his old companions, Sulu, Uhura, and Scott, steal the *Enterprise* and embark on a daring and forbidden quest to recover Spock's body. Spock is found as a mindless child, wandering about on the Genesis planet, the site of a Federation "life from lifelessness" experiment to which his funerary vessel had been sent. Spock is taken to the planet Vulcan where, in a rare and dangerous ritual of "re-fusion," McCoy places his own life at risk in order to restore Spock. The strength of this tale of resurrection lies not only in the literal rebirth of Spock after his own very real death but in the weaving of this theme into a larger tapestry of life and death, aging and rejuvenation, decay and restoration as complementary aspects of a reciprocal movement or cycle. Not only is Spock restored to life, but by the same process, Kirk and his companions are spiritually rejuvenated.

Although this pair of feature films is *Star Trek*'s most sustained treatment of the resurrection theme, it is by no means the only one. In TOS's "Amok Time," Captain Kirk goes into a deathlike state to rescue Spock from the impossible situation of having to fight Kirk to the death; in TNG's replay of this strategy in "Code of Honor," Yareena really does die before being revived by Doctor Crusher. In TNG's "Tapestry," Picard dies during surgery following an injury to his artificial heart. He enters an afterworld presided over by the supremely annoying Q, who eventually restores him to life on Doctor Crusher's operating table. In VGR's "Coda," Captain Kathryn Janeway is killed during a mission to a remote planet and finds herself wandering about the ship in spirit form while an incorporeal being posing as her father's ghost tries to coax her into the "afterworld." Only after she firmly refuses the offer is she able to reenter her body, enabling her desperate companions to revive her. In DS9's "The Visitor," young Jake Sisko sees his father dematerialized in a terrible accident aboard the *Defiant*; he becomes obsessed with the recurrent vision of his father's "ghost" (Captain Sisko trapped in another dimensional reality) and eventually manages to alter events in such a way as to restore his father to life.

Some of the above-mentioned episodes broach another theme by which *Star Trek* and other science fiction can approach the mortality question—that of multiple parallel existences. In *Trek*, alternate universes are similar enough to provide common points of reference (e.g., recognizable characters and places) but different enough so that a person who is dead in one "reality" might well be alive in another. For example, when Benjamin Sisko visits the "mirror universe" (DS9's "Through the Looking Glass" and "Shattered Mirror") he finds that his wife Jennifer is alive there. In DS9's "Visionary," Chief Engineer Miles O'Brien dies, but he is soon replaced by another version of himself from an alternate time line just a few hours into the future, and the death of *Voyager*'s Ensign Harry Kim is similarly repealed in VGR's "Deadlock." Security Officer Natasha Yar is killed in the year 2364 during a mission on the planet Vagra II (TNG's "Skin of Evil"), but she is encountered in a later episode (TNG's "Yesterday's *Enterprise*") when another *Enterprise* from the year 2344 of an "alternative time line" unexpectedly appears.

The alternate universe or time line is only one of the *Star Trek* narrative devices by which a person has more than one existence and can, therefore, be both dead and alive. Another is the frequently encountered theme of the double or clone, discussed earlier in this chapter. In DS9's "Whispers," the audience shares the final hours and moments of Miles O'Brien as he is hunted down and killed in cold blood by his Starfleet companions, who seem to have gone altogether mad. Only at the end do we learn what the central character did not know—that he is "only" a duplicate of the "real" Chief O'Brien, subliminally programmed to commit acts of terrorism. The clone thinks he is O'Brien and thus experiences O'Brien's death (as does the audience); yet O'Brien lives. In TNG's "Rightful Heir," Commander Worf encounters a clone of the ancient Klingon hero Kahless; Worf's recognition of the clone's claim to "be" Kahless suggests that, in some cases at least, cloning can amount to resurrection.

In the present age of burgeoning information technology, we seem increasingly inclined to label the intangible aspects of the person as "mind" and to reduce mind to a complex set of information patterns. Since we are well accustomed to the idea of the rapid, massive transfer of information as invisible impulses flowing through tiny circuits or even through empty space, the possibility that the mental aspects of a human being might be instantly transferred to a new physical location may seem a reasonable extrapolation from phenomena that we already accept as routine. If the mental element could be transferred from one physical location to another, the result would be something strikingly similar to the phenomena of spirit possession and transmigration of souls that people of diverse cultures have believed in for thousands of years.

We have already noted the many *Star Trek* episodes that seem to replay the traditional idea of the migration of the spirit into a different physical body. If we add to the notion of migratory minds the idea that the body itself is defined by information (arrangements of molecules into patterns guided by DNA),[10] we can pose a startling theoretical question: If I am the sum of my body plus my mind, and the integrity of both body and mind consists essentially of patterns of information, and these information patterns can be infinitely duplicated, transmitted, and preserved, what becomes of mortality? The soul would not be, as Yeats put it, "fastened to a dying animal."[11] In TNG's "The Schizoid Man" a doomed human, Dr. Ira Graves, takes over Data's android body until, realizing that he hasn't the self-control necessary to manage such superhuman powers, he places his memories into a computer. The premise of transferring the mind of a mortal human into a potentially immortal android body is central to *The Original Series* episodes "Requiem for Methuselah" and "Return to Tomorrow." In TNG's "Inheritance," Data meets his "mother," Dr. Juliana Tainer, the former wife and scientific co-worker of his maker Dr. Noonien Soong, and he discovers that Soong had transferred her mind from her dying organic body into an android one. Although the android Juliana Tainer has been programmed to age as an organic being would, Soong could presumably have chosen to make her as immortal as her "son."

The holographic projection provides another medium through which the information patterns constituting a "mind" could be joined with an artificial human form. In DS9's "Doctor Bashir, I Presume," Starfleet's Doctor Zimmerman recruits Bashir as the personality prototype for a newer and more realistic holographic medical program, claiming that it offers him "a shot at immortality." In DS9's "Our Man Bashir," several crew members are nearly lost in a transporter malfunction, and their lives are saved only through the expedient of storing their "body" patterns in one part of the ship's computer system, while their "minds" enter the holodeck's computer where they temporarily become actors in Bashir's spy-thriller holographic program. If this situation were extended indefinitely, the human crew members might easily transcend death, aging, and illness by assuming a holographic existence.

Another, very different way of dealing mythically with death is the narrative strategy—a very ancient one at that—of "normalizing" mortality by presenting it as a necessary and even beneficial aspect of human existence. Such a theme is developed on a secular plane in TOS's "The Mark of Gideon," in which the inhabitants of the planet Gideon have so prolonged human life through technological advance that they are desperate to introduce an epidemic disease on their miserably overcrowded planet. Similarly the story of Flint in TOS's "Requiem for Methuselah" relates that this ancient human, who had lived many illustrious lives in such identities as Brahms and Da Vinci, has eventually become bored with it all and migrates to the planet Holberg 917G, where his immortality is nullified. The immortal Q shows up on *Voyager* in VGR's "Death Wish" as a refugee from the Continuum and petitions for the Continuum's permission to become mortal so that he can end the boredom of his existence. In TNG's "Time's Arrow," Data is faced with his own death in a most tangible way when the *Enterprise* team finds his disembodied head among the remnants and artifacts of nineteenth-century San Francisco. Although this death is later erased in one of those time-paradox escapades for which *Trek* is noted, Data in the meantime has an opportunity to consider the meaning of his mortality, and he confesses that he is comforted by the thought that this not only relieves him of the bleak prospect of outliving his human friends but brings him closer to the human condition.

We have suggested here that a coherent delineation of the self does not arise automatically from the raw data of experience and observation; on the contrary, there are many kinds of experience that seem to contradict the notion of a stable, bounded self marked by continuity over time. *Star Trek* uses a variety of narrative devices to stabilize the boundaries of the self against these challenging anomalies and disruptions; some of these devices have broad cross-cultural parallels, while others are unique to *Trek*, or at least to science fiction that shares in its narrative premises. Through the use of spells, invasive spirits, soul loss, spirit doubles, and divided psyches, *Trek* positions the self in semiotic opposition to various nameable disruptions or discontinuities, thus allowing us to confront and deal with those disruptions as externalized things while reinstating the essential reality of an ultimately stable, bounded self. In the case of mortality, on the other hand, *Trek*'s mythos has the opposite task of softening and destabilizing a boundary—that of life and death—which in ordinary perception is all too stark. In each case, the effect is to preserve the sense of an integral self in the face of recurring human experiences that might call it into question. Thus, *Star Trek*'s mythos has managed to preserve something corresponding to the idea of the soul, with its singularity, boundedness, and potential transcendence of the physical body, even in the absence of religion in the traditional sense.

CHAPTER 5

CELESTIAL FEMININITY

Gender in the *Star Trek* Cosmos

Worlds may change, galaxies may disintegrate, but a woman always remains a woman.

—Captain James Tiberius Kirk
"The Conscience of the King" (TOS)

As every Trekker knows, NBC decisively rejected *Star Trek*'s original pilot episode, "The Cage," on the grounds that it was "too cerebral" for the American viewing public. The network invited the show's creators to submit a second pilot but admonished them to get rid of the "Martian" (Spock) and, above all, to dump the female first officer. Subjects in a test screening, it seems, hated the character called "Number One." Women as well as men thought it inappropriate to have a female in a command role, characterizing her as "annoying" and "pushy" despite the restraint with which she is portrayed in the episode.[1] Spock stayed, but the network prevailed in its opposition to the female first officer.

It is interesting to speculate how *Star Trek*'s treatment of gender roles might have unfolded if Roddenberry's original intentions had prevailed. One can see hints of the possibilities in the dialogue of "The Cage." Captain Pike is needlessly stern with the attractive young Yeoman Colt, confessing afterward to Number One that he is uneasy with a woman on the bridge. In response to her questioning look, he awkwardly explains that she, of course, is different. The tension in this exchange could have set the stage for an exploration of Pike's reluctance to see Number One simultaneously as a woman and as a fellow officer, as well as the corresponding inner conflicts on Number One's part. Later in the episode, the Talosians, discouraged by Pike's refusal to be seduced by Vina, present him with a choice of Yeoman Colt and Number One as consorts, pointing out the former's "strong feminine instincts" and the latter's intelligence as two contrasting assets from which he might choose—again juxtaposing the conflicting standards by which men judge women. The continuation of Captain Pike and Number One as the two main figures on the bridge of the *Enterprise* might have foregrounded issues of "femininity" and achievement and could have suffused the series with an examination of gender that would have been far ahead of its time.

But that is not what happened. Deprived of key characters and premises that might have drawn *Star Trek* toward a more precocious exploration of gender, the series drifted with the prevailing cultural currents, reflecting America's unexamined gender assumptions more often than it challenged them.[2] Roddenberry's intent to present women as serious participants in the *Trek* adventure did not find expression until the later series, where the treatment of gender takes on a more complex character.

WEARING THE INTERPLANETARY PANTS

The Starship *Enterprise* that America came to know through *The Original Series* is a man's world. Yeoman Rand, who in the first few episodes seems to show some promise as Kirk's love interest, is meekly vacant and disappears after a few episodes. From then on, the only woman to appear as a regular on the bridge is the communications officer, Lieutenant Uhura. Uhura's role rarely allowed for more than the most perfunctory one-liners ("Hailing frequencies open, sir"), and one classic bit of *Star Trek* lore concerns Nichelle Nichols, the multitalented African American actress who played Uhura, who was persuaded by Dr. Martin Luther King Jr. to continue in the role despite her frustration over its limitations.[3]

Women from off the *Enterprise* are fair game for Kirk's dalliances, while the women aboard the ship (within the extended family, so to speak) are chaste and demure, rarely seen and more rarely heard. When the women of the *Enterprise* crew do anything on their own initiative, it is likely to be some predictable feminine folly, such as falling under the romantic spell of a dangerous outsider and becoming his unwitting accomplice, as Lieutenant Carolyn Palamas does with Apollo in "Who Mourns for Adonais" or Lieutenant Marla McGivers with Khan in "Space Seed." While they seem inordinately vulnerable to seduction from outsiders, however, the *Enterprise*'s women are virtually asexual in their relations with other crew members. Women from the outside, by contrast, are sexually aggressive and often threaten the moral order of the ship. In "The Conscience of the King," the young Shakespearean actress Lenore Karidian so enchants Kirk that he never suspects she is a deranged killer bent on eliminating him and others who might incriminate her father for past atrocities. "Elaan of Troyius" centers on Kirk's taming of the shrewish Elaan, the "Dohlman" of planet Elas whom the *Enterprise* must deliver to a politically important wedding. Just as Elaan's arrogant and barbaric manners seem about to soften under the firm tutelage of Captain Kirk (particularly after he threatens to spank her), she causes one of her tears to touch him, sending him into a state of helpless infatuation for which even Dr. McCoy has no antidote. Elaan does this not so much to gain power over Kirk as to achieve her one most frustrated wish in an otherwise privileged autocratic existence—to be loved by the man of her choosing who is also, as it happens, the one man able to put her in her place.

Stories like these owe much to tradition. "Elaan of Troyius," besides its obvious parallel to Shakespeare's *The Taming of the Shrew* (as well as folk tales and ballads with the same theme) and its transparent reference to the fatefully irresistible Helen of Troy, also contains less overt parallels to Homer's Circe and other mythic figures who charm men into perilous befuddlement. Here, too, is the ancient notion of women's physical secretions as a powerful source of magical pollution that can be the undoing of virile pursuits. Notions about women from outside the "tribe" as having the potential either to be dangerous (often magical) sexual aggressors, or conversely, the objects of sexual conquest, are pervasive in patriarchal cultures. Present also is the corollary idea that the women of one's own social group are either chaste or, should their chastity fail, traitors who pollute and endanger the group through their intimacy with, and submission to, the outsider. The Elaan of Troyius story also exemplifies the recurrent theme of the reassertion of patriarchy over rebellious women who are by nature unable to handle power without abusing it.[4] In these and other ways, *Star Trek*'s portrayal of women in TOS plots resonates strongly with traditional patriarchal motifs.

The original *Enterprise* not only carries Western gender roles to the far reaches of the galaxy, but it discovers them wherever it goes. In one star system after another, women are depicted—when they are depicted at all—as alluring, scantily clad objects of the erotic male gaze. They are seldom the holders of legitimate authority. When not playing the role of silent helpmates, they are likely to be dangerous ensnarers and usurpers of men. Of course, *Star Trek* is not the only television show to depict this orthodox Western gender ideology, but in the *Trek* context the implications are profoundly different than in, say, a situation comedy, because *Trek* self-consciously challenges the limits of our imagination about humans and sentient life in general, and it does so in a hypothetical setting of cosmic diversity when humanity has supposedly progressed beyond arbitrary prejudices.

Of the three episodes conceived as possible pilots for Roddenberry's second attempt to sell the series in 1966, the two not selected, but aired early in the first season, deal centrally with gender issues. One episode, "Mudd's Women," hints at an attempt to raise cogent issues about gender, but it too ends up affirming more of conventional wisdom than it problematizes. The *Enterprise* overtakes the lovable charlatan Harry Mudd, whose "cargo" consists of three breathtakingly beautiful women intended as brides for lonely but wealthy men in remote mining settlements. The women's charms are such that the *Enterprise* crew men are enchanted almost beyond self-control. But their beauty is dependent on an illegal "Venus drug" supplied by Mudd. Without the drug, the women become "ugly" (in their "ugly" mode, actually, they look like rather attractive women in their thirties instead of lavishly made-up twenty-year-olds—a visage that they, and later their prospective husbands, find repugnant). The issue of feminine beauty reaches its culmination when one of the women, refusing to take her beauty pill, instead cooks breakfast for a lonely miner and then asks him whether he really prefers a woman who can cook for him, sew for him, and cry with him, or a vain and "useless" beauty. The story thus broaches an important question as to what men really want, but the question of what women want is never considered: in this story, women want men to want them. The outcome of the story is philosophically anticlimactic: to illustrate her point about vain bimbos, one of the women pops her Venus pill and regains her beauty, only to discover that Kirk has slipped her a placebo and that her beauty is, as he explains, a matter of believing in herself. The husband-to-be never has to confront her question of whether male expectations are self-defeating, since it turns out that a woman who believes in herself can satisfy the full spectrum of a man's wishes. Although the episode cavorts near the brink of a discussion as to whether there is more to a woman's life than being attractive to men, it never makes the leap.

HEGEMONIC ESSENCES

As myth, *Star Trek*'s ability to justify prevailing cultural concepts of gender entails going beyond the mere imitation of the familiar. The hegemonic power of myth lies in its ability to naturalize and essentialize social facts, that is, to remove them from the contingencies of human-made history and to represent them as timeless and intrinsic, inseparable from the very nature and plan of the cosmos. The essentialization of social roles through myth is sometimes subtle, a subtext of the mythic narrative whose meaning is only implied or is left to the vicissitudes of diverse readings of the text. But while TOS's message concerning the universality of orthodox gender norms suffuses every episode in at least a subtle way, there are times when—lest the message be mistaken—we are explicitly informed that gender as we know it is not only a highly dependable feature of the cosmos but indeed one of its most basic characteristics.

In TOS's "The Conscience of the King," the coquettish Lenore Karidian, after tantalizing Kirk with double entendre, comparing him with the *Enterprise*'s "surging and throbbing" power, entreats him: "Tell me about the women in your world—has the machine changed them, turned them into just people instead of women?" Kirk's reply, quoted above, is classic: Whatever else may change, explains the Captain, "a woman always remains a woman." The full meaning of this exchange becomes clear when one recalls that "the machine" is used throughout the series as a metaphor for the hyperrationality of modern life and its potential for dehumanization. Turning women into "just people" is a transparent reference to the feminist agenda that was conspicuously entering the mainstream of public discourse in the late 1960s. It is paradoxical that while men are fully human as "just people," the characterization of women by this phrase seems somehow to reduce and dehumanize them. As Simone de Beauvoir argued in *The Second Sex*, the essence of women in the patriarchal worldview lies in their "otherness."[5] Men are just people, but women are the exotic "other," and to deprive them of this otherness is to rob them of their substance. Kirk's comforting reassurance is that the essential otherness of femininity will survive the onslaughts of rationalist humanism in general and feminism in particular.

Cosmic femininity applies not just to Terrans or even humanoids but to all intelligent life-forms, including incorporeal ones. In this connection, the episode "Metamorphosis" is a quintessential study in TOS's poetics of gender. The Starfleet shuttle craft *Galileo*, on a mission to transport the seriously ill Assistant Federation Commissioner Nancy Hedford for urgent medical treatment, is diverted by a cloudlike entity and forced to land on Gamma Canaris N. There the crew of *Galileo* meet Zefram Cochrane, a renowned scientist, who had launched himself into space at the age of 85 in order to die in privacy. Cochrane has been "rescued" and restored to youth and health by a cloudlike being called the Companion, who provides for all his needs. The Companion has waylaid the *Galileo* shuttle because it senses Cochrane's need for human company. When Kirk communicates with the Companion by means of a universal translator, the voice they hear is feminine. Kirk explains to a perplexed Cochrane that "the ideas of male and female are universal constants . . . the Companion is definitely female." Cochrane is outraged to learn that he has unwittingly been the Companion's "lover." Kirk mediates, counseling Cochrane to be more open-minded but also trying to persuade the Companion that she is too different from Cochrane to understand his needs as a lover must.

Meanwhile, Nancy Hedford, nearing death, confesses that her successful diplomatic career has been a poor substitute for the one thing she really wanted: the love of a man. "I've been good at my job, Doctor," she says, "but I've never been loved. What kind of a life is that? Not to be loved—never! And now I'm dying. And he [Cochrane] runs away from love!" The Companion apparently concurs, and she makes the irreversible decision to give up her incorporeal form to join with Nancy in her body, committing them both to a renewed but finite existence. They cannot, however, leave the planet from which the Companion's energy emanates. Cochrane, realizing that he owes his life to the Companion and that she would die of loneliness without him, accepts her love and remains on the planet with her.

The story "Metamorphosis" is, if read along a certain axis, a progressive parable about the importance of overcoming prejudice against the unfamiliar—a triumph of reason and compassion over bigotry. But on the level of gender, the message is one of immutable essentialism. Even as TOS pushes the boundaries of what we can imagine as possible, it also establishes certain limits of imagination that cannot be transgressed. Gender is portrayed as the very loom on which all intelligible experience is woven, and as something that can not be transcended anywhere in the universe. Not surprisingly, within this immutable structure of gender there is much that can easily be recognized from our own culture. While Cochrane is dependent on the female entity for the practical ways in which she serves him, the female entity is dependent on Cochrane for entirely emotional reasons. What she requires from him is nothing more or less than his love and the knowledge that he is happy. While the male has a drive toward unhampered self-expression and freedom from entanglement, the female is driven by the need to be loved and to see herself through the eyes of her lover. The relinquishing of her immortality is but a small sacrifice "to touch the hand of the man." The Companion has given up all her power and all her uniquely self-defining qualities in order to win Cochrane's love. When Kirk beams up, Scotty inquires what happened on the planet. "Not very much in the end," he replies with an impish smile, "only the oldest story in the world."

The "oldest story" makes sense only if we take for granted our own familiar gender polarities. Reverse them, and the story becomes implausible and incoherent. Neither does the plot remain compelling if one sets aside the equation of love with heterosexuality. Logically, the Companion could have satisfied her own need for love as well as Nancy Hedford's by saving Nancy's life and becoming her platonic "lover," just as she had previously done for Cochrane—thus saving him the difficult choice of relinquishing his desire for freedom. But in *Star Trek* the necessity of heterosexuality, even for incorporeal beings, goes without saying.

That the cosmic status of orthodox gender roles *does* need affirming in

TOS is surely related to the fact that, during the 1960s, feminist theories that proclaimed gender to be an arbitrary social construct were becoming a prominent part of our society's internal dialogue. An optimistic vision of the human future must posit either that this difficult issue will be addressed and transcended or that it will fade away like a bad dream. What TOS provides is, for the most part, a reassurance of the latter.

SUCCUBI AND DEVOURING WOMEN

In "The Man Trap," one of the episodes considered for the 1966 *Star Trek* pilot, the *Enterprise*'s landing party arrives on planet M-113 with supplies for archeologists Robert and Nancy Crater. Nancy, with whom Dr. McCoy was once romantically involved, appears differently to each crew member according to his or her own inner thoughts and desires. After several crew members die mysteriously, it emerges that Nancy had long ago been killed and replaced by a shape-shifting creature that lives by draining the salt from its victims' bodies. Robert, out of scientific interest and a need for companionship, has knowingly adopted the creature as his companion, but Kirk has no interest in communicating with it—he simply hunts it down and kills it.

The salt vampire of "The Man Trap" is reminiscent of the folkloric succubus that appears in men's dreams to have intercourse with them. Although "succubus" comes from the Latin root meaning "to lie beneath" rather than the Anglo-Saxon "suck," the notion of men being diminished by the loss of their semen or other fluids is part of a widespread mythic motif of the polluting and debilitating power of female sexual predation. In European tradition, the succubus served, especially for celibate monks and priests, to displace blame for men's nocturnal fantasies. Men were not, after all, violating women (or their own monastic vows) in their dreams, but were the victims of sexual violation by predatory female apparitions. Thus men's desires were projected onto feminine fiends whose sexuality posed a mortal danger, and the reprisal directed against women suspected of these mystical sexual activities was severe. Instead of saving the being (providing it with salt would, presumably, have rendered it harmless) and reconciling the relationship as he did in "Metamorphosis," Kirk kills the creature with a grim zeal. The creature appears in death as a hag (another avatar of the demonic female night visitor of traditional folklore) with suction cups on its fingertips and a huge, round sucking mouth with teeth inside.[6]

Perhaps even more important here than the sexual connotation is the matter of nurturing versus parasitic femininity. Unlike the Companion of "Metamorphosis," this shape-shifting being depletes rather than nurses, takes rather than gives—thus it embodies men's fears of the "negative" side of intimacy. The fact that the monster assumes the appearance of McCoy's old flame points to the need to overcome longings for personal intimacy and to renounce romantic attractions that could sap the vitality from the male brotherhood of the *Enterprise*.

In patriarchal mythology, women who fail to fit the nurturing role seem inevitably to slip into the opposite one—the devourer of men. The premise of the third season episode "Spock's Brain" is that a bevy of exasperatingly stupid women from the planet Sigma Draconis VI steal Spock's brain in order to use it to control the high-tech underground world that they have inherited from their more intelligent ancestors. The men of their planet are forced to inhabit the frozen surface, where they live in dread of the pain-inducing devices used by the women (the givers of "pain and pleasure") to control them. (As with English-speaking Terrans, incidentally, the word for women, *eymorg*, is a derivative of the word for men, *morg*.) The females have managed the feat of stealing a brain only by acquiring a temporary state of intelligence by using a special helmet bequeathed by the ancestors, but Spock's brain is needed for the continuing control of the life-support and other routine functioning of their world. The story gives no explanation, other than their unnatural isolation from male influence, of how the eymorgs evolved into such bubbleheads. When Kirk catches his first sight of the brain-stealing beauties, he asks for the person in charge so that he may speak to "him." Once he becomes fully aware of the distastefully unnatural order of things on this planet, he easily overcomes the tearful, dim-witted matrons, returning the planet to a more acceptable arrangement in which men are men, women have no contrivances for controlling them, and people have to fend for themselves without pilfered brains.

The final episode of TOS seems aimed directly at the burgeoning feminism of the 1960s. In this story, "Turnabout Intruder," Kirk becomes the victim of a scorned and frustrated woman. Janice Lester, driven to insanity by the pain of being jilted by Kirk years earlier and by her frustration at being barred from becoming a Starship captain, uses a device to switch bodies with the captain and to assume his identity. "Now you will know the indignity of being a woman," she tells Kirk. Although she claims that her main motive is envy of Kirk's status and power as a captain, she also hints that her longing for "male" achievements is really a substitute for her deeper desire to be loved by a man. "It is better to be dead," she explains to the helpless Kirk-within-Lester, "than to live alone in the body of a woman."

Lester's scheme does not go well, however; for despite her years of planning and preparation, she immediately begins to behave in a decidedly uncaptainly manner—indecisive, incompetent, vindictive, peevish, paranoid, wildly overemotional and, finally, murderous. From the beginning, her unstable condition attracts attention. Scotty remarks that "I've seen the Captain feverish, sick, drunk, delirious, terrified, overjoyed, and boiling mad—but up to now I have never seen him red-faced with hysteria." The choice of words is interesting, since "hysteria" was a nineteenth-century medical term for psychosomatic disorders afflicting anxious or assertive women and supposedly originating in the uterus, for which the treatment of choice was "hysterectomy." In sum, Janice Lester is not so much a villain as a victim of a peculiarly feminine disorder resulting from rebelliousness against her gender role—what Kirk calls her "intense hatred of her own femininity." Like so many overreaching women in TOS, Lester is shown finally in tears, being led away—not to be punished so much as patronized. Kirk laments that "her life could have been as rich as any woman's, if only . . . if only." If only, that is, she had accepted her limitations instead of coveting male privileges.

"Turnabout Intruder" nicely sums up the conservative currents in TOS's portrayal of women. The *Enterprise* often encounters male beings who command genuine power—sometimes legitimate and good, sometimes willful and evil—but females do not straightforwardly hold power of either kind. Instead, they have wiles; they cheat, and they use tricks. In the end, these women break down and are led away to be placed under benevolent male care.[7] Not so much evil as insane, they have forsworn male protection and inevitably succumb to weaknesses of mind and emotion to which their unprotected state exposes them. Women are not naturally people of action in the world but creatures driven by emotional needs and dependencies, vulnerable to irrational whims and bad influences. One does not fight them the way one fights male villains but takes them in hand and gives them firm paternal guidance. By projecting this view of femininity onto a cosmic plane, TOS generally functions as a patriarchal hegemonic mythology that coincides historically with, and counters, the increasing visibility of feminism in American politics during the 1960s.

Important as this pattern is, it is not seamless. "The Cloudminders" (TOS) depicts a society divided between oppressed subterranean "Troglyte" miners and cloud-dwelling aristocrats; the *Enterprise* proves the catalyst for a revolutionary change in this order, but the change is actually brought about through the courageous vision of two women who seem naturally suited to leadership of the two factions. But far more significant, in terms of the overall *Star Trek* mythos, is the muted but revealing countertheme that emerges in connection with Spock and the Vulcans. In "Elaan of Troyius," Kirk concedes to Spock that Vulcan is the only planet in the Galaxy whose women are rational. When Vulcan society is glimpsed for the first time in the episode "Amok Time" (TOS), its presiding figure turns out to be a matriarch named T'Pau. What makes this premise especially interesting is that the Vulcans' apparent matriarchy is little remarked upon and does not present any particular difficulties, nor does it influence the direction of the plot. It simply is not a problem, even for Kirk. The significance of the Vulcans' surpassing aberration should not be underrated in view of the symbolic role that Spock and his people play in TOS. On the one hand, the Vulcans are the quintessential aliens, the perennial exception to Kirk's parochial views about humanoids across the galaxy; at the same time, they are us—the very embodiment of the ideal of rationalism that has formed the core of Western humanism since Socrates, the culmination of European Enlightenment idealism and the exemplars of peace, justice, civic responsibility, tolerance, reason, scientific curiosity, and all the rest.

And so, in the matter of gender as in the issue of utopia discussed in a later chapter, Spock appends the question mark, the quizzically raised eyebrow, to Kirk's confident pronouncements about cosmic human nature. This countertheme provides an element of philosophical open-endedness that counters the clearly ideological elements also present in the original *Trek* and that hints at the complex genius of *The Original Series*, as well as the possibilities for an expanding vision of gender in the later series.

FROM JANICE TO JANEWAY

In Greek mythology, the god Janus was the double-faced deity of doorways and transitions. It is perhaps a poetic coincidence that Captain Kirk's women are framed by Yeoman Janice Rand, the silently subservient beauty who disappears after a half-dozen TOS episodes,[8] and by the pathetically ineffectual man-eater Janice Lester of the series' last episode. These women do not represent an evolution of the feminine image from the beginning to the end of the series, but rather the two sides of the traditional patriarchal construction of femininity: the good-submissive-nurturing and the bad-assertive-devouring.

To anyone who has seen even one episode of *The Next Generation, Deep Space Nine*, or *Voyager*, the departure from the gender assumptions of the first series will be immediately apparent. For one thing, women are everywhere visible in positions of genuine leadership. The crew of TNG has a woman doctor, counselor, and chief security officer. DS9's primary officers include as many women as men. VGR's Captain Kathryn Janeway finally surpasses even the role envisioned for Number One in the original pilot. It is not only the liberal-minded Federation of Planets that features women in positions of command and leadership in the later series but also their archenemies, the Romulans, as well as the Federation's newfound but largely unreconstructed allies, the hypermacho Klingons. In fact, it's hard to find people anywhere in the galaxy who have not discovered the virtues of gender equality. From one star system to the next, women turn up as prominent scientists, diplomats, military officers, terrorists, and even as the ultrapowerful Borg queen. Even the language of Captain Picard's opening voice-over reflects a change from the original *Star Trek*: "To boldly go where no *one* [not *man*] has gone before."[9]

Another, equally dramatic, pangalactic discovery is that women do not necessarily have to wear sexually titillating costumes, or for that matter any special costume unique to their gender. By stages, even the alluring Deanna Troi, counselor of the *Enterprise D*, eases from low necklines and miniskirts into something closer to the regulation Starfleet uniform that the other crewwomen have worn from the beginning.[10] Gone are the days when *Star Trek* actresses had to have their precariously minuscule costumes taped to their bodies at strategic locations in order to get past the network censors.[11]

This is not to say that traditional gender ideas have disappeared from *Star Trek*, but their expression is more subtle and has shifted to other levels of abstraction. Picard's *Enterprise*, unlike Kirk's, has women on the bridge who actually wield expertise and authority and whose opinions count. In its first season, the eight principal characters of the series include three women: Chief Medical Officer Beverly Crusher, Ship's Counselor Deanna Troi, and Chief Security Officer Natasha Yar. Certainly, these characters represent a conception of women's capabilities that is different from TOS, but it does not mean that the deeper premises about gender have altogether changed. In TNG's scheme of things, a triad of women forms a matrix of protection not unlike that which maternal mammals provide for their young and for which, some might argue, we never outgrow our longing. Security Officer Tasha Yar guards the crew members against attack, Doctor Crusher preserves them from injury and illness, and Counselor Troi rescues them from psychological distress.

Of these functions, the most interesting departure from the original *Enterprise* is the presence of the Counselor Troi, a descendant of an empathic race, whose therapeutic role is to provide crew members (it seems that her clients are predominantly male) with encouragement and understanding. Deanna Troi's role as ship's counselor not only hints at the growing status of "therapy" in American culture, but, as pointed out by various commentators, her role draws on such stereotypic "feminine" traits as nurturance and sensitivity.[12] As Lynne Joyrich puts it, "she embodies rather than performs" her work, a calling in which femininity and the receptive capacity are "occupationalized."[13] Guinan, an alien bartender and confidante also has advisory and listening functions that overlap with Troi's and that some commentators identify with an "archetypal wise-woman" or "African matriarch" image.[14]

The umbrella of safety, health, and psychological security provided by the female matrix echoes the functions once associated with home and hearth and, especially since the nineteenth century, with women of the middle class. (Even the *Enterprise* herself is symbolically female and speaks with the voice of "*Star Trek* mother" Majel Barrett.)[15] Men, nurtured and protected in this secure feminine haven, can range into the larger world to conduct the business of technological mastery, political leadership, strategic dealings with the larger world, and the general pursuit of the community's ultimate aims and mission. Women meanwhile maintain the matrix, the frame within which the thoughts, feelings, and actions of the men stand for the human drama, the drama of everyman as everyperson.

Outward changes and continuities in the depiction of gender roles are important in themselves, but so is a deeper shift in the philosophical stance as to why gender roles exist at all. The later series, beginning some twenty years after the original *Star Trek*, reflects not just new ideas about social equality, fair hiring, and promotion practices, or concern for sexual modesty, but rather a whole new mythos of gender. At the root of this change is the rise of a social constructionist perspective. While *The Original Series* went out of its way to essentialize familiar gender patterns as timeless, universal, and immutable, the three later series entertain the idea (shared by radical feminism in particular and contemporary social science in general) that gender is a social construct whose meaning is almost infinitely flexible depending on the vicissitudes of cultural variation and that neither our own system nor any other has an automatically privileged claim to being more "natural" or laudable than others.

The social constructionist view of gender roles in the late series is not, as we have already seen, consistently developed, and anyone expecting a random distribution of behavioral traits among "male" and "female" in the *Star Trek* universe of the twenty-fourth century is in for a disappointment. Nevertheless, the point is repeatedly made that our gender constructs are anything but necessary. In the DS9 episode "Sanctuary," the Skreeans, a group of refugees from the Gamma Quadrant, have a social order dominated by women who are quite amused at the quaint idea of men in leadership positions since, as they allege, men are by nature too emotionally flighty to handle such responsibilities (they are, of course, useful as helpmates and sexual concubines). The most significant feature of this episode is that these radically different gender roles, which would have shocked Captain Kirk and forced him to intervene, are taken in stride by the DS9 crew. The Skreean gender norms are not integral to the main dramatic tension of the plot, which has to do with the Skreeans' plight as refugees. In short, the socially constructed nature of Skreean (and by implication our own) gender roles is used only to add a touch of local color to the episode, and no moral issue is made of it. Had such people appeared in TOS, a righteous denouement, surely bringing about a reversal of this travesty, would have been required.

TNG's "The Outcast" not only treats gender roles as social constructs, but it even goes so far as to question the necessity of gender distinctions of any kind. The J'naii are a race that has long ago done away with social gender roles and with heterosexual activity as well. Fetuses are incubated extrasomatically after being inseminated by two parents. Those few who still retain any vestige of gender identity or any sexual longings are regarded with disgust and are obliged to undergo therapy, as Riker tragically discovers when he and a J'naii named Soren fall in love. Although Soren makes an eloquent speech on behalf of tolerance for people like herself (but not for their particular superiority or naturalness), she later expresses gratitude for the therapeutic "cure" forced upon her, leaving Riker and the rest of us to wonder how we can tell right from wrong, choice from coercion, or the natural from the unnatural, when radically different cultures collide.

One of the few rigid gender codes to become an integral part of an ongoing story line is that of DS9's Ferengi, whose laws demand that women remain isolated in the home, naked and uneducated, excluded from business or other worldly activities, required to chew their sons' food for them, and so on. Since the Ferengi are buffoons also known for their avarice, deviousness, cowardice, and general boorishness, perhaps we should not be all that surprised to find that they are also, as Kira Nerys puts it, "misogynistic little trolls." The joke, it seems, is on them. Or at least, on some of them. Quark, a DS9 resident Ferengi of more decent character than he likes to admit, grudgingly becomes a secret accomplice of certain Ferengi females who defy the limit, including a woman who falls in love with him while masquerading as a man ("Rules of Acquisition"), as well as Quark's own mother who is put on trial for openly scorning custom by making an impressive profit in surreptitious business enterprises—and, shameless as she has become, wearing clothes in front of her grown sons ("Family Business"). Although Quark's prejudices run so deep that he is genuinely shocked by these women's behavior, he does not turn against them but cleverly manipulates Ferengi patriarchal conceits in order to help them avoid punishment. Apparently, traditional Ferengi notions of gender are almost too silly even for some Ferengi. In fact, it seems that Quark finds non-Ferengi women increasingly appealing: in "House of Quark" and "Looking for Parmach in all the Wrong Places," Quark finds himself in a politically mandated temporary marriage with a Klingon woman (Klingons are possibly the most assertive females in the *Trek* universe), and he becomes quite taken with her. In "Profit and Loss," Quark is reunited with a Cardassian ex-lover who is pursued by the Cardassian authorities as a firebrand dissident. In short, the exposure to a more cosmopolitan array of possibilities seems to move Quark toward a fascination with assertive women.

The Ferengi case illustrates the later *Star Trek*'s mediation of the issue of socially constructed versus essentialist views of human behavior. Peoples across the galaxy may be culturally different, but it is repeatedly suggested that these differences tend to become overridden by convergent "evolution" toward an ideal human condition (in this case, gender equality) that is everywhere the same. This message is most explicitly laid out, in connection with gender roles, in TNG's "Angel One." Arriving at the planet Angel One in search of survivors from a Terran ship, the *Enterprise* encounters a society ruled by an elected council of female oligarchs. At first, this social system evokes no disapproval aboard the *Enterprise*; Troi says that it reminds her of her home planet Betazed, and Worf remarks that Klingons, too, "appreciate strong women." When the away team pays their diplomatic respects to the ruling council, Riker proves willing not only to appear in the skimpy costume worn by the men of Angel One but even to be seduced by the planet's chief matriarch (all for the sake of diplomacy, of course). However, the planet's social system begins to appear more sinister as the *Enterprise* team realizes that the men of the planet are not only the mentally, physically, and politically weaker sex but that this supposedly "natural" order is maintained when necessary by the use of brute force—in this case, against the dissident Terran survivors and the outcast women of Angel One who have chosen to be with them. The Terrans and their wives, whose location is accidentally revealed during the action, face execution until Riker persuades the council that development toward gender equality is an irresistible "evolutionary" trend. Perhaps swayed by the fact that she finds Riker more attractive than the submissive males of her own world, the leader agrees to allow the dissidents to continue their lives in a remote part of the planet, thus slowing but not blocking the inexorable humanoid "evolution" toward gender liberation.

The most intriguing signs of changing American perceptions of male and female, however, are not necessarily the self-conscious attempts to grapple directly with gender issues but the cases where the plot and the casting treat male and female characters as personalities with no particular regard for their gender. For example, TNG's "Starship Mine" features an old-fashioned action struggle between Captain Picard and a band of ruthless terrorists led by a woman, culminating in the obligatory fistfight wherein Picard's adversary dishes it out like the hardened thug she is. In all three of the later series, it is quite often the case that a given character could have been cast as male or female with little or no resulting difference in the story—something that would have seemed out of place in TOS. In TNG's "The Best of Both Worlds, Part I," Riker contends with a brash, upwardly mobile young officer who sees him as lacking in ambition and aims to take his job. While the audience may read the character in a particular way because of her being female, the character is written and played in a manner that would make equally good sense had she been cast as a male; she does not show any of the wiles, paranoia, indirection, or pushiness that were employed in the earlier *Star Trek* to show that power and ambition were "unnatural" for women. It is true that the episode validates the camaraderie of the ship over the misguided ambitiousness of this young officer, but it does so in a way that could just as well have employed a male character.

Similarly, the fact that *Voyager*'s captain is a woman seldom affects the story lines in any significant way. Janeway's command of the conglomerate crew is the result of her rank in Starfleet and of the crew's recognition of her superior leadership abilities; thus by virtue of both institutional recognition and personal ability, she is undisputedly in command and worthy of the job. The only person with the stature to dispute her authority is Chakotay, now second in command but formerly the captain of an opposing Maquis vessel, and his loyalty is steadfast. Although it might be said that Janeway at times shows a bit more sensitivity and concern for the crew's personal feelings and interpersonal relations than Sisko or Picard might, and her relations with her first officer are sometimes complicated by their latent sexual attraction, the episodes seem to go out of their way to depict Janeway as every bit as tough, decisive, and professional as any other Starfleet captain. Janeway is *Star Trek*'s long-awaited answer to Janice Lester.

TINFOIL BIKINIS AND POLITICAL CORRECTNESS

The opening episodes of the 1997–98 VGR season ("Scorpion, Part II," "The Gift," "Day of Honor") introduce a new character, a recovering Borg called Seven of Nine, whose initially precarious costumes recall the famously titillating creations of TOS costumer Bill Theiss. Commentator John Hiscock attributes this development to a perception on the part of VGR's production team that the series has become "too prudish" and that ratings might be boosted by a return to the TOS tradition of "tin foil Bikinis." Hiscock quotes VGR creator Rick Berman to the effect that the series has lost some of its sexual spice because it has placed too much emphasis on being "politically correct."[16]

If "political correctness" means a sensitivity to feminism and other left-liberal political views, it is probably too simplistic to blame it for the decline of the "sexy" *Star Trek* female. More likely, the trend is caused by a complex interplay between progressive cultural change and certain thoroughly traditional notions about female sexuality. The liberal left is not necessarily antisexual (in fact, it is often accused of being libertine), but it is critical of the power-laden symbolism of women as the sole object of the sexual gaze, with men doing all the gazing. This criticism has undoubtedly influenced *Trek*'s far-from-consistent trend toward downplaying the sexual objectification of women. It would be just as "politically correct," and perhaps more interesting, to portray both men and women as sexually allured and sexually alluring. However, in our discussion of religion we suggested that one of the reasons for emphasizing sexual moderation (even for the notorious Captain Kirk) is to counter the allegation that, without religious scruples, people would be reduced to lusting beasts.

There is, however, a traditional prejudice about female sexuality that may influence *Star Trek*'s characterizations. In patriarchal traditions, men are permitted, even expected, to be both autonomous and sexual. Women's sexuality, however, is a benign force only when it is responsive, and accountable, to the male—that is, imbedded in a context of a "serious" relationship that a woman sees as leading potentially to marriage and parenthood. A woman who is self-directedly, autonomously sexual may be suspected of misusing her sexuality to gain illegitimate power. Therefore, a woman who holds legitimate authority is in a bind: if she is "responsively" sexual, she compromises her image of authority; if she is autonomously sexual, she casts doubt on the benevolence of her power; if she is asexual, she casts doubt on her "womanhood." Captain Janeway, whose authority and benevolence must remain beyond question, is constrained to take this last path; and as a consequence, she is seldom able to "let her hair down." "I'm the Captain," Hiscock quotes Janeway as saying; "There's no time to jump in the sack."[17] Time, however, probably has little to do with it.

The mediation of femininity, sexuality, and legitimate authority is a theme on which *Star Trek* narrative often plays, but cultural constraints prevent the play from going far. Although the sinister anti-Kira of the mirror universe is a sex kitten, Major Kira Nerys of DS9 confines her sexuality to "serious" relationships. Interestingly, one of the more serious of these is her chaste infatuation with Miles O'Brien when, through high-tech immaculate conception, she is pregnant with his (and Keiko's) child. Jadziah Dax seems to have some sexual flings prior to her marriage with Worf, but Jadziah is not all woman; as a joined Trill she is a sort of serial hermaphrodite and, over time, a bisexual person in the most far-reaching sense.

This brings us back to Seven of Nine. It is surely no accident that a profoundly category-defying character has been chosen for what VGR executive Brannon Braga calls an "infusion of sexuality."[18] Seven of Nine is sexually alluring but is alien to sexuality. With her cold Borg bravado, her superstrength and who-knows-what residual Borg appliances lurking in her body, she is rather too fierce to be approachable by men. Yet beneath the arrogant Borg facade is a little girl once assimilated against her will, waiting to be rescued by the maternal Janeway or perhaps wooed and softened by a nurturing male. The difficulty of placing Seven of Nine within the familiar semiotic polarities of gender, power, and sexuality is what gives her such an engaging potential for mythic explorations of these polarities.

CHAPTER 6

THE PERFECT MATE

Family, Sexuality, and Male Bonding

> Let us not forget that our lack of imagination always depopulates the future. . . . But the humanity of tomorrow will be living flesh. . . . New relations of flesh and sentiment of which we have no conception will arise between the sexes; already, indeed, there have appeared between men and women friendships, rivalries, complicities, comradeships—chaste or sensual—which past centuries could not have conceived.
>
> —Simone de Beauvoir
> *The Second Sex* (1949)

In the audio narration provided for the Smithsonian Institution's early 1990's exhibit on *Star Trek*, William Shatner and Leonard Nimoy remark with some regret on *The Original Series'* consistently negative portrayal of marriage and family life. In fact, TOS departed more substantially from traditional notions of monogamous fidelity and nuclear family cohesion than it did from patriarchal ideas of gendered social roles and personality traits. At the same time, *Star Trek* has, throughout the more than thirty years of its development, idealized and spiritualized the bond of friendship—especially male friendship—as the center of its vision of emotional intimacy, the basic unit and building block of true human sociability.

FEDERATION FAMILY VALUES

The antimarital bias of *The Original Series* should not be altogether surprising. In the milieu of the late 1960s, marriage was high on the list of social institutions that came under fire from a broad variety of social critics, including radical psychologists, Marxists, feminists, and various other prophets of the counterculture. It was widely believed that freedom from "repressive" and "possessive" monogamous restrictions not only would bring a release of positive psychosexual energies but would also foster a more healthy lifestyle that would in turn lead to a more equitable relationship between the sexes. In retrospect, it is clear that freeing sexuality from the constraints of monogamy and traditional morality, on the one hand, and freeing women from the burdens of male domination, on the other, are two different issues that are only tangentially related to one another. As the original *Star Trek* series illustrates in an unintended way, some classic patriarchal notions can thrive even in a world with little overt restriction of sexuality.

The twenty-third-century society envisioned in the original *Star Trek* idealizes the behavior of humans unfettered by traditional sexual restrictions. Nobody, apparently, believes in God or sin anymore, and never is it suggested that sex is harmful or immoral. Sexually transmitted diseases and unwanted pregnancies are, one may assume, things of the past. It is understood from the beginning that people are free in this future world to have sexual relations when and with whom they choose, without its becoming much of a moral issue. Yet somehow, despite the lifting of restraints, despite the acres of exposed female flesh, and despite Kirk's legendary irresistibility to women, life in space is anything but orgiastic. In fact, the most striking thing about most aspects of sexual relations in the twenty-third century is how little has changed—a point to which we shall return momentarily.

One thing, however, has changed radically. In keeping with TOS's antimarital bias, marriage and the family have all but vanished from the twenty-third-century universe. No central character aboard the original *Enterprise* has a spouse or permanent partner either on or off the ship, although some may have left a few failed relationships behind them. Neither do they have children, siblings, or parents who play significant roles in their lives. Captain Kirk has a brother, who appears only briefly as an already-dead body (played by Shatner himself in TOS's "Operation: Annihilate!"), and three nephews about whom no more is said. Although most of the cast has a moment or two of romantic involvement at some time during the series, these relationships always end—sometimes tragically—and the subject of marriage seldom comes up. Gene Roddenberry acknowledges the antimarital premise of *Star Trek* in an interview: "Marriage in the form that it is now cannot possibly continue into the future," he explains. "That's why we have so little of it in *Star Trek.*"[1]

Marriage, when it does appear, is often portrayed as an escape, a digression, or perhaps a punishment. Captain Pike is reunited with Vina in "The Menagerie," but only because he too has been horribly disfigured by an accident, and the life of illusion offered by the Talosians is the only prospect left for him. When McCoy thinks he is terminally ill in "For the Earth Is Hollow and I Have Touched the Sky," he decides to stay on a remote planet and get married; but as soon as his health is restored, he bails out. Captain Kirk finds marital bliss with the Indian maiden Miramanee while in a state of amnesia ("The Paradise Syndrome"), but she and their unborn child die just as he recovers the knowledge of his true identity. Spock falls in love while under the influence of mind-altering spores in "This Side of Paradise," but he is living in a fool's paradise, alienated from his true self and his genuine mission in life, and his love affair terminates the instant he comes to his senses. On the other hand, when the ruthless superman Khan is banished to a remote planet, his fate includes marriage to a crew member whom he has seduced ("Space Seed"). The unscrupulous Harry Mudd, who has surrounded himself with sexy androids, is punished for his many crimes by being marooned with multiple android copies of his nagging wife ("I, Mudd").

In the wake of the 1960s there was a cultural rehabilitation of the ideal of marriage and family life, and this change was clearly reflected both in political rhetoric and in media fantasies. Themes related to the affirmation of family life—for example, the reconciliation of estranged spouses, children, and siblings and the challenges of fatherhood—have become standard fare for television and film plots. Reflecting this trend, the characters in the later *Star Trek* series have a virtual army of parents, siblings, children, spouses, ex's, and so forth, all of whom sooner or later seem to find their way into a story or two. The characters thus acquire definite childhoods, off-ship loyalties, and the other complicating baggage of personal history. Picard has a brother with a family whom he rather envies; Deanna Troi, a domineering mother; Will Riker, a demanding father. Dr. Crusher and DS9's Sisko, O'Brien, and Quark all have family members on board. Even TNG's one-of-a-kind android, Commander Data, has someone he calls Father (Dr. Soong, the scientist who created him), Mother, (Dr. Soong's wife), Grandfather, (Dr. Soong's mentor), as well as an android evil twin "brother" Lore, a "daughter" Lal (Data's own creation), and a "lover," Tasha Yar. The functions of child care, schooling, and other necessities of ordinary domestic life are carried out in DS9 and aboard the *Enterprise D*. The premise of the VGR series is that loved ones are a lifetime's journey away—and yet, it is largely the pull of longing for them that keeps the crew striving, Odysseus-like, to reach home (in this way, the *Voyager* series recaptures aspects of the simpler adventure format of *The Original Series* while paying homage to 1990s family values). If the vision of space explorers freed from marriage and family made a certain kind of sense in the 1960s, the pendulum has since swung in the other direction.

Even in the more favorable environment of the later series, however, there are factors that keep the intensity of family and romantic couple relationships somewhat muted. First, there is the overriding importance of the larger community of the ship, which is central to Roddenberry's guiding ideas. The *Enterprise* is idealized as a utopia, with a nearly perfect reconciliation of community and individuality and diversity. Commentators on historical utopian societies have noted that these close-knit societies often develop institutions, such as celibacy or free love, whose purpose is to discourage romantic and familial attachments that might compete with the community.[2] In *Star Trek*, love relationships and familial ties may be significant plot elements, but they are also held in check. Potential lovers such as Deanna Troi and Will Riker, or Beverly Crusher and Captain Picard, maintain stoic restraint in the expression of their feelings; Doctor Crusher and DS9's Commander Sisko and Chief O'Brien are faced with the delicate task of reconciling parental responsibility with the knowledge that their communal responsibilities must come first.

Family ties are also limited by narrative conventions concerning the mythic hero and the heroic quest. In order to undertake the heroic quest, the archetypal hero must quit the comfort of hearth and family, or be forcibly deprived of them, or never really have had them to begin with (often the hero is a foundling or orphan, or originates in mysterious circumstances unlike those of a normal family). Domestic and personal comforts are, at least until the quest is completed, dangerous distractions and temptations. It should not come as a surprise, then, if the central characters in *Star Trek* do not enjoy secure, comforting intimate relationships.

There are strong hints of contemporary American social realities, too, in the *Star Trek* heroes' desire to avoid entangling relationships that might interfere with their ability to operate as free agents (e.g., Riker's choice of his career over his relationship with Deanna Troi). This theme of avoiding the inconveniences of intimacy may also help make sense of the propensity of *Trek* males to fall in love with imaginary, synthetic, or disposable women.

PLASTIC WOMEN

In his Epistles to the Corinthians, the Apostle Paul renounces many of the old Hebrew laws; but of the traditional codes that he does reaffirm, few are more clear than the imperative that women submit to men, "for neither was the man created for the woman; but the woman for the man" (I Corinthians 11:9). However, as Paul himself acknowledges, no sooner was woman created "for the man" than she started behaving inconveniently, causing man's fall from divine grace. Since social realities tend to fall short of the patriarchal dream of women who are molded to suit male needs, our narrative fantasies are likely to portray and mediate the resulting dissonance. Greek myth tells of the Cyprian sculptor Pygmalion who, disappointed with the women of his native land, created his own lover:

> Pygmalion knew these women all too well;
> Even if he closed his eyes, his instincts told him
> He'd better sleep alone. He took to art,
> Ingenious as he was, and made a creature
> More beautiful than any girl on earth.[3]

Pygmalion prayed to Venus for a woman as perfect as his own creation, and eventually, Ovid recounts, the goddess took pity on him, turning his artifice into a living bride.

Star Trek's science fiction world, with its androids, genetic manipulations, and holographic people, allows for the narrative possibility of creating humanoids to any specifications, and this possibility has frequently been exploited to conjure up artificial women who embody male fantasies. Flint creates an android lover in TOS's "Requiem for Methuselah," as do Harry Mudd in TOS's "I, Mudd" and Roger Korby in TOS's "What Are Little Girls Made Of?" and Kirk enjoys his virtual lover Ruth in TOS's "Shore Leave." Rhonda Wilcox draws attention to the use of computer holographics to create "synthetic women" who suit the fancies of TNG's men. Although women seldom if ever show an interest in creating synthetic males, she points out, the men have a "fascination with synthetic women as opposed to real ones—in particular, with holographic, computer-created women." Wilcox touches on several examples, including the holographic image of the late Lieutenant Natasha Yar that Data keeps in a drawer, Barclay's secret holodeck fantasy of Troi as his "Goddess of Empathy," and Geordi La Forge's infatuation with a hologram of scientist Leah Brahms whom he initially summoned up for technical advice. The centerpiece of Wilcox's discussion, however, is "the beautiful Minuet," who appears to Riker in a holodeck nightclub as a distraction to keep him from discovering a plan by the humanoid/computeroid "bynars" to commandeer the ship's computer (TNG's "11001001"). Riker says admiringly of Minuet, "She already knows what I want her to say before I'm aware of it myself." When Riker asks Minuet how real she is, she replies, "As real as you need me to be." But Minuet's face goes blank when she is not being addressed by men; her very existence is a function of male needs. She is, as Wilcox observes, "the ultimate convenience female."[4]

Although Wilcox's observations center on TNG, synthetic women appear in the other later series as well. The DS9 episode "Our Man Bashir" depicts Doctor Julian Bashir's spy-thriller holographic program featuring

Bashir as a James Bond-style secret agent with a voluptuous "valet" named Mona Lovsit, who is everything that a would-be ladies' man like Bashir could want. In VGR's "Alter Ego," a lonely alien female from a nearby outpost poses as a holographic woman in a *Voyager* holodeck program and, using the same be-whatever-they-want tactics as Minuet, manages to get first Harry Kim and then Tuvok to fall in love with her (when they discover that there is a real person behind the illusion, their interest in her disappears). In VGR's "Blood Heat," the holographic Doctor creates an enticing (but strangely mute) Vulcan maiden in a vain attempt to help the Vulcan crew member Vorik through the dangerous sexual phase of Pon Farr. These examples serve to reinforce Wilcox's perception that, in *Star Trek*, the ideal woman is often the objectified embodiment of male desire with no inner self to complicate the so-called relationship that a man may have with her.

Emily Hegarty makes a similar point in her commentary on the TNG episode "The Perfect Mate," which involves not a hologram but an "empathic metamorph" whom the *Enterprise* is to deliver as a diplomatic "gift" to cement an alliance between two warring worlds. The metamorph, Kamala, describes herself as having "the ability to sense what a potential mate wants, what he needs, what gives him the greatest pleasure, and then to become that for him, until I reach the final stage of bonding, when I must imprint upon myself the requirements of one man."[5] (The gender assumptions behind such a statement become obvious the moment one tries to imagine a man saying it!) Kamala, like "Mudd's Women" (TOS), has a disruptive effect aboard the ship, driving the male crew members to a state of almost desperate sexual desire, not only by the chemicals she exudes but also by the accommodating traits she adopts for each man whom she encounters. The reduction of woman to a commodity that serves male needs is powerfully expressed not only in Kamala's pliant behavior but also in what Hegarty calls her "objectified status as a diplomatic gift/slave."[6] Although Kamala is a supposedly willing participant in this objectification, she admits that she has never really been offered much choice in the matter. Comparing Kamala to Harry's Mudd's commodified mail-order brides in TOS's "Mudd's Women," Hegarty points out that Mudd's women, at least, were able to reflect upon who they were, but Kamala has no true self—she is what various men want her to be. Her only act of real choice is to "bond" with Captain Picard instead of the diplomatic groom chosen for her, but it is a worse-than-futile gesture, since in the end she is obliged to go through with a loveless political marriage and to give up all hope for personal fulfillment.

In a parallel argument, Karin Blair's 1977 book *Meaning in Star Trek* takes up the theme of "disposable women" who are "conceived as the embodiments of male fantasies." Such women are, in Blair's Jungian terms, projections of the male psyche's "anima," or female image. One reason for Blair's depiction of these women as "disposable" is their apparent expendibility in the service of the goals defined by male protagonists. In TOS's "The Mark of Gideon," for example, Odona's life is offered for sacrifice by her own father in order to bring a cleansing epidemic to their overcrowded planet. Odona is, as Blair puts it, "hardly real except in her utility, . . . serving as a function of the masculine will." Similarly, Edith Keeler in TOS's "The City on the Edge of Forever" is consigned to death in order to restore cosmic order and allow Kirk et al. to continue in their privileged historical time line. The Indian princess Miramanee, whom Kirk marries in TOS's "The Paradise Syndrome," is described by Blair as "the link, the prize—her life circumscribed by male agendas." Mr. Flint's android dream girl Rayna in TOS's "Requiem for Methuselah" dies from emotional upset when two men fight over her (as does Data's daughter Lal when Data and a Starfleet official contend for her in TNG's "The Offspring"). Even when these women are not killed off in the stories, their presence seems to terminate once their ephemeral dramatic usefulness ends, and most are seen only for an episode—which, as Blair argues, connotes another kind of disposability. Blair's discussion is limited to TOS and early films; and while the later series do have women who are neither "disposable" nor strictly a function of male needs, the male-fantasy woman continues to have a special irresistibility for *Star Trek* men.[7]

From the "synthetic" holographic women, to the empathic metamorph Kamala, to Vina in TOS's "The Cage" and the Companion in "Metamorphosis," *Star Trek*'s plastic women are able to fulfill the ideals of male desire by virtue of their having no independent self. One has only to try and imagine a reversal of this theme—men whose personhood is defined by the whimsies of women—to see the degree to which *Trek*, and the culture that produced it, still adheres to Paul's assumptions about gender.

THE SACRED MARRIAGE OF MALES

In an award-winning 1986 essay, April Selley attributes *Star Trek*'s enormous appeal to its stature as "the quintessential American romance."[8] Selley uses the term *romance* not only in the literary sense of a heroic adventure set in an exotic place but also in the more colloquial sense of a love story. If the love between man and woman in *Trek* is often shallow and always ephemeral, love between men is another matter. Drawing attention to the spiritual significance of male bonding in American fiction, Selley quotes Leslie Fiedler's *Love and Death in the American Novel*, in which Fiedler characterizes "an archetypal relationship which . . . haunts the American Psyche: two lonely men, one dark-skinned, one white, bent together over a carefully guarded fire in the virgin heart of the American wilderness; they have forsaken all others for the sake of the austere, almost inarticulate, but unquestioned love which binds them to each other and to the world of nature which they have preferred to civilization."[9]

"Nature undefiled," says Fiedler, "is the inevitable setting of the Sacred Marriage of Males." In Selley's view, the relationship between Kirk and Spock, in particular, fits this archetype of the American male romance. Separated from history, family, and race, Spock and Kirk have forsaken the comforts of civilization for "space, the final frontier." For Selley, D. H. Lawrence's characterization of the bond between Natty Bumppo and Chingachgook in the novels of James Fenimore Cooper might as well have been written of Kirk and Spock: "Each obeys the other when the moment arrives, and each is stark and dumb in the other's presence, starkly himself, without illusion created." Selley suggests that the Vulcan mind-meld, which takes place between Spock and various other characters, including Kirk, symbolizes "the fleshless Sacred Marriage of which Fiedler speaks." It is significant that *The Final Frontier*, a film that foregrounds the Kirk-Spock-McCoy relationship, begins and ends with the three men's sharing the camaraderie of a campfire in Yosemite. In that same film, Kirk shares with Spock and McCoy his premonition that he will die alone—which is taken to mean that he cannot die as long as these friends are with him (indeed, he dies a century later in the presence of Captain Picard—an ally but not an intimate friend).[10]

In the context of sacred male bonding, the influence of women can only be a disruptive force. Here again, Selley draws a parallel between *Star Trek* and the American romance as represented in Cooper's novels, where women are regarded with suspicion and even a "secret vindictiveness." In *Trek*, Selley observes, women from outside the *Enterprise* are "dark ladies" whose power over men poses a danger. Women's sexuality in *Trek* is often, as Emily Hegarty puts it, "voracious."[11] While a man's dark thoughts are usually of violence, a woman's malevolence in *Star Trek* is, Amelie Hastie argues, "played out primarily in terms of female heterosexuality gone haywire."[12] The depiction of women's sexuality as a devouring, irrational, antisocial force appears to be a widespread male preoccupation, expressed in such mythic themes as the Zuni Indians' Toothed Vagina Woman or the sirens and laurelei of Greek and European mythology.[13] The Borg Queen of *First Contact*, arguably the most powerful and purely evil villain yet to appear in the *Trek* universe, melds the Borg's project of taking over the universe with her own personal desire to seduce (and come between) Data and Picard. Even "innocently" attractive women like the celibate Starfleet officer Ilia (*The Motion Picture*), Mudd's Women, Elaan, or Kamala are disruptive influences aboard the *Enterprise*. When *Trek*'s women are sexual, it is sometimes a sign that they are under an evil influence or are themselves evil. In the twisted "mirror universe" of DS9,[14] male counterparts of familiar characters are aggressive and violent, while female counterparts tend to be wily, treacherous, and sexually "naughty." Indeed, the one female *Trek* protagonist who is best able to be heartily sexual when the occasion calls for it is Jadziah Dax, and it is probably no coincidence that she is also the most ambiguously female, since her personality as a joined Trill contains elements of Curzon and other previous male "hosts."

Sexual women are not only voracious seducers and devourers, but they are inherently given to stealth and concealment. They are time and again shown to be something different, and more dangerous, than they seem. In *The Undiscovered Country*, for example, the male heroes are betrayed by the scheming female Vulcan officer Valeris and are nearly delivered to their deaths by the shape-shifting siren Martia. The theme of women as deceivers who conceal their true nature is so endlessly repeated in *Star Trek* as to defy listing.[15]

The surest antidote for the spell of woman is the reassertion of male friendship. It is the bond of male brotherhood, for example, that saves both Data and Picard from the Borg Queen in *First Contact*, that La Forge uses to free the neurotic Lieutenant Barclay from his addictive holographic fantasies of Deanna Troi in TNG's "Hollow Pursuits," that rescues Spock from Leila's enchanting unreality in "This Side of Paradise" and from his sexual frenzy in "Amok Time," and so on. In TNG's finale "All Good Things," Worf and Riker learn that, despite Worf's constant fretting over Riker's feelings about his courtship of Troi, rivalry and grief over Deanna Troi may ruin their friendship in a possible future time line. This revelation seems to upset them more than the foretelling of Troi's death; and in the final scene, Riker and Worf implicitly resolve never to let this (the destruction of their friendship, that is), come to pass. In VGR's "Parturition," Paris and Neelix's divisive jealousy over Kes is transcended when the two go on an away mission during which they have a baby together—that is, they help deliver and nurture an infant nonhumanoid being on this remote planet. The experience cements Paris and Neelix's friendship, and Kes is all but forgotten in their quasi-marital exuberance. In VGR's "Alter Ego," the relationship between Harry Kim and Mr. Tuvok is strained when each of them falls in love with the same holographic woman; but when they realize that they are being courted by a real alien woman who is taking the form of a holographic female, they lose interest in her and concentrate on their own friendship. In the final scene of the episode, Kim and Tuvok decline the attentions of another holographic temptress who might distract them from the pleasures of one another's company.

Even if the woman in question is not evil, she is a potentially disruptive influence that calls for the reassertion of male friendship. In TOS's "The City on the Edge of Forever," the gesture by which Kirk forsakes the love of his life, the saintly Edith Keeler, is that of embracing McCoy so tightly that McCoy becomes helpless to prevent Keeler's death. As Kirk's determination melts into grief, his embrace with McCoy changes from one of forcible restraint to one of intimacy and solace.

Child psychiatrist Ilsa Bick charges that *Star Trek*'s preoccupation with the "circle of men" represents an expression of the "latency" stage of Freudian psychodynamic development—that is, the preadolescent stage characterized by (among other things) "the inability to successfully negotiate sexuality" and "an insistence upon woman's 'otherness.' "[16] In its "persistent focus on latency-age concerns," Bick suggests, *Trek* resembles other latency narratives, such as *The Wizard of Oz*, which ultimately emphasize a return to home and sameness rather than the liberating changes of more mature "adolescent" narratives. When Picard finds himself in the circle of card-playing friends at the end of the final TNG episode "All Good Things," he is, according to Bick, simply "discovering what the latency-age child has known all along: friends are at the center of the universe."[17] The claim that *Trek* reflects and reinforces a "developmental stuckness" at the preadolescent level depends, of course, not only on the acceptance of Bick's particular interpretation of *Trek* texts but also on the validity of the neo-Freudian developmental paradigm itself. Those of us who take a more agnostic view of Freudian theory may be uncomfortable with an interpretation that attributes such naiveté (if not perversity) to the postlatency women and men who enjoy *Trek*. Furthermore, Bick's reading of the textual "evidence" is subject to debate. Selley, for example, seems to anticipate Bick's argument when she denies that the American romantic hero is a "perpetual boy," arguing instead that he is a "sad and conscientious" figure who represents "prelapsarian virtue in a postlapsarian world" and is "his brother's keeper."[18]

Any discussion of male bonding as an emotionally powerful force—and particularly one that invokes such phrases as "the Sacred Marriage of Males"—must inevitably confront the issue of whether *Star Trek*'s intense male-male relationships are in some sense homosexual. Even the *Trek* text itself circumspectly refers to this possibility at times, as when Kirk starts to embrace Spock as they are reunited in *The Final Frontier* and Spock protests: "Please, Captain—not in front of the Klingons!"

Star Trek's male friendships, beside which most male-female relations pale, do have a romantic quality; and in recent scholarly writings on *Trek*, it has become fashionable to use the term *homoerotic* in reference to these relationships. Hegarty, for example, arguing that the "homosocial" and the "homosexual" are only differing intensities of the same thing, seems to read virtually all social relations between *Trek*'s men as in some sense homoerotic. Elyce Helford writes of the "homoerotic implications" of Kirk and Spock's reunion at the end of "Amok Time," suggesting that "Kirk can be read as sexually motivated to extricate Spock from his vow to T'pring." Moreover, according to Helford, the fact that Spock "teases" Yeoman Rand about the evil Kirk's attempt to rape her in TOS's "The Enemy Within" suggests Spock's "homoerotic attraction to the man who wields the power."[19] Bick not only sees "homoerotic" elements in the Vulcan mind-meld, but she also suggests that when Kirk and Spock "resort to violence, each literally beating the other" in TOS's "The Naked Time," it shows that "this is the only way in the master narrative that homoerotic elements can be consciously expressed."[20]

Contemporary scholarship on *Star Trek* seems to have a remarkable ability to detect not only homoeroticism but also homophobia. Helford, for example, refers to a "homophobic" scene at the end of TOS's "Turnabout Intruder" in which Kirk, recently rescued from a woman's body, is reassured of his masculinity by his ability to cast his "sexist gaze" on a crew woman.[21] Hegarty's analysis of TNG's "The Perfect Mate" attributes to Picard the unspoken sentiment that Kamala's betrothed, Alric, is "not man enough" for her, from which Hegarty deduces a "homophobic" attitude on Picard's part, a deduction that supports her conclusion that *Trek* is a purveyor of "misogynistic and homophobic" readings of Shakespeare.[22]

Arguments such as these draw attention to the complex sexual messages of *Star Trek*, including the role of ephemeral male-female liaisons in establishing the "manly" heterosexuality of the male protagonists, which in turn sets the stage for a portrayal of chaste, selfless, and deeply spiritual bonds between men. However, it is reasonable to question the usefulness of terms like "homoerotic" and "homophobic" when they are applied so loosely that one can see homoeroticism in a fistfight and homophobia in a sexual glance. It is not necessarily far-fetched to discern certain homoerotic or homophobic elements in *Trek*, but these needn't be as profound or as esoteric as some critics claim.

A different approach to the meaning of *Star Trek*'s male friendships can be seen in Jungian- and structuralist-influenced writings of the 1970s and 1980s, which centered on how the different characters (mainly in *The Original Series*) express the interplay, or structured opposition, of masculine and feminine gender traits in the various male characters. Blair's 1977 work *Meaning in Star Trek* associates Spock with the Jungian masculine or "animus" archetype, Doctor McCoy with the feminine "anima," and Kirk with the mediation of male-female.[23] Others cast Kirk and Spock, respectively, as feminine and masculine, citing Kirk's use of intuition as opposed to Spock's logic.[24] However, Rhonda Wilcox points out that the Vulcan sexual frenzy of Pon Farr, a hormone-driven periodicity that incites uncontrollable emotions, evokes cultural conceptions of the feminine in association with Spock.[25] Of the many ruminations about the masculine versus feminine traits reflected in *Trek*'s males, Elyce Helford's recent analysis is the most appealingly complex. Helford sees each character as displaying a complex mixture of traits (e.g., Kirk's independence and power; but also his intuitiveness, expressiveness, and inferior physical strength relative to Spock) that reflect our culture's complex explorations of what it means to be masculine.[26] But even at their best such arguments do not always make it clear whether the "gendered" nature of such traits as "intuitiveness" are constructs of the *Trek* narrative, of American culture, or of the scholar's own analytical framework. The emphasis on Kirk-Spock over *Trek*'s other male friendships, and the critics' drive to genderize and sexualize this friendship (even when they disagree on how it should be done), suggests the powerful pull of a theoretical undercurrent on the part of *Trek*'s academic critics—an undercurrent that may stem from the peculiarities of Western "depth" psychology.

Depth psychology in both its Jungian and its Freudian forms has left a general imprint on scholarly thought, an influence that promotes the notion of human attractions as deeply gendered and sexual. Jung emphasized the male and female components within each individual personality, and he posited an unconscious longing for the unification of these elements. Commentators like Blair who follow this approach tend to accept these archetypes of gender as immovable fixtures of the human psyche rather than as cultural artifacts that need to be explained and critiqued, and they use them as explanatory devices to show why, for example, Kirk-Spock-McCoy form a unity. Freud, on the other hand, was more interested in the erotic character of unconscious human drives. According to Freud, all human attraction and motivation comes ultimately from the libido (Id), as sublimated and redirected by the reality principle (Ego) and the conscience (Superego). For Freud, humans are "naturally" libidinous but antisocial; or to use a distinction we have employed in other connections, Eros is natural to humans, while Philia is artificially (i.e., socially) imposed.

Even for non-Freudians, this influential notion of the sexual/genderal foundation of the psyche has left a legacy of unexamined suppositions. Perhaps a society whose preoccupations were different from ours might have developed a view of the psyche in which sociality or Philia was assumed to be the most fundamental impulse, and such a view would not necessarily be less compatible with anthropological evidence about human behavior. The persistent sexualization and genderization of *Star Trek*'s male friendships in scholarly writings may say as much about our theoretical predilections, which fail to recognize sociality and friendship as a fundamental human motive, than about *Trek* or about people as such.

EROS, PHILIA, AND TALES OF *PON FARR*

Star Trek's conventions of intertextuality often lead to the continuation or revisioning of earlier *Trek* tales in much later episodes, sometimes in different series. One such case is the memorable tale of the Vulcan mating frenzy called Pon Farr in the TOS episode "Amok Time," which is mirrored and revisioned thirty years later in the 1997 VGR story "Blood Heat." Apropos of the preceding discussion of Eros, Philia, sexuality, and friendship in *Trek*, these episodes are interesting for their complex play upon these very themes.

"Amok Time" begins with Spock's behaving mysteriously out of character: he puts his own purposes before those of the *Enterprise* and its crew, hijacking the ship to take him to his home planet of Vulcan. As the story unfolds, we learn that Spock is under the sway of *Pon Farr*, a mating frenzy that overtakes Vulcans every seven years, at which time he must return home to mate. The situation turns out to be more grave than expected, since Spock's betrothed has taken the option of challenging Spock's right of marriage. Worse yet, she chooses Captain Kirk as her champion to engage Spock in a combat to the death. The ritual is binding upon Spock, who has no choice (especially in his desperate condition of *plak tow*, or blood fever) but to fight Kirk until one of them is dead. Spock's betrothed, T'pring, is actually in love with another Vulcan, and she has taken advantage of the ritual protocols to place Spock in a situation that will, whatever its outcome, destroy him and leave her free to take her paramour. The combat ends with Spock the victor; and after Kirk's lifeless body has been beamed back to the *Enterprise*, Spock utters one of his most famous lines in response to the Vulcan matriarch T'Pau's ritual farewell, "Live long and prosper": "I shall do neither," says Spock, "I have killed my captain and my friend." A doleful Spock beams aboard the *Enterprise* to find Kirk alive and well, his death having been simulated by Doctor McCoy's subterfuge. In the classic scene that follows, Spock, clearly on the verge of an emotional outburst at the sight of his friend, restrains himself with great difficulty and offers unconvincing denials of his elation.

VGR's "Blood Heat" also begins with an erotic disruption of community, when the Klingon-Terran Chief Engineer B'Elanna Torres finds herself the object of unwelcome sexual advances from the young Vulcan officer Vorik. When Torres rebuffs Vorik, he impulsively clamps her face in his hands. Afterward, the holographic Doctor surmises that Vorik has entered his first Pon Farr. Since they are some seventy years' travel from the Alpha Quadrant and the planet Vulcan, the Doctor must approach Tuvok, the only other Vulcan aboard, for advice. Tuvok, however, is reluctant to discuss Pon Farr, even with his younger Vulcan shipmate. The Doctor, thrown upon his own resources, attempts to ameliorate

Vorik's potentially lethal "blood heat" by creating a holographic Vulcan maiden. Meanwhile Torres, on an away mission with Paris and Neelix beneath the surface of a nearby planet, starts behaving irrationally. Vorik has unknowingly passed his condition along to Torres when he forcibly held her; and since the effects of Pon Farr on the Klingon-Terran physiology are unpredictable, Torres may be in more peril than Vorik.

In the subterranean caves, Torres is possessed by unbearable sexual urges and begs Paris to relieve her suffering. Paris, who has long sought her attentions, respectfully declines because, he explains, she is not really herself and would regret it later. Just when it seems that Paris has no choice but to do his duty and save Torres' life, Vorik appears to claim his "mate." Torres, however, surprises everyone by challenging Vorik's claim and naming herself as his adversary in ritual combat. Before long the two of them, alive but somewhat the worse for wear, lie exhausted on the field of battle. Their sexual urges have been rechanneled into aggression, and Pon Farr has abated. Later, Torres lets Paris know that he had done the right thing by resisting her sexual demands made under the influence of her unusual condition.

The differences between these two Pon Farr stories are revealing. In "Amok Time" the woman in question, T'Pring, shows no sexual inclinations herself. She does not act on her own behalf, but cunningly manipulates both tradition and male action to achieve her goals. Even in this matriarchal society, T'Pring is an object to be won, and she can avoid total objectification only by using indirection and feminine wiles. Torres, on the other hand, takes the initiative in sexuality, physical combat, and the generally straightforward assertion of her interests. The climax of the story, in which Torres batters Vorik in return for his unwelcome sexual advances, plays upon social issues concerning sexual harassment and coercion.

On another plane, however, these stories illustrate a pervasive pattern in *Star Trek*'s treatment of Eros and Philia. The primary motivation that drives *Trek* heroes, at least when their true natures prevail, is Philia—the emotions of loyalty, affiliation, selflessness, and friendship. Eros, in a muted and communal form, does play a role in the human quest for adventure, challenge, and growth. But strongly intoxicating and personalized Eros is portrayed in the *Trek* mythos as an intruder, a temporary state of bewitchment that threatens the integrity of the *Trek* crew both as individuals and as a collectivity. Paris, despite his sexual interest in Torres, instinctively recoils from a sexual encounter based on raw Eros because he knows that it would demean Torres' integrity and ultimately destroy their friendship. Eros-as-sexuality is closely allied (both in these stories and in Freudian psychology) with Eros-as-aggression, and each of these stories employs the device of redirecting sexual Eros into aggression and allowing it to come to a climax that averts harm to the community; hence, order is restored and the temporary triumph of Eros gives way to the return of stable Philia in the form of friendship and group loyalty.

AS TIME GOES BY

When it comes to marriage, family, gender roles, and sexuality, *Star Trek* has constructed a cautiously liberal rather than a radical vision of the future. It portrays a cosmos in which the values of America's liberal middle class are fulfilled, rather than one in which they have been radically reexamined and transformed.

Since radical social experiments are not presently in vogue, it might be useful to refocus our mental framework by considering the range of radical experimentation in America, where the nineteenth century witnessed viable alternatives to orthodox marriage and family life—for example, the group marriage practiced in New York's Oneida Colony, the polygamy of the Mormons, and the Shakers' highly successful practice of celibacy and gender equality. Over a century later, in the 1960s, America saw its most recent round of radical experiments involving free love, chastity, and various other patterns ranging from the anarchistic to the totalitarian and from the reactionary to the recklessly innovative.[27] Viewed in this American historical context of social experimentation—to say nothing of the global diversity of sexual and family arrangements—the timidity with which *Star Trek*'s twenty-fourth century has approached these matters is striking. In TNG's final episode "All Good Things," Picard travels into the future and meets another Captain Picard—that is, Captain Beverly Picard (formerly Beverly Crusher), who has married Jean-Luc, divorced him, and gone on to become a Starfleet captain. As with Jennifer Sisko, Benjamin's wife who has died before the beginning of DS9 (but whom Benjamin meets several times in an alternative future), we see that women who marry take their husbands' names and keep them after they have become estranged, gone their separate ways, and become independently successful. Although such practices are far from universal in our own time, they are taken for granted in this vision of the twenty-fourth century. Male protocols, too, will apparently retain the stamp of a time when women were objects of male possession: when Worf becomes interested in Deanna Troi, he asks another man (Troi's former lover Will Riker) for permission to court her. Why, one might ask, is it necessary to consult Riker, and if it is necessary, why is it a matter between two men rather than the two former lovers, or all three parties? The question of what Deanna Troi might want does not come up until Deanna herself raises it.

On the *Enterprise D* and the DS9 station, one encounters patterns of male-female relations that 1960s radicals would have associated with

their parents: monogamy, sexual fidelity, sexual jealousy, paternal authority, the nuclear family, and women as primary child care providers.
Chief Engineer Miles O'Brien's wife Keiko, a competent scientist, has
followed Miles to his assignment on the dreary station and finds herself
mostly hanging around their quarters in a traditional wife/mother role.
O'Brien is distressed over her restlessness, but aside from a token effort
at teaching school (a classically female occupation) and a few temporary
off-station assignments, husband and wife are unable to imagine any
viable alternatives.

Despite the common perception of Captain Kirk as an interplanetary
ladies' man, the sex lives of *Star Trek* heroes are wholesome if not prudish by current American standards. One might expect that, in a future
where sex is not "sinful" and has no unwanted physical consequences,
people would engage in a great deal of it. The characters in all the *Trek*
series, however, are closer to the chaste knights and ladies of Arthurian
fantasy than to the libertines with whom they share prime television
time. Even James Kirk, for all his flirting and muscle flexing, seems to
have a fairly tame sex life. The aliens who hang around Quark's establishment may frequent his virtual-reality brothels, but DS9's heroes snort
disdainfully at any such notion (Quark himself would be a bit out of
character if he partook). Nice people do not do nasty things on the *Enterprise D*'s holodeck either; the shy, neurotic Barclay arouses great indignation when the others catch him enjoying sexy flirtations with a
holodeck image of Troi in TNG's "Hollow Pursuits" (Kira Nerys takes
a more direct approach, threatening to kill Quark for attempting to use
her image in a holosuite fantasy for one of his infatuated clients). Those
who might indulge in sex for sheer pleasure, such as Harry Mudd with
his female androids in TOS's "I, Mudd," are liable to get their come-
uppance. Unbridled promiscuity, orgies, and group sex are scarcely to
be found in the *Trek* universe, even on the most exotic and unsavory
planets (although some exceptions are hinted at, as in the pleasure planet
of TNG's "Justice" and the delights available to the guests at Quark's
DS9 "establishment").

Neither does the *Star Trek* galaxy have room for gay relationships. If
a significant portion of humanity throughout earth history has been gay,
this fact is either altered in the future or kept very well hidden. Everyone's heterosexual credentials are established early in each series, as in
"The Naked Time" (TOS) and "The Naked Now" (TNG) when the web
of suppressed heterosexual attractions within each crew member is revealed under the influence of an inhibition-destroying toxin. It is probably no accident that Mr. Data and Tasha Yar, arguably the two most
androgynous characters on the TNG crew, are the only ones actually to
consummate these longings. Odo, a shape-shifter whose human form
(and thus his gender?) are arbitrary illusions, might also be suspect were

it not for the fact that various episodes establish his attraction for Kira and his attractiveness in turn to Deanna's mother Lwaxana Troi; in the 1997 DS9 episode "A Simple Investigation," Odo finally has an actual sexual affair with a humanoid woman.

Some titillating brushes with homosexuality do occur, as when a Ferengi woman, disguised as a man, falls in love with Quark and kisses him (DS9's "Rules of Acquisition"). When "he" attempts later to explain, the embarrassed Quark insists that it did not happen. A still more indirect approach can be seen in TNG's "The Outcast," when Soren makes an impassioned plea for tolerance of sexual "deviance" (in this case, her heterosexuality in an asexual society) that unmistakably echoes the arguments of contemporary gay apologists. The lesson of tolerance for sexual preferences is clear, but a direct treatment of homosexuality is artfully avoided.

One the best known "exceptions" to *Star Trek*'s avoidance of homosexual themes is the 1995 DS9 episode "Rejoined," which involves two joined Trills, Jadziah Dax and Dr. Lenara Kahn. The two had been husband and wife in previous host-symbiont joinings, and their discovery that they are still in love places them in opposition to a strict Trill law against "reassociation" (regardless of whether the hosts in question are of the same or different sexes). Jadziah urges Lenara to accept banishment, and hence the eventual death of their symbionts, so that they can be together. Lenara finally decides otherwise, but not before the two engage in a passionate woman-to-woman kiss whose infamy rivals Kirk and Uhura's "first interracial kiss on television" almost thirty years before. But however the "kiss" scene may look when viewed out of context, it is part of what is defined, within the narrative frame, as a heterosexual relationship. In that sense, the premise of the incident is only a little more daring than TNG's "The Host," in which Beverly Crusher reluctantly chooses to end her love affair with a Trill after "he" passes into a new host body that happens to be female.

Even though the kiss in "Rejoined" is not really lesbian, it nevertheless goes farther than *Star Trek* would likely go in physical relations between men—no matter how good the extenuating explanation. The taboo against gay male sexuality is strong in *Trek*, and it is only in a few framebreaking, self-parodying moments that homosexuality is indirectly suggested: for example, in Spock's "Please, Captain—not in front of the Klingons!"[28] or in *First Contact*, when Troi finds Data and Picard caressing the side of an erect missile as they discuss the tactile element of human understanding and she asks them whether they would like to be alone. It may or may not be the case that the American viewing public, or at least those who control the content of television, are more tolerant of lesbian than gay male sexuality. But as we have suggested, gay male sexuality would also run counter to the theme of idealized and spiritu-

alized male friendship that is so central to *Trek*. While *Trek* is not especially erotic, it is deeply devoted to creating a mythos of Philia—
particularly its expression through male friendship.

Why has *Star Trek* failed to exploit the possibility of enhancing the
mythos of friendship/Philia by developing deep friendships among
women? After thirty years, there are still no female friendships that carry
anything like the emotional depth or the elements of self-transcendence
that one sees in male friendships. It is hard to offer any explanation other
than the most painful one: that *Trek* has remained so wedded to patriarchal notions of the "otherness" of women and their sexual (as opposed
to social) nature that it has proven unable to take its own central mythos
as far as it might. At least, not yet.

The late 1997 DS9 episode "You Are Cordially Invited" marks an event
of no small significance: the first-ever marriage of two central *Star Trek*
characters. This episode provides an occasion for some summing up of
Trek's mythos of gender and family after three decades of storytelling.
As the big day approaches, the groom, Worf, frets endlessly about guest
lists and details of the ceremony, while bride-to-be Jadziah Dax indulges
him with a cheerful but pragmatic let's-get-it-done attitude. Dax's pre-
nuptial celebration is a wild party, while Worf goes into somber retreat.
Thus, the story plays with role reversals at the level of personal style.
On the cultural and social level, however, the events surrounding the
wedding depict a gender asymmetry that could hardly be more conservative. The story centers largely on the trials through which Dax is put
by her future in-law, the formidable "Mistress of the House of Martok."
Dax is so humiliated by her hazing that she almost backs out of the
wedding, but Sisko argues that, in agreeing to marry Worf, Dax had
accepted the necessity of conforming to Klingon custom and ritual. Although the Trill are known to have abundant rituals and customs of their
own, these are never so much as mentioned. Dax is entering Worf's
"house" and not vice versa; submissiveness to in-laws and minute conformity to Klingon culture is all part of the passage.

Meanwhile Sisko, Bashir, and O'Brien are taking part in Worf's "bach-
elor party," a heroic trial in a holodeck wilderness complete with self-
torture and lurking death ("sounds like marriage," quips Bashir). The
sacred marriage of males around an austere campfire amounts to a reaffirmation of the male brotherhood in the face of this new relationship.
The pageantry of male bonding is accompanied by a reassertion of important male-female friendships, including a reconciliation between the
temporarily estranged Odo and Kira and a heart-to-heart talk between
Dax and Sisko. But there is no corresponding celebration of female-
female bonds—and indeed none worth celebrating.

Insofar as myths are the stories we tell ourselves about ourselves, they
have a wonderful capacity to surprise us when we look at them unflinch-

ingly. In retrospect, *Star Trek's* portrayal of gender roles and relations has evolved from the doggedly essentialist viewpoint of *The Original Series* to a more liberal, but nonetheless far from radical, outlook in the later series. Given its unique opportunity to stretch our imagination about human relationships, *Trek* has stretched farther in some directions than in others, and there are some instructive patterns in what *Trek's* immensely popular vision of the future has given us. While technology has advanced exponentially and traditional religious morality has all but vanished, the notion of a woman fully retaining her identity after marriage, or managing her relationships without the guidance of patriarchal conventions, seems further out of reach in the twenty-fourth century than it did for many visionaries of the past. The liberating changes apparent in the sexuality and gender roles of the *Trek* universe are biased in favor of those that remove irrational barriers to male freedom, male friendship, and male fulfillment.

This unevenness in the reach of *Star Trek's* imagination reveals important partialities in our own time and world. It may well point to the strength of cultural forces that drive gender hegemony. As Simone de Beauvoir argued a half century ago, our lack of imagination concerning the future of gender should come as no surprise, since gender essentialism is one of our most deeply embedded cultural constructs. Paradoxically, it is *Trek's* earnest attempt to explore the unrealized possibilities of gender within human relations that leads us to a recognition of how far we still have to go.

CHAPTER 7

THIS SIDE OF PARADISE

Utopian Visions

A map of the world that does not include Utopia is not even worth glancing at, for it leaves out the one country at which Humanity is always landing.

—Oscar Wilde
The Soul of Man Under Socialism (1895)

What is utopia, after all, but a narrative of an ideal way of life? Whatever moral values people hold, they are often struck by the disparity between their ideals and the realities of human existence with its undeserved privilege and suffering, its pointless conflict and cruelty, its troubling gap between motive and conscience. It is as though life were a jigsaw puzzle with the pieces cut in shapes that cannot connect. The utopian is someone who envisions how the various facets of personal and social needs might be made to fit together harmoniously. Utopian myths, and the societies modeled upon them, vary greatly in their approach to problems of achieving this "fit." Utopias may be hierarchical or democratic, repressive or expressive, religious or secular, high-tech or rustic, large or small, self-promoting or reclusive, open or closed to change. Utopia may be framed as a return to the primordial state of Paradise or as a new age of unprecedented enlightenment. Yet the central defining trait of utopia, as George Kateb proposes, is the idealization of harmony:

Are we not entitled to speak of utopia as that system of values which places harmony at the center: harmony within the soul of each person, harmony of each person with all others, harmony of each person with society at large; as that system of values which would hold social life to be perfect if between appetite and satisfaction, between precept and inclination, between requirement and performance, there fell no shadow? Is not this the vision of utopianism through time; is not this the substance of the longings of common humanity? Is not utopianism the moral prepossession of our race?[1]

If the utopian myth is the expression of humanity's yearning for harmony, it is ironic that utopias can provoke such virulently disharmonious opposition as they do. Vehement objections to utopian visions are as old as the notion of utopia itself, going back at least to the critics of the philosophically perfect society depicted in Plato's *Republic*.

Thus, while Oscar Wilde may be right in his claim that humanity is continually "landing" in utopia, not everyone who lands there likes what they find. Anyone acquainted with the original *Star Trek* series will recall various episodes in which the *Enterprise* encounters a planet where people live a peaceful, orderly, and effectively planned existence that they find pleasant and fulfilling. Despite Starfleet's unequivocal rule against interference, Captain Kirk finds it necessary to destroy this "Paradise," taking the opportunity to lecture on the undesirability of a life of effortless happiness. As the episode ends, Kirk and the *Enterprise* reembark on their voyage of discovery, leaving the survivors of the broken utopia to find their way in the healthier milieu of individualism, competition, and strife, while Spock raises a pointed eyebrow in puzzlement at human irrationality.

It is easy enough to dismiss *Star Trek*'s cautionary "Paradise" tales as conservative diatribes against the dreams of the utopian left—as briefs for the "Middle American" ideals of individualism and competition. Indeed, some of Captain Kirk's speeches, taken by themselves, invite such a reading. However, there is more to the *Trek* mythos than is covered in Kirk's occasional "storm and struggle" soliloquies. The dissenting voice of Mr. Spock and the Vulcan ethos, the evolving discourse of *Trek* in the 1980s and 1990s, and the frankly utopian character of the Starship community contribute to making *Trek*'s utopian dialogue one of the richest mythic projects ever developed on commercial television.

We have said that myths are a people's deep stories, whose purpose is to confront cultural ambivalences and to place experience into cosmological context. *Star Trek*'s narratives of utopia reflect and mediate issues on a number of different levels, ranging from the rise and aftermath of the 1960s' "peace and love" counterculture, to the broader American discourse on individualism and community, to the most deeply rooted philosophical inquiries on the human condition (Plato wrote *The Republic* not to inspire a social experiment but to explain justice). A good place to begin, perhaps, is to situate *Trek* in relation to the modern Western dialogue on utopia.

The nineteenth century was the great age of Euro-American utopianism. The foundations had been laid in the preceding centuries—for example, in the imaginary utopias of Renaissance literature, including the 1516 work by Thomas More that gave us the word *Utopia* itself, a pun exploiting the similarity of the Greek words for "good place" and "no place." The forebears of nineteenth-century utopias also included radical Christian movements devoted to reclaiming the ideal of a simple, selfless, and loving community based on the lives of the early Christian Apostles. By the nineteenth century, the literary and sectarian facets of the utopian movement were in full flower. They were joined by a plethora of social theories (including some that were foundational to modern sociology) that spelled out visions of a more harmonious society based on modern reason and science; such theories gave rise to scores of actual communitarian experiments.[2]

If the nineteenth century was the heyday of utopia, the twentieth century has seen the rise of the dystopia. A "dystopia" is a narrative construct of a false utopia—not simply a bad or evil society, but one that is evil in spite of, or specifically because of, its utopian claims. The false utopia as a literary type first became prominent as part of the backlash against the warm utopian vision of Edward Bellamy's popular novel *Looking Backward* (1888). The continuing strength of the dystopian theme in literature draws upon certain ominous trends in modern society, including not only the rise of the totalitarian regimes of the communist left and the fascist right but also the cultlike veneration of corporate conformity, hedonism, and sterile efficiency in modern capitalist industrial societies. Dystopian fiction takes for granted at least a vague awareness of the utopian narrative form, since it ironically depicts societies that lay claim to utopian status but that are very obviously (from the author's perspective) contrary to human good. Among the well-known dystopian narratives of this century are Eugene Zamiatin's *We* (1920), Aldous Huxley's *Brave New World* (1932), George Orwell's *Nineteen Eighty-Four* (1949), and Kurt Vonnegut's *Player Piano* (1952), to name only a few. This is not to say, however, that utopian writings have ceased. *Walden Two*, written in 1955 by psychologist B. F. Skinner, is one of the most noted utopias of all time and has become the inspiration for a number of societies in the United States and elsewhere. Even Aldous Huxley, author of the infamous dystopia *Brave New World*, penned the 1962 utopian work *Island*. Utopia has not been displaced by dystopia; rather, the two have become voices in a conversation about the good life.[3]

Just as utopian narratives implicitly criticize the status quo, some of the hostility directed against utopia has been based on an unreflective conservatism that holds that familiar social arrangements are mandated by nature, or by God, or by self-evident canons of propriety—in short, by forces that lie outside the proper domain of human choice. But there is another, more thoughtful line of critical dialogue about utopia that often surfaces in *Star Trek*. Some critics of utopia may in fact be sympathetic to utopian ideals but may nevertheless see those ideals as vulnerable to misdirection, or even as inherently self-defeating. Such critics insist on probing the deep issues behind utopia—issues such as the nature of happiness, the moral relationship of the individual to society, and the problem of reconciling order with freedom.[4] We shall return to these issues after a glimpse at some of *Trek*'s most infamous utopias.

HELLISH HEAVENS

Stardate 3156.2: The U.S.S. *Enterprise*, under the command of Captain Kirk, has been sent to the planet Beta III to investigate the fate of the U.S.S. *Archon*, a Federation ship that had disappeared there a century before. The landing party runs into trouble, and Sulu is retrieved in a trancelike state, smiling beatifically and murmuring about a "paradise" of "the sweetest, friendliest people in the world." Kirk and the others beam down to find a society whose style of dress and speech are reminiscent of late-nineteenth-century America, with hints of a lobotomized version of communal harmony styled on the popular image of Quakers and similar Christian sects. Spock comments on the aura of "mindless, vacant contentment" among the people, but the bland ritual greetings of "Joy to you, friends" are interrupted when the clock tower chimes the hour and the people are seized by what turns out to be a twelve-hour seasonal orgy of lust and violence called "festival." When Kirk and his companions question what is happening, their hosts perceive that these strangers are "not of the body," and one of the locals runs off to inform the so-called Lawgivers. Monklike enforcers arrive to announce that the visitors "will be absorbed." Spouting such slogans as "The good is all" and "Landru is gentle," the enforcers kill one of Kirk's hosts for his reported irreverence to the Lawgivers.

The enforcers are befuddled to a standstill when Kirk's team flatly refuses to accompany them to the brainwashing "absorption chamber." The *Enterprise* team escapes and, after dodging a lethal mob mobilized by an unseen hypnotic force, is guided by one of their hosts to a hideout of the resistance movement. The team learns that the present regime was established thousands of years ago by a leader named Landru, who saved the planet from self-destruction by restoring the culture to the ways of "a simpler time" of "peace and tranquillity." Landru appears to Kirk and Spock in a holographic projection and explains that this is "a world without hate, without fear, without conflict: no war, no disease—none of the ancient evils." Landru, the hologram explains, "seeks peace for all, the universal good." Kirk and his companions, however, have "infected the body" by sowing the seeds of doubt. "You will be absorbed," Landru's image intones. "Your individuality will merge into the unity of the good, and in your submergence into the common being of the body you will find contentment and fulfillment; you will experience the absolute good." Such was, apparently, the fate of the so-called Archons, the rebellious survivors of the U.S.S. *Archon* who evidently did succeed in planting some lasting seeds of resistance. The resistance movement helps Kirk and Spock escape "absorption," but the dissenters' wavering resolve is tested when Kirk demands to be taken to Landru. In Landru's chamber, Kirk and Spock's suspicions are confirmed: Landru is a computer, programmed with the original Landru's social designs but not with his "wisdom" or his "soul." Ignoring the computer's protest that it has successfully maintained harmony, Kirk causes it to destroy itself by confronting it with the contradiction between its programmed ends (protection of the "body") and its actual means, which have denied freedom and creativity and therefore stifled the "full potential of every individual of the body." "Without freedom," Kirk says, "there is no creativity; without creativity there is no life. The body dies; the fault is yours." Landru obligingly erupts into smoke and sparks.

At one point in the story, Spock objects that the destruction of Landru would be a violation of Starfleet's Prime Directive of noninterference. Kirk dismisses the objection, saying that the rule applies only to "a living, growing culture." Again, at the end of the story, Spock seems haunted by doubt, noting "how often mankind has wished for a society as peaceful and secure as the one provided by Landru." "Yes," responds Kirk, "and we never got it—just lucky, I guess!"

As they leave Beta III, the *Enterprise* crew members receive a report from Mr. Lindstrom, the sociologist who is supervising Beta III's return to a "normal human" culture following Landru's demise:

Kirk: How are things going?

Lindstrom: Couldn't be better! Already this morning we've had half a dozen domestic quarrels and two genuine knock-down drag-outs. It may not be Paradise—but it's certainly human.

The episode just described, entitled "The Return of the Archons," employs a basic formula that is repeated, with some variation, in many of *Star Trek*'s later dystopian encounters: (1) a utopian—or rather, dystopian—community of peace and harmony is encountered on a newly discovered planet; (2) members of the *Enterprise* crew are drawn into the midst of this social order and (3) find their freedom jeopardized until (4) they finally reemerge from this constricting social order by asserting their freedom of thought and action and (5) liberate the members/victims of the dystopia, (6) returning them to a more "natural" path of development, justified in (7) a concluding soliloquy about the shortcomings of "Paradise."

The same plot formula underlies a rather different dystopian tale in TOS's "This Side of Paradise," which aired only three weeks after the "Archons" episode. A landing party beams to the planet Omicron Ceti III, where the party expects to find no survivors of the deadly "Berthold" rays bombarding the site of an agricultural colony. To their surprise, the members of the party encounter the colony's leader Elias Sandoval and others in perfect health, and they find the members of the colony mysteriously stubborn in their refusal to leave the planet. Spock encounters Leila Kalomi, a woman whose love for him in a previous meeting had been unrequited. She shows him the secret of the colony's survival—plants whose spores bestow not only immunity to the deadly rays but perfect health and happiness as well. After a painful struggle, Spock succumbs to the euphoria induced by the spores. The ensuing encounter between a puzzled, still-normal Kirk and a Spock intoxicated with joy, childlike whimsy, and romantic love is one of the great moments of the series. The colonists praise their life as a "return to a simpler time," a "perfect world" of peace, love and harmony, a world without sickness, death, need or want. Spock concurs: "It's a true Eden, Jim—there's belonging, and love."

Soon all the *Enterprise* crew, including the recalcitrant Captain, have come under the influence of the spores and are making preparations to abandon their ship. Just as Kirk is about to beam down, he experiences a wave of anger and remorse at betraying his duty. The agitation frees Kirk from the spell, causing him to realize that the influence of the spores is nullified by strong emotions. Kirk lures Spock onto the ship and he taunts him into a violent rage. Spock, having come to his senses, helps devise a plan (involving anger-inducing sonic vibrations) to free the others from the influence of the spores. As Sandoval suddenly recovers his sanity, he looks around at his utopia of health, happiness, and social harmony and declares, "We've done nothing here—no accomplishment, no progress."

Back aboard the *Enterprise*, McCoy observes, "That's the second time that man has been thrown out of paradise." Kirk's reply is classic:

> No—this time we walked away on our own. Maybe we don't belong in Paradise, Bones. Maybe we're meant to fight our way through. Struggle. Claw our way up, fighting every inch of the way. Maybe we can't stroll to the music of lutes, Bones—we must march to the sound of drums.

Asked his opinion of Omicron Ceti's "Paradise," Spock replies, "I have little to say about it, Captain, except that, for the first time in my life, I was happy."

The standard dystopian plot formula is employed again during the second season episode "The Apple," in which the references to Judeo-Christian mythology are even more clear. In this story, the gentle, child-like primitive inhabitants of Gamma Trianguli VI enjoy perfect health, contentment, and social harmony, protected and nurtured by Vaal, a machine that punishes wrongdoers with deadly lightning bolts. The people, who call themselves the Feeders of Vaal, must make offerings of food (easily available rocks) to meet the computer's energy needs. Threatened with destruction by Vaal, the *Enterprise* uses its phasers to annihilate it, setting the people on a path of development more palatable to Kirk's taste. Vaal is represented by the huge carved head of a serpent, and its name bears a striking resemblance to a biblical reference to false gods, or Baal (plural, Baalim). But in this case it is, as Spock points out, Captain Kirk who plays the role of the serpent, offering human freedom and human knowledge (and incidentally, sex) in place of eternal perfection and virtual immortality, destroying the people's obedient faith and causing them to be driven from Eden. In defense of these actions, Kirk and McCoy argue that the Edenic existence is not "real" and that they have simply "put those people back on a normal course of social evolution."

"I, Mudd" is a comedy featuring the rascal Harry Mudd, hundreds of voluptuous female androids, and a good dose of slapstick. At its core, however, is a variant of the dystopian plot formula. The *Enterprise* is hijacked to a world of superhuman androids who offer the crew members the fulfillment of their every desire—even immortality—in exchange for their freedom. The androids are not going to take no for an answer, for their intent is to commandeer the *Enterprise*, maroon its crew, and eventually to place the whole "dangerous" human race under its watchful care. The crew members team up with their erstwhile adversary Harry Mudd to confuse the androids with insistent proclamations that they cannot bear a life of perfect happiness. They do this mainly because they know that this "irrationality" (together with some other creative nonsense) will cause the bewildered androids to blow their circuits, but this seemingly paradoxical aversion to total happiness is actually very much in keeping with what is said in the other dystopian stories.

In another variant of the dystopia plot, *The Original Series* episode "The Way to Eden" features a group of young refugees from a damaged ship. They are seekers of the legendary planet Eden, led by the deranged charismatic visionary Dr. Sevrin. These communal utopians are clearly modeled on the "Flower Children" of the 1960s, and their childlike faith finds outlet in sensual spontaneity. Spock is strangely drawn to them and they to him; it seems that they "reach" one another. He joins them with his Vulcan harp in a jam session, and he even goes so far as to help them find the planet Eden. In the end, however, their vision is as ill-fated as that of other utopians. The planet Eden turns out to be poisonous, Adam dies with the deadly fruit of Eden in his hand, and Sevrin stubbornly commits suicide by biting into it in defiance of all warnings. Spock offers the only words of encouragement after their tragic failure: "It is my sincere wish that you do not give up your search for Eden. I do not doubt but that you will find it—or make it yourselves."

PARADISE MISPLACED

Hardly anyone would seriously oppose the project of making a better life for themselves and their neighbors. The question is, How can we tell genuine improvement from dangerous illusions? Perhaps we are all uto-pians in the final analysis; but in the shorter run, Western social thought tends to divide those who believe that we should take a direct approach to righting the wrongs of society from those who fear that a head-on approach to social improvement may have unintended consequences quite contrary to the goals of reformers. To the former (the so-called utopians) the skeptics may seem to lack moral courage and vision; to the skeptics, the utopians may appear naive and overly literal in their ap-proach to human problems. The debate between these two positions is a long-standing one in the Western cultural tradition; but in order to grasp *Star Trek*'s particular approach to these issues, we must consider it within the specific context of its time and cultural milieu.

The romantic primitivism of the 1960s counterculture, with its empha-sis on a rustic life of peace and harmony, its flirtation with visionary gurus, and its interest in pleasure-inducing elixirs, provided the most immediate cultural backdrop against which TOS's utopian meditations were projected. The premises of the counterculture, however, are imbed-ded in the broader discourse of American cultural history. Americans have, for good reasons, often seen their nation as an unprecedented uto-pian social experiment—as Lincoln put it, "the last, best hope of earth." This self-appointed prophetic mission has confronted America with a fundamental issue regarding human improvement: Should we create a better society—a New Jerusalem, so to speak, and trust it to produce better individuals? Or shall we put our faith in the unfettered, freely self-perfected individual, the New Adam, and let society follow as it will? Does moral priority go to the individual or to society? Although Amer-ica's mythos openly venerates the individualist side of the scale, we remain deeply ambivalent. The force of this ambivalence has waxed and waned through different periods of our history.

The 1840s, for example, was a time of heightened American soul searching that illustrates the historical depth of our ambivalence about the New Jerusalem versus the New Adam. The French writer Tocqueville had recently coined the term *individualist* to describe the new American character, and the 1840s was the decade when Ralph Waldo Emerson published his celebrated essay "Self Reliance" and when his neighbor Henry David Thoreau sought the purifying solitude of Walden Pond. It was the decade when James Fenimore Cooper published the last two of his Leatherstocking novels, and it witnessed the culmination of two decades of mythmaking about Daniel Boone and Davey Crockett, which brought into popular focus the mythic icon of the virtuous, natural, self-created frontiersman.[5] At the same time, the 1840s was also the century's great decade of commune building, when scores of communal and cooperative social experiments tried to set reformist examples for the world to follow. These experiments included not only religious societies like the Amana and Shaker colonies but also the American followers of the French communitarian theorist Charles Fourier (including Horace Greeley of "Go West, young man" fame) and even some of Emerson's New England transcendentalist associates. In his critique of his communalist colleagues, Emerson made it clear that he and they were following very different paths.[6]

The 1960s was marked by a storm of cultural self-contradiction over many of the same issues. For the two preceding decades, sociologists and cultural critics had been turning out alarmist critiques that warned of America's loss of traditional individualism in an age of corporate organization and social conformity.[7] It is probably no accident that this period also produced, in the "Western" genre of film and television, a plethora of morality tales in which the interplay of order versus freedom, society versus self, and the cultural versus the natural "man" were played out. The 1950s popular-culture revival of Davey Crockett as a mythic figure helped bring about a renewed focus on the American Adam. In the 1960s, with the impetus of the antiwar and civil rights movements, America's turmoil boiled up a so-called counterculture that was widely seen, from both sides of the fence, as a rejection of traditional American values. In retrospect, however, it is clear that some very traditional American themes and contradictions emerged in the mythos of this supposed counterculture. The commune building of the 1960s surpassed even that of the 1840s, but along with the much-touted ethos of harmony, peace, and community there coexisted strong themes of "do-your-own-thing" individualism and the romanticization of the "natural" person, the eccentric vagabond loner, the rebel who listened to a "different drummer'' and thus provided a rejuvenating spark for a decadent, conformist society. The original *Star Trek* concept had ties to the mythos of the American Western (in his initial proposal, Roddenberry compared Trek to a then-popular Western series when he referred to it as a *"Wagon Train* to the stars''); and like the Western, *Trek* focused on the quintessential American dilemma of social order versus individual freedom.

The prophets of the counterculture were good utopians in the sense that they believed humanity can "have it all"—that there is no inherent contradiction between true individuality and community, harmony, depth of experience, and so forth. Paradise, according to such a view, is possible if only we possess the courage and the imagination to build it. In this particular sense of utopianism, *Star Trek* has presented a generally anti-utopian, or at least a deeply cautionary, perspective. *Trek* is anti-Paradise. *Trek*'s utopian narratives posit that the utopian pursuit of happiness, community, harmony, and peace, while not necessarily wrong in itself, cannot be followed very far without incurring substantial human costs.

Star Trek's dystopian tales suggest that "perfection," once achieved, demands stasis—that the more perfect a society is (or considers itself to be), the less its need (or tolerance) for change. Kirk justifies his intervention against the social order of utopian societies in "Return of the Archons" and "The Apple" on the grounds that those utopias are stagnant and unchanging, and therefore inauthentic, societies. Faced with an unexpected development (e.g., the arrival of visitors), these ultraplanned societies are unable to cope; they are thrown into a state of utter confusion. Any new element must be rejected, killed, "absorbed," or otherwise neutralized—and if that is not possible (as proves to be the case in the stories), the entire fabric of the society may unravel simply from the effects of being questioned. Not only is this state of affairs inimical to the survival of the society itself, but, according to *Trek*'s narratives, such a state fails to provide individuals with the challenges that give meaning to their lives. In "This Side of Paradise," Kirk angrily counters Sandoval's claim of a "perfect world," saying that "man stagnates if he has no wants, no ambitions, no desire to be more than he is." Against the arrested cultural development of the Feeders of Vaal, or the deliberate primitivism of a return to a "simpler" life in "The Return of the Archons" and "This Side of Paradise," *Trek* suggests that people have a responsibility to their species' collective project of growth and change. Perfection, insofar as it is conceived of as a state of *being* rather than a project of *becoming*, is detrimental to the health of the individual, the society, and the species. By a cruel irony, utopians are doomed to live eternally in their constricted situation unless someone else intervenes, for utopia enervates people and deprives them of the drives that, in the usual course of things, would lead to growth and change.

Utopias, according to these classic *Star Trek* narratives, are not only stagnant but tyrannical as well. Insofar as perfection requires orderly planning, it requires either voluntary submergence of the individual mind into that of the group and/or the rule of some oligarchy, dictator, machine, or other authority. The latter occurs in many of *Trek*'s utopian narratives, often in combination with the former. But power, we are cautioned by these stories, inevitably becomes caught up in maintaining itself. The good of the society becomes wholly identified with the will of Landru or Vaal, and all dissent—indeed, all expression of individual conscience—is by definition antisocial. Perfection, in other words, implies repression—which explains why *Trek*'s utopias are usually fear-ridden.

This brings us to one of the most striking themes in *Star Trek*'s utopian dialogue: the politics of emotion. The people in *Trek*'s fictional utopias are typically "happy" in the restricted sense of "vacant contentment" that Spock discerns in the followers of Landru and the slack-jawed Feeders of Vaal. Throughout *Trek* there runs a consistent message that mindless, artificially-induced pleasure is a stunted, truncated emotion. The term *passion* might describe part of what is missing from such "Paradise" scenarios as those discussed above. Passion is a spontaneous, unruly emotion. It cannot be planned or spoon-fed; rather, it is inherently connected with authentic inner experiences arising from the sensate body and the ineffable spirit. These, however, are the very elements from which dwellers in Paradise are most alienated. The Feeders of Vaal in "The Apple" have no knowledge of sex and, apparently, no sexual urges until they observe a romantic encounter between humans from the *Enterprise*. In "Return of the Archons," the people of Landru, despite their ritualized references to "joy," show an obvious deficit of feeling. Their bland everyday behavior is offset by a carefully circumscribed orgy of pointless violence and sex during the ritual of "festival"; but this too is prescribed by Landru, and it comes and goes with all the mechanical orderliness of the chiming of a clock. Even in "This Side of Paradise," where there is no oppressive political apparatus, the pleasant sensation of euphoria induced by the spores seems to make people placid rather than passionately joyous or inspired. According to the dystopian myths of *Trek*, to accept a life of pure happiness is to reject the range, depth, and meaning of genuine human experiences that must, by definition, be rooted in the adventurous uncertainties of real life and in awareness of the physical and psychic self in all its manifestations, not just the pleasant ones.

The dystopias of *Star Trek* are depicted as pursuing placid, orderly Philia by suppressing the more chaotic and self-oriented passions of Eros. Utopia does to society what the transporter malfunction did to the "nice" Kirk in "The Enemy Within": it excises Eros, the sort of disorderly but impassioned drives that make Kirk able to function as a leader and a man of action. Eros is very literally forbidden to the nonsexual Feeders of Vaal and carefully circumscribed for the followers of Landru presumably because erotic sensations might lead them to listen to their inner feelings rather than the voice of social authority. It is surely no coincidence that personal romantic or sexual attraction is taboo in such classic literary dystopias as Orwell's *Nineteen Eighty-Four*, Huxley's *Brave New World* and Zamiatin's *We*. This is not to say that sexual activity is necessarily suppressed; it may simply be trivialized and alienated from the natural body and from deeply personal meanings and affections. Sex is abundant in these three fictional dystopias, but to fall in love (or even into unregulated lust) is to commit treason against the state.

The expressions of Eros that dystopias suppress include not only sexuality but passionate or self-directed emotions of every kind, including aggression, ambition, and striving. When Kirk's *Enterprise* encounters a people who are altogether gentle, pacifistic, and oriented toward the collective good, it is a forgone conclusion that certain fundamental human emotions have atrophied. Conversely, the introduction of Eros is portrayed as restorative and empowering for the victims of dystopia. It is anger and strong passion that frees the crew from the effect of the spores on Omicron Ceti III, destroys Vaal, and portends a bright future for the liberated subjects of Landru. In a broad sense, anger and conflict are portrayed as a humanizing force in these narratives precisely because a one-sided pursuit of harmony and peace has become the vehicle of dehumanization.

In this regard, the episode "This Side of Paradise" is an interesting case because it is not easy to find fault with the well-adjusted colonists, who have no oppressive political system and who seem quite genuinely happy and free. They seem able to feel and express sexual affection and romantic love without falling into the extremes of mindless lust or numbing celibacy seen in the servants of Landru and Vaal. The telling characteristic that betrays the falseness of their Paradise, however, is the fact that (with the unexplained exception of Kirk) strong emotions are foreign to them, and if those emotions are forced upon them their spell of happiness is broken. Once their banal bliss is displaced by more authentic feelings, the crew and colonists show little interest in regaining Paradise.

Although the concepts of Eros and Philia can illuminate some dimensions of these narratives, *Star Trek*'s utopian discourse is rich enough to overflow the mold of any neat binary opposition. For example, while the smothering dystopian society demands Philia toward the social body as a whole, it treats the more tangible Philia of concrete interpersonal relations, including those of family and friends, with the same disdain that it directs toward romantic love. Collectivists may claim to care for one another, but their devotion is dutiful, generalized, passionless; their "caring" is nothing more than a submission to the sterile abstraction of the collectivity. While under the influence of the spores on Omicron Ceti III, Spock is affable toward Kirk, but Spock loses touch with the deep personal attachment, loyalty, and responsibility toward his friend—feelings that he regains only after the spell of the spores is broken.

Another, complementary motif in *Star Trek*'s anti-Paradise rhetoric is the necessity of moral challenge and vexing choice. Without difficult moral choices, the followers of Vaal and Landru cannot mature, and so they remain childlike and "innocent" in the darkest possible sense: they are morally obtuse, unable to protest or resist even such patently evil acts as murder when commanded to do them in the name of the collective good. In the totalizing utopia where misbehavior is virtually impossible, moral choice is unnecessary. Consequently, every action is unproblematic. There is no soul-searching agony behind the utopians' decision to violate their visitors' autonomy by shooting spores at them, or even to chase them around with bludgeons. Their codes of conduct, together with their systems of socialization, are so comprehensive and well-tuned as to erase all the ambiguity, doubt, and pain from moral choice. There are no pangs of conscience because the conscience is not needed; everyone does what is "right" by training and inclination. We often talk as though this is the condition for which we strive, but to imagine its actual attainment is, ironically, a frightening prospect. When choice becomes painless, it may be a sign that choice has in fact disappeared.

In *The Final Frontier*, the religious visionary Sybok gains followers by subjecting them to a form of one-minute psychotherapy that brings them into direct contact with their most painful memories and inner conflicts. Once Sybok's recruits confront their pain therapeutically, they are relieved of it. Thus, they achieve inner harmony and become Sybok's grateful disciples, willing to renounce all principles of personal conscience in order to follow his quest. Kirk, however, refuses to undergo this process, claiming that he needs his pain—that his pain is vital to his self-identity. Spock, who does submit to Sybok's treatment, is not impressed. Apparently Spock has also, in his own way, successfully integrated his pain into his personality and does not care to be "relieved" of it.

The possibility that humans have an irrepressible and legitimate need for pain, suffering, challenge, ambiguity, and difficult moral choice—in short, a need for disharmony—strikes at the very heart of utopian thinking. One of the most memorable dialogues in dystopian literature occurs in *Brave New World*. The Savage, Huxley's protagonist, is an outsider to the rigidly hierarchical technological utopia where all human needs are either effortlessly quenched or drowned in drug-induced euphoria. His dialogue with the expositor of this dystopia, Mustapha Mond, is the philosophical climax of the book. "What you need," says The Savage, "is something with tears for a change. Nothing costs enough here." The uncomprehending Mond explains that they have succeeded in doing away with life's inconveniences to make way for a life of pure comfort. The Savage retorts:

> "I don't want comfort. I want God, I want poetry, I want real danger, I want freedom, I want goodness. I want sin."
> "In fact," said Mustapha Mond, "you're claiming the right to be unhappy."
> "All right then," said The Savage defiantly, "I'm claiming the right to be unhappy."
> "Not to mention the right to grow old and ugly and impotent; the right to have syphilis and cancer; the right to have too little to eat; the right to be lousy; the right to live in constant apprehension of what may happen tomorrow; the right to catch typhoid; the right to be tortured by unspeakable pains of every kind."
> There was a long silence.
> "I claim them all," said The Savage at last.
> Mustapha Mond shrugged his shoulders. "You're welcome," he said.[8]

In "The Apple," Spock plays the role of Mustapha Mond to Doctor McCoy's Savage in a strikingly similar exchange:

> *Spock*: Allow me to point out, Captain, that by destroying Vaal, you have also destroyed the people of Vaal.
>
> *McCoy*: Nonsense, Spock! It will be the making of these people. Make them stand on their own feet, do things for themselves. They have a right to live like men.
>
> *Spock*: You mean they have a right to pain, worry, insecurity, tension . . . and eventually death and taxes.
>
> *McCoy*: That's all part of it. Yes! Those too!

The dominant theme in TOS's stories of Paradise is that the cost of such a life is prohibitively high and that once in Paradise we will become trapped there, imprisoned in our own creation and denied the highest rewards of human existence. Paradise is a form of cowardice, by which we give up our freedom of thought and choice, our individuality and our capacity for passion—all in exchange for safety, security, and ease. However visionary it may be in its beginnings, Paradise degenerates into a life unexamined and therefore not worth living.

UTOPIA RECONSIDERED

Although *Star Trek*'s original series does present a strongly cautionary view of utopia, that view is not a totalizing dogma but part of a complex conversation that also involves, as its most prominent dissenting voice, Mr. Spock. Spock recognizes some shortcomings in the dystopias encountered in the episodes described above, but he is uneasy about Kirk's impulse to destroy them. In defense of the Feeders of Vaal, Spock not only cites the Prime Directive but also characterizes their society as "perfectly practical" and "a splendid example of reciprocity." Landru's dystopia on Beta III, which Spock admits is "a soulless society . . . no spirit, no spark," nonetheless wins his recognition as a "marvelous feat of engineering." He alone regrets the fate of these societies. He alone has a good word to say about his experience on Omicron Ceti III, and he alone sympathizes openly with the ill-fated idealists of "The Way to Eden." Of course, Spock, with his scientific curiosity and his veneration of "infinite diversity in infinite combinations," is more tolerant than Kirk or McCoy—but there is something more substantial behind his utopian sympathies. Spock's Vulcan culture actually violates many of Kirk's pronouncements about what "people" (including those on Beta III or Gamma Trianguli VI) can or should do. Vulcan culture emphasizes Philia in the form of duty and service, while containing sexuality and banishing the other disruptive emotions of Eros. The Vulcan ethos asserts the moral priority of the group ("The needs of the many outweigh the needs of the few"). While Kirk poses as a rebellious, self-made individualist, Spock openly reveres his culture and traditions. In short, Vulcan culture upholds much of what Kirk finds distasteful in utopia.

Although Kirk's proclamations on "human" nature seem directed at any and all humanoids, the half-Terran Spock is allowed to play the devil's advocate against this galactic humanism. To complicate matters further, we know that the Vulcans once behaved in the way more in keeping with Kirk's sermons but have since "evolved" to a more "advanced" state. Does this not undermine some of Kirk's claims as to what we are capable of? It is unlikely that Spock's cultural deviations from Kirk's grandly "human" ideals are simply, like his ears, an alien eccentricity—or that *Star Trek*'s writers have carelessly overlooked the fact that a central, well-loved character was contradicting Kirk's all-American views. Although the stories foreground Kirk's and McCoy's interpretations, it is reasonable to interpret Spock's agnosticism on these issues as an important part of the dialogue. Spock's understated counterpoint adds a vital dimensionality that distinguishes *Trek*'s critique of utopia from a mere defense of some earthbound bourgeois "status quo."

During the late 1960s, the presence of a self-conscious "counterculture" with a leftist social agenda deeply affected the issues dealt with in

Star Trek, leading to many clearly allegorical episodes that dealt not only with utopia but also with pacifism, race relations, and other concerns of the time. By 1987, when *The Next Generation* premiered, the social context had changed significantly. The "counterculture" was but a memory and the Cold War was winding down. Cultural imperialism was going out of fashion, and multicultural understanding was coming in; anthropologists were chagrined to hear the "natives" talking back to them. Accordingly, Picard's interpretation of the Prime Directive becomes more scrupulous and his speeches less ethnocentric than Kirk's. "Utopias" are still encountered and are often found wanting, but their inhabitants are not under a hypnotic spell; and though it may take an unexpected encounter to make them aware of some problems, utopian societies can change without renouncing their principles.

Early in its first season, *The Next Generation* aired an episode called "Justice," in which the *Enterprise D* encounters a society of seemingly perfect harmony and contentment. The people, known as the Edo, never have to do anything "uncomfortable," and their main activity seems to be recreational sex. It is only when Dr. Beverly Crusher's son, Wesley, stumbles accidentally upon an arbitrary "forbidden zone" that the *Enterprise* crew learns the secret of this Eden: the death penalty is inflicted for the smallest infraction of the law. Picard, who takes the Prime Directive seriously, considers it beyond his authority to intervene. Finally, he agrees to rescue Wesley forcefully, only to find that the god-machine that rules this planet will not permit them to leave. But instead of commanding the machine to destroy itself, as Kirk would undoubtedly have done, the urbane and articulate Picard reasons with it. The godlike machine claims to know what is best for its "children," having saved them from their own once-violent ways by imposing this simple, regimented life of "law" and "tranquillity." Picard, however, persuades the machine to consider his argument that the laws cannot be truly just when they are so rigidly enforced (a possible reference to the 1980s movement toward mandatory sentencing and harsher criminal punishments). Picard is able to have it both ways: he has the conviction and the courage to confront the machine, but in the end he is able to reconcile his intervention with the Prime Directive because he and the machine have had a productive philosophical discussion.

In later episodes, the rulership of utopia passes from computers to human idealists. The transitional TNG episode "When the Bough Breaks" takes the *Enterprise* to the planet Aldea, a "dream world of mythology" so elusive that its very existence has been widely dismissed as legend. A mysterious blessing has enabled the Aldeans to conceal their planet from marauding outsiders and to develop a life devoted to artistic and musical achievement. There is only one problem: the Aldeans are stricken with an illness that prevents them from reproducing. They have lured the *Enterprise* there in order to steal its most artistically inclined children, so that the Aldean culture may continue. Although the Aldeans prove to be loving adoptive parents and excellent teachers, and they command enough power to cast the *Enterprise* into a distant part of the galaxy, the kidnapped children and the *Enterprise* crew refuse to accept the situation. Wesley Crusher, the eldest of the children, learns the secret of Aldea's powers. The Custodian, a computer designed by the people's "progenitors" during the "days of strife," now provides for the inhabitants' needs and "regulates" their lives. Working surreptitiously together, Wesley and his mother, Dr. Crusher, are able to determine that the planetary cloak created by the computer has damaged the planet's ozone layer, exposing the people to radiation that causes their disease and infertility. It seems that the Aldeans have so thoroughly given themselves to the arts that they no longer understand how their computer works and consequently have not monitored its activities. As Picard puts it, "Your Custodian has controlled you so completely that you have lost even the desire to question it." The Aldeans take the lesson, disable their protective cloak, and give up their legendary isolation. But the *Enterprise* is also changed—the children come away with a heightened awareness of their gifts, and the parents are more inclined to respect and cultivate those abilities. Each society has learned from the other.

In TNG's "The Masterpiece Society," the crew members of the *Enterprise* are surprised to find a secretive Terran colony on a planet that is threatened by the approach of a stellar core fragment. The colonists, who are reluctant to allow outside contact even under such emergency circumstances, explain that their society is a "perfect" one, a "paradise" based on genetic engineering, with each individual bred for a specific social role. So perfect is their society that, as they themselves predict, the smallest disruption is enough to throw it out of balance. Ironically, it is the technology of Geordi's visor (his prosthesis for a visual impairment that would never have been allowed to occur in this genetically perfect society) that provides the model for a technology that Geordi and colony scientist Hannah Bates use to save the planet. However, Hannah and twenty-three other colonists, having had a taste of the larger world, wish to leave the colony despite the leaders' argument that it cannot function in the absence of even one member.

The inherent problem of this "perfect" society is reminiscent of TOS's message, in that the colony's rigidity and predictability disallows for the kind of creativity and flexibility that would permit a society to adapt and grow. On the other hand, the problem of how outsiders (or insiders, for that matter) should deal with such a society has taken on new dimensions. Despite the fact that Picard is every bit as outraged by the idea of genetic engineering as Kirk would have been, and the fact that the Prime Directive does not actually apply to these Terran colonists,

Picard is torn by pangs of conscience over the fate of the colony. He counsels the dissidents to consider their decision carefully, even offering to return after six months to allow them more time, but the disaffected colonists will not delay. Although the colony's leader predicts that the society will manage to adapt, Picard regrets the harm done by the *Enterprise*'s visit.

Another classic dystopian encounter occurs in DS9's "Paradise," when Commander Sisko's away team attempts to rescue the survivors of a Federation ship marooned on the planet Orellius, only to discover that the survivors have created a communal colony to which they are fully committed and which they have no intention of leaving. Stranded by what appears to be a natural energy field that blocks their means of transportation and communication to the outside, Sisko and O'Brien seem at first to get along well enough as guests of the colony. However, friction with the commune's autocratic leader Alixus erupts into a confrontation after O'Brien defies the community's strict rules against modern technology by attempting to access Starfleet medical equipment in order to save the life of a dying colonist. Sisko is held responsible and is tortured by being exposed to the sun's heat in a metal box. He resolutely accepts more torture rather than give in to Alixus's demands that he shed his Starfleet uniform and get into the spirit of the place. At the climax of the episode, O'Brien and Sisko reveal that Alixus has deceived her people into believing that they were accidentally marooned on the planet, when in fact she had planned the colony's existence there from the beginning and had artificially created the technology-disabling energy field that has kept them there. This revelation, combined with the harshness of the punishments inflicted on Sisko simply for defying authority, leads to a crisis of faith for the people of the colony.

In an impassioned speech, Alixus accepts responsibility for her abuse of power, agreeing to be placed under arrest by Sisko. But she also argues that her ends—the colonists' satisfying social existence—have justified the means. The people are given the choice of leaving; and although they are dismayed at the leader's excesses, they choose to stay and apply these lessons toward the improvement of the communal life they have chosen. Imperfect as it is, this utopian colony is not presented as fundamentally wrong or even hopelessly flawed. Its continuation is a legitimate, clear-eyed choice on the part of the colonists. "Paradise," like TNG's "Justice," "When the Bough Breaks," and "The Masterpiece Society," embraces many of the same criticisms of utopia—such as stagnation, lack of freedom, abuse of leadership power—that are seen in *The Original Series*. But in these later stories, the utopias are depicted as having both "good" and "bad" aspects; and once the members gain insight from their contact with the *Star Trek* heroes, they are able to change while maintaining some of their utopian distinctiveness. Above all, the citizens of these later utopias claim the right to make their own cultural choices free from outside intervention.

ALMOST HEAVEN

In TNG's "Thine Own Self," Lieutenant Commander Data, suffering from amnesia and wandering about on Barkon IV, is taken into a home where he befriends a young girl named Gia. She tells Data that, according to her father, her departed mother has gone to "a beautiful place, where everything is peaceful, and everyone loves each other, and no one ever gets sick." She asks Data, "Do you think there's really a place like that?" Data gazes out the window at the stars and says, quietly but with conviction, "Yes, I do." The scene leaves little doubt that Data is referring to his home on the *Enterprise*.

Whether or not *Star Trek* is utopian depends on one's definitions. If utopia is a banal paradise from which all struggle has been banished, then *Trek*'s predominant voice is anti-Utopian. If, on the other hand, utopia is a vision of an ideal human fellowship, then *Trek*'s mythworld is utopian beyond a doubt. In fact, *Trek*'s rejection of bland paradisic collectives helps set the stage for *Trek*'s own utopian mythos.

Unlike *Star Trek*'s fictional robotic societies in which individuality and will are submerged in the collectivity, the *Trek* fellowship is (with all the paradox the phrase implies) a community of individualists. Each person's contribution is contingent on his or her freely given loyalty, individual temperament, and personal conscience. One's freedom does not end with the act of joining the community, but instead the community preserves freedom and creativity within its protecting embrace. In this genuine utopia there is no trace of the stock motivating forces of dystopian societies: fear, mindless indoctrination, or suppression of personal feelings.

Although the sense of a shared mission of human discovery whose value transcends personal interest is a potent force holding this voluntary utopia together, the core of the *Enterprise*'s moral and social system, the element that links personal conscience with durable social ties, is friendship. Friendship is impossible for anyone who has surrendered their personal conscience and feelings, and the latter traits are intolerable in a totalitarian society. Therefore, the totalitarian dystopia cannot rely on friendship or heartfelt interpersonal loyalty to keep people committed, and this leaves it no choice but to use other methods, such as fear, coercion, and indoctrination, that demean the human spirit. In the *Star Trek* mythos, this is the crucial difference between utopia and dystopia.

The difference between collectivism and true fellowship is brought into focus by *Star Trek*'s depiction of the Borg as the quintessential collectivist hell. The cybernetic Borg are *Trek*'s ultimate unredeemable dystopian society. The Borg Collective hungrily assimilates whole worlds, promising them "perfection" but erasing all diversity, all individuality, and all feeling. Although individual Borg are oriented only to the "hive mind," they have no feelings for one another; they step calmly over the bodies of fallen "drones," retrieving them only to salvage their usable parts. The Borg have done away with both Eros and Philia, or rather, they have reduced them to their cadaverous core: the will to conquer and submission to a group mind. The Borg are the collectivist negation of *Trek*'s creed of fellowship.

It is not only collectivists, of course, who are incapable of fellowship. *Star Trek* broaches the problem from the other direction as well—that of unbridled egocentrism. Harry Mudd, the scamp of outer space, can think only of his own self-interest in the narrowest terms; thus, he deprives himself of all benefits of friendship, community, and mutual loyalty. Khan and other "supermen" are similarly defeated by their self-imposed isolation. If *Trek*'s communal paradises represent an overvaluation of Philia at the expense of Eros, its arrogant and unprincipled loners represent the opposite possibility. Between these two extremes, the utopia of the *Trek* crew is situated as the mediating ideal.

While the depiction of the *Star Trek* fellowship as an ideal community is characteristic of all four series, the challenges to this fellowship become progressively more complex. In keeping with the growing social recognition of diversity and pluralism, the characters' personal, political, and cultural differences tend to become more deeply problematic. Community continues to triumph and the notion of the crew as a utopian fellowship remains central to *Trek*'s mythos, but at the same time there is an expanded vision of the diversity—even conflict—that must be dealt with in this community.

Anyone who takes *Star Trek*'s utopian future as a form of social realism or a blueprint for building a new world will find it exasperatingly lacking in particulars. The process by which *Star Trek*'s Federation of Planets has eliminated intolerance, exploitation, greed, war, and materialism (and thus become a utopian society in its own right) is never quite spelled out. The sweeping character of these changes is made explicit in a dialogue between Deanna Troi and Mark Twain (TNG's "Time's Arrow, Part II"), but though the reforms are said to have occurred "a long time" before the twenty-fourth century, no further explanation is offered. The film *First Contact* only adds that these changes were somehow inspired by contact with other worlds in the late twenty-first century. In the end, these thoroughly utopian achievements are established through the narrative equivalent of waving a magic wand.

Similarly, the fellowship of the Starfleet crew is constructed through narrative devices that simply cut through the Gordian knot of complex human issues. Such problems as alienation, inequality, power, and exploitation are solved by the simple expedient of omitting the trouble-making areas of social life from the picture. The fellowship of the crew has none of the problems that Marx and other social critics have addressed because it is a society without political decision making, without production or reproduction, without exchange, without property—indeed, almost without economic consumption. Amongst the *Enterprise* crew members there is no substantial internal conflict; friendship is universalized so that there are no cliques, no exclusion, and no enmity. Families, couples, or permanent love interests seldom divide the group loyalties of the crew. Cultural identity has only a positive side; it rarely leads to denigration of other groups. Diversity is always a source of mutual respect. The repartee—even outright friction—between diverse personalities turns out, when the chips are down, to mask a deeper affection. Any conflicts that may arise between duty, personal integrity, and loyalty to friends are superficial and soluble. There is no alienation from work; everyone is doing exactly what he or she loves to do. True, the harmony implied by these premises is sometimes destabilized for purposes of plot development, but only within the strict limits of what can be reconciled by the end of an episode.

Some potentially non-utopian implications of the *Star Trek* mythos are placed aside lest they obstruct our view of this ideal community. For example, little is made of the premise that the crew members are bound by a strict chain of command. All around the loyal and mutually devoted cadre of the officer elite, hundreds of ordinary crew members go largely unnamed and unnoticed, follow orders without notable expression of free thought, and are treated as somewhat expendable. These aspects of the narrative are expedient staging devices that allow the central fellowship of the *Trek* heroes to occupy the spotlight. In sum, then, much of what makes *Trek*'s vision of future society so scintillating is its depiction of an idyllic human community whose appeal is achieved through narrative devices that cause stubborn human problems miraculously to vanish. In this sense, *Trek* is within the utopian literary tradition at its most idealistic.

If utopia is defined as a state of paradise that smothers the spark of growth and change, then the cosmology of *Star Trek* is profoundly anti-utopian. If, on the contrary, utopia is conceived as a process of movement along a path of human self-transcendence, *Star Trek*'s very conception of humanity is quintessentially utopian. In the *Trek* cosmos, societies that strive to stay the same—or, worse still, those that attempt a primitivist return to a "simpler life"—deny the imperative of growth and exploration that defines humanity and its place in the cosmos. As we shall see, the celebration of growth as the greatest good, and of humanity as the prime exemplar of this good, lies at the heart of the *Star Trek* mythos.

CHAPTER 8

UP THE LONG LADDER

Evolution, Progress, and Destiny

For I dipt into the future, far as human eye could see,
Saw a Vision of the world, and all the wonder that would be;
Saw the heavens fill with commerce, argosies of magic sails,
Pilots of the purple twilight, dropping down with costly bales;
Heard the heavens fill with shouting, and there rain'd a ghastly dew,
From the nations' airy navies grappling in the central blue;
Far along the world-wide whisper of the south-wind rushing warm,
With the standards of the peoples plunging thro' the thunder-storm;
Till the war-drum throbb'd no longer, and the battle-flags were furl'd
In the Parliament of man, the Federation of the world.
There the common sense of most shall hold a fretful realm in awe,
And the kindly earth shall slumber, lapt in universal law.
 —Alfred Lord Tennyson
 Locksley Hall (1842)

Until the moment of its surprise ending, TOS's "Errand of Mercy" promises to follow the false-utopia plot formula described in the previous chapter. Captain Kirk and Mr. Spock arrive on the planet Organia to offer their help in fighting off an impending invasion by the ruthless Klingons (seen for the first time in this episode). According to Starfleet's information, Organian culture is at a primitive level, "a D-minus on the Richter scale of culture" as Spock explains with a perfectly straight face. When they beam down, Kirk and Spock are surprised to find that the Organian delegation, a committee of affable old men, politely declines their offer of military protection, technological tutoring, and cultural instruction. The rebuff seems all the more incomprehensible when Spock informs the Captain that, according to his tricorder readings, Organian society is not "making progress toward mechanization" but is "totally stagnant," not having changed substantially for tens of thousands of years (fancy it—the tricorder as a progress-o-meter!). Kirk is shocked at this news: "It doesn't seem right," he exclaims.

Placid as ever, the Organians reiterate that they require no assistance but are concerned about the danger the Klingons might pose to the *Enterprise* officers. Their fears are justified: the Klingons suddenly seize control, and Kirk and Spock are obliged to disguise themselves as civilians. Soon Kirk and Spock are attempting to stir the Organians to resistance by mounting a two-man guerrilla campaign against the Klingon occupation. To their dismay, the Organian leaders stand calmly by and urge both sides to cease their conflict even as the Klingons execute hundreds of unresisting Organian citizens in retaliation. Kirk shares the Klingon commander Kor's contempt for the passive and compliant Organians, and even the normally tolerant Spock seems vexed.

This episode appears late in TOS's first season, and any viewer familiar with the season's earlier offerings, particularly "Return of the Archons" and "This Side of Paradise," might expect a dramatic climax marked by a stirring speech in which Kirk instructs the Organians on the value of progress and freedom gained through struggle. Instead, the consummation of the battle is interrupted when the Organians use their unsuspected powers to render the combatants harmless. "We are terribly sorry that we have been forced to interfere, Gentlemen," the Organian spokesman Ayelborne patiently explains, "But we could not permit you to harm yourselves." "We find interference in other people's affairs most disgusting," they continue, "but you, Gentlemen, have given us no choice." Using powers beyond the understanding of humans, the Organians disable both sides' weapons of war. Kirk and Kor sputter with righteous indignation, protesting that this is none of the Organians' business. "We have the right . . ." Kirk fumes. "To wage war?" Ayelborne interrupts. "To kill millions of innocent people? To destroy life on a planetary scale? Is that what you're defending?" "Well," Kirk responds sheepishly, "Of course, nobody wants war, but . . . Eventually, I suppose, we . . ." "Yes, eventually you would make peace," Ayelborne counters, "but only after millions had died. We are bringing it about now. The fact is, in the future you and the Klingons will become fast friends."

The chastening of the humanoid antagonists becomes complete when the Organians ask them to leave because "the mere presence of beings like yourselves is acutely painful to us." They explain that they were once corporeal humanoids not unlike the Klingons, Vulcans, and Terrans, but they have progressed millions of years beyond the need for physical bodies and have evolved into dazzling beings of "pure thought." All the physical manifestations of Organian life had been illusions created for the sake of the visitors. Mr. Spock sums up the evolutionary status of the Organians as follows: "I should guess that they are as far above us on the evolutionary scale as we are above the amoeba."

"Errand of Mercy" seems to reverse certain recurrent plot conventions of *Star Trek*. The superbeings who limit human freedom are not at all like those of the four series pilots or the many other episodes in which godlike aliens are exposed as mean tyrants. The Organians restrict human freedom for good reasons and only after considerable provocation. Their tranquillity and their seemingly "arrested" society are marks of a genuinely superior existence, not a false Paradise. Kirk's contempt for the Organians and his condescending offer to protect and educate them are utterly misguided. In the end, *Trek*'s heroes stand humbly before the Organians like unruly children. For once Kirk and Spock get it really wrong, they lose the moral high ground and have to listen to someone else's righteous pronouncements. Score one for nonhumans.

On a deeper level, however, the episode actually upholds the basic premise on which human superiority and Starfleet's missionary/colonial charter is based. By dramatizing the notion of a necessary developmental hierarchy through which all beings are destined to progress, the Organians have made their point. They then conveniently disappear never to be seen again in the *Star Trek* universe, and the Terran-centered Federation of Planets, with the original *Enterprise* as its exemplar, is left to bear the standard of cosmic progress.

"Errand of Mercy" is rooted in a cosmology of progress that suffuses the original *Star Trek*, and in a more complicated way, all the *Trek* corpus. So deeply does this cosmology resonate with contemporary Euro-American assumptions about time and change that it may be difficult to appreciate how historically recent it is—for it is essentially a product of the eighteenth and nineteenth centuries—or how strongly it has come under increasing attack from the "postmodern" perspective that we shall examine later on. In order to delve into the deep metaphors and mythic themes of episodes like "Errand of Mercy," it is necessary to consider briefly the development of the Western mythos of progress.

TIME AND COSMOS

The cosmologies of most small-scale, nonliterate societies portray an essentially static universe. In such a cosmos, time has a sacred center in the eternally present moment of creation, and change is a disruptive departure from this perfect equilibrium, for which the cure is an "eternal return" to mythic time through the ritual reenactment of Creation.[1] Even in cultures that recognized change over time, the conception of change has more often been one of degeneration than of progress. When the early Greek writer Hesiod described endless cycles of declining stages, each going from Golden to Silver and Bronze Ages, through regressive Iron Ages (exemplified by his own time) to eventual senility and decay, he was expressing cosmological views shared by Hindu and Chinese philosophers.

Judaism and its offshoots helped to establish the idea of linear historical time with a definite beginning, marked by unique events such as the Creation, the Fall, and the Flood, and leading toward a finale when the moral plan of the Creator is fulfilled and historical time comes to an end. These elements, however, do not necessarily add up to a conception of progress in the sense of worldly human betterment. The Christian European view prior to the eighteenth century portrayed earthly history as the chronicle of degeneration from original perfection, and the existence of heathen "savages" was taken as evidence that some had fallen farther than others from this original high estate. In this cosmology, the condition of Fallen Man can be improved only through the working out of God's plan for salvation, and human pursuits in this world can only distract us from the faith required for redemption in the next.

Whatever ultimate structures of time they envisioned, traditional cultures were mostly concerned with maintaining, rather than changing, basic social arrangements and customs in a world that was already about as good as it was going to get (at least, until the end of time). The Christian West's premodern philosophy of a static, divinely ordained cosmos was manifested as early as the twelfth century in the idea of a "Great Chain of Being." According to this conception, the flawlessness of God's creation is reflected in the unbroken hierarchical continuum from the lowliest forms of life through beasts, men, and angels to the Creator—a chain in which no possible link is absent and in which each creature has its necessary place. It was a cosmology in which the greatest good was to know one's place and stay there.[2] As an idea, the Great Chain of Being grew in strength through the seventeenth century and became one of the key cosmological premises of the eighteenth century. But it was the concept of progress, which came to fruition in the nineteenth century, that supplied a new cosmic context for the Chain of Being.

Whether or not people wished to recognize the fact, the post-Renaissance world of the eighteenth and nineteenth centuries was a time of enormous change in human social life. The growth of colonial empires, contact with other cultures, the beginnings of the Industrial Revolution, rapid urbanization, the decline of traditional aristocracy and the growth of the business class, advances in science, and other factors combined to impress upon people the fact that their society was in an unprecedented state of flux. Unlike the Renaissance thinkers who saw themselves largely as imitators of a superior Greco-Roman culture, philosophers of the European Enlightenment of the eighteenth century began to picture the human enterprise as an inexorable march of improvement brought about by the growth of reason and science. This confident view of human progress, based on the notion that both the natural world and the essential character of humankind are objectively knowable through universally valid methods of observation and reason, is sometimes called *modernism* (a term promulgated by "postmodern" critics, to whom we shall refer again). The term *progress* refers here to the modernist idea of movement toward a better, higher, more desirable state of being. Europe in the eighteenth century saw the rise, perhaps for the first time in documented human history, of an overarching mythos of the human enterprise as a path of universal intellectual and moral improvement—in short, a modernist cosmology of progress.

THE COSMIC ESCALATOR

While the modernist mythos of orderly human progress has its roots in the Enlightenment, it came to full fruition with the rise of industry and science in the nineteenth century. During the first half of that century, advances in geology and archeology led to the growing realization that the earth and humankind had a past far more distant than that of Biblical history. The naming of ages or epochs of the past helped to formalize that belief into a narrative structure. In archeology, the mid-nineteenth century saw the appearance of the concept of "prehistory," as well as the widespread acceptance and archeological documentation of a Stone Age-Bronze Age-Iron Age sequence of cultural stages, which was shown to have occurred throughout much of Europe and beyond. (Note how profoundly this tale of human progress has inverted the meaning of the Greek view, in which the Iron Age represented a steady decline from the excellence of the Golden, Silver, and Bronze Ages). Building upon this cosmology of universal progress and using the data of "primitive" cultures to reconstruct the past of "advanced" ones, the formal discipline of anthropology began in the 1860s to speculate about the changes in religion, family, marriage, economy, law and political organization through which all peoples presumably would have passed as they moved from (to use one of the more popular nomenclatures) savagery to barbarism to civilization. World cultures were thus organized into a hierarchy from primal savages to the Euro-American peoples (and especially their "refined" social classes), who represented the vanguard of moral and intellectual advancement. In an age of sweeping social changes that entailed the hardships of the working classes under early industrial capitalism, as well as the sometimes brutal European conquest and domination of peoples across the globe, the idea of progress as a natural law governing history—an article of faith among Western social theorists by midcentury—placed these tumultuous changes within an overarching mythic narrative of human improvement.

The Great Chain of Being was not abandoned; rather, it was wedded to the notion of progress. The previously static cosmic ladder became—to use an image from twentieth-century technology—an escalator. According to this view, every species or culture strives to better itself and, though some may fall by the way, the overall "law" of the universe is to produce ever greater advancement in terms of complexity, intelligence, and other desirable traits. In the realm of culture, an orderly pattern of cultural "evolution" would produce a parallel developmental sequence of customs, beliefs, and social institutions among the diverse peoples of the world, even though some (i.e., Western Europeans and Anglo-Americans) had obviously come farther than others. The cosmology of orderly progress, wherein the present of "backward" peoples is comparable to our own past, and wherein our present portends their future, made European colonialism and the elite domination of the "backward" classes appear not only inevitable, but even benevolent—a helping hand up the ladder of improvement.

The first significant attempts to frame an evolutionary theory in biology appeared in the late eighteenth century. These were, essentially, efforts to work out the details of the "progress" cosmology within the realm of scientific biology. Jean Baptiste Lamarck and Erasmus Darwin (Charles's grandfather) each proposed theories of biological change that relied on notions of directed effort and individual striving that logically paralleled the human quest for betterment. Such theories, though cosmologically correct, were scientifically unconvincing. When Charles Darwin's 1859 masterpiece *The Origin of Species* finally succeeded in providing a scientifically plausible mechanism of biological change, it was widely hailed as a triumph for the cosmology of progress. In retrospect, nothing could be farther from the truth.

What is most remarkable about Darwin's theory of natural selection, as well as the contemporary evolutionary biology based upon it, is that it departs so radically from the cosmology of progress that we have been discussing. Darwin's insight was that, from such commonplace and undeniable facts as reproduction with variation, the tendency of organisms to produce more offspring than can survive, and the fact that the individuals most suited to survive in their particular circumstances will be most likely to reproduce offspring like themselves, one can logically deduce that populations would change, or "evolve," over time. Darwin himself put it this way: "If variations useful to any organic being ever do occur, assuredly individuals thus characterized will have the best chance of being preserved in the struggle for life; and from the strong principle of inheritance, these will tend to produce offspring similarly characterized. This principle of preservation, or the survival of the fittest, I have called Natural Selection."[3] More than a century after Darwin penned these words, it would be hard to find a better bare-bones summary of the process of evolution. Biologists have since learned a great deal about the mechanisms of genetics, the source of new traits through random mutations, and various other nuances, and they have also developed a rich vocabulary for talking about these matters. Still, the elements of today's evolutionary biology are all present in Darwin's writing, including the influences leading to divergence of species, the idea of ecosystems and ecological niches, and so on.

Despite (or perhaps because of) the revolutionary nature of Darwin's ideas, many of those who welcomed Darwin's theory in his time, as well as many who accept it today, have misunderstood it. Ever since Darwin's day, the lay understanding of evolution—what might be called "pop evolutionism"—has amounted to something quite different from Darwinian-based evolutionary biology. At its core, pop evolutionism is a continuation of the pre-Darwinian mythos of the "cosmic escalator" discussed above. Let us now consider a half-dozen particular points on which a genuinely Darwinian biology differs from pop evolutionism:

Teleology. Popular thinking about evolution is suffused with the pre-Darwinian idea that natural change is guided by purpose and therefore works toward a goal, or at least toward movement in a preordained direction. Such goal-orientation is sometimes referred to as *teleology,* from the Greek *telos,* or "purpose," which in Greek philosophy was as much a characteristic of nature as of human action. The most revolutionary achievement of Darwin's evolutionary biology was to show that complex organisms and ecosystems could develop *without* teleology—that is, without the guidance of any preordained purpose or preexisting design. Evolutionary changes do not occur by design; they are simply the accumulated aftereffects of a blind process, of some variants reproducing more than others. The difference is cosmologically profound.

Destiny and contingency. Pop evolutionism tends to embrace a concept of biological destiny, which assumes that each species—and life in general—is moving along a predetermined path. Hence, it is commonly assumed that the evolutionary processes of countless worlds would produce beings very much like ourselves. Evolutionary biology, however, recognizes the contingency of evolutionary paths—that is, it views them as the chance result of an interaction between innumerable, largely unpredictable variables. If, for example, the dinosaurs had not been eliminated by a cataclysmic geological event (possibly the earth's collision with a comet or asteroid) 65 million years ago, the proliferation of mammals might not have occurred. Similarly, if global cooling had not occurred 15 million years ago, or if the African Rift Valley had not formed a few million years thereafter, hominids would probably not have evolved. To imagine that bipedal apes like ourselves would evolve repeatedly across the galaxy is to believe in a cosmology of human destiny that has little in common with evolutionary biology.

Progress. One of the central premises of pop evolutionism is that "evolution" is the same as "progress." From a scientific perspective, however, the process of natural selection has no connection with progress in the generally accepted sense of "betterment." The fact that a particular organic variant flourishes has nothing to do with its being somehow "better" or "higher," or even, for that matter, more biologically "complex." The evolution of viruses and parasites, for example, not only fails to display any discernible trend toward moral or aesthetic improvement, but it generally entails a decrease in complexity relative to ancestral forms. To offer a different sort of example, the total extinction of humanity would be a fairly unremarkable event from a biological perspective, given that the vast majority of species that have ever lived on the earth are now extinct. For that matter, it is not hard to imagine scenarios that would lead to the extinction of all but the simplest life-forms (several mass extinctions of almost this magnitude have already occurred in our planet's past). Although these episodes would be as "natural" and as "evolutionary" as other biological changes in earth history, one would be hard put to defend them as "progress" in any meaningful sense of the term. Despite the popular tendency to equate the two, evolution and progress are utterly different concepts built on different metaphysical bedrock.

Descriptive and Prescriptive Laws. Given its assumptions about destiny, design, and betterment, it is not surprising that pop evolutionism tends to interpret evolutionary "laws" as statements about how things are "supposed" to happen. Here again, popular thought diverges radically from the scientific evolutionary perspective. Scientific laws, such as the law of gravity, are descriptive rather than prescriptive. If certain objects do not fall as expected, we have to revise our "laws," not admonish the objects for behaving inappropriately or intervene to make them do as they "should." Similarly, evolution is not "supposed" to do anything in particular or go anywhere special—it does what it does, and it is science's task to understand how and why.

Chains and Trees. Since pop evolutionism is inclined to see all change as following a master trend or design, it often portrays diverse types of organisms as stepping stones toward that goal. Even in popular science books, one can occasionally find various species arranged in a chart as though they were stations along a path leading to humanity. This mode of thinking is rooted in the medieval "Great Chain of Being" or, more specifically, in the evolutionary version of the Chain of Being that we called the Cosmic Escalator. Of course, most people know better, and if pressed they might admit that a "tree" with diverging branches is probably a more suitable image than a chain leading from bacteria through salamanders and opossums to ourselves. Many biologists, however, would go farther still and replace the "tree" image with a more complex "bush," in which the vast majority of "twigs" lead to extinctions. The trend in evolutionary biology is toward more complicated evolutionary scenarios with countless branches and dead ends, while pop evolutionism clings to the notion of simple and direct paths leading to necessary outcomes.

Biology and Culture. Where humans are concerned, evolutionary biologists may disagree on the question of just how (and how much) biology and culture influence one another, but they are generally agreed on the importance of distinguishing the two. Biological processes of change involve alterations in genetic codes, while cultural changes are brought about through the learning and teaching of new behavior patterns. Culture, like genetic information, can "evolve," in the sense that it can change gradually through the action of adaptive pressures. It is, however, thoroughly unscientific to muddle biology and culture. Pop evolutionism, unfortunately, plays fast and free with this distinction, as though cultural phenomena were the expression of genetic codes and vice versa. In this way it collapses the complex and elusive interplay of culture and biology into a more cosmologically elegant (but scientifically misguided) picture of "evolution" as a single process that improves body, mind, and lifestyle all in one grand sweep.

In sum, then, popular evolutionism since Darwin's day has invoked the prestige of biological science to justify ideas that not only are pre-Darwinian but are quite difficult to reconcile with the tenets of scientific evolutionary biology. Darwin's revolutionary ideas were absorbed, in large part, into a preexisting cosmology according to which all things advance inexorably along a predestined path. Why are these popular interpretations of evolution so tenacious despite their questionable scientific status? Certainly not because scientific evolutionism is hard to understand; on the contrary, its basic ideas are easily grasped. One reason may have to do with the fact that pop evolutionism fits well with some conservative ideological agendas—for example, with the doctrine misnamed "Social Darwinism," which employs the above-mentioned premises to justify the exploitation of the weak by the strong. There are, however, other less sinister reasons for the tenacity of pop evolutionism.

Although Darwinian evolutionary biology provides a framework for organizing and explaining biological phenomena, it lacks other crucial elements of a cosmological vision. Popular conceptions of evolution thrive because they intuitively supply the narrative scope and moral depth required of a comprehensive mythos. *Star Trek* takes the grand narrative implied in pop evolutionism and makes it explicit, using the secular language of science to instill the human enterprise with a heroism, destiny, and cosmic centrality at least as majestic as that provided by any traditional cosmology.

THE EVOLUTIONARY BIOLOGY OF *STAR TREK*

Why are there so many people in the *Star Trek* universe? This is not the same as asking why there is intelligent life, which could take many forms. Why are there so many *people*—that is, beings so similar to us that the great classifier Linneaus, had he encountered them, would surely have included them in our own genus *Homo*, and even our own species *sapiens*? Furthermore, why is it that these "people" are (compared with the diversity of Terran cultures) so behaviorally similar in every part of the galaxy? Perhaps it is for the same reason that the Navaho trickster Coyote speaks and acts in ways intelligible to the Navajo: if he didn't there could be no story. The task of mythic exploration into the human condition requires that our narrative characters balance the qualities of "like us" and "not like us" at just that point where the tasks of myth can best be undertaken. Another, more mundane, consideration is the limit to how much difference can be coherently portrayed in a one-hour television show, and to what production budgets will allow. Still, it is hard to shake off the niggling sense that *Trek* takes greater liberties with biology and anthropology than production consultants or nit-picking viewers would easily permit in matters of physics and engineering. The implausibility of *Trek*'s biological and anthropological premises are not simply the result of carelessness, but stem instead from *Trek*'s faithful adherence to its modernist-humanist mythmaking project.

In *The Original Series*, the *Enterprise* crew members so routinely encounter human look-alikes in other star systems that they seldom find the fact worthy of comment. Such aliens are often referred to as "humanoids" or simply "humans," with seldom a hint that there is anything remarkable about the evolution of the same species on more than one planet. Only rarely (e.g., when a group exhibits cultural forms nearly identical to those of recent earth history) do the Starfleet heroes feel obliged to throw in a remark about "parallel evolution." In point of fact these aliens are, biologically speaking, depicted as members of our species: not only can "we" Terrans mate with them, but these matings can produce viable offspring—for example, (Vulcan-Terran) Spock, (Betazoid-Terran) Deanna Troi (TNG), (Klingon-Terran) B'Elanna Torres (VGR), and (Klingon-Romulan) Ba'el (TNG's "Birthright"). In biological terms, this reproductive compatibility *by definition* makes all these so-called "humanoids" variants of *Homo sapiens*. It would seem to follow that these extraterrestrial humanoids are also members of our larger taxonomic groupings as well—Family: Hominidae; Order: Primates; and so forth—and that this network of biological relatives implies a sequence of geological and bioevolutionary contingencies virtually identical to those of our planet. To say that this scenario downplays the contingency of evolutionary paths would be an understatement.

Granted, the phenomenon of "parallel evolution" from different ancestral forms is well documented for terrestrial species. The continents of Australia and South America (prior to its connection with North America) independently evolved an array of marsupial mammals from the same ancient mammalian stock that gave rise to the placental mammals of Eurasia, Africa, and North America. Both the marsupial and the placental lineages produced strikingly similar-looking forms based on their adaptation to equivalent ecological niches—for example, the marsupial and placental saber-toothed "cats" and a twin pairing of marsupial and placental "moles." Their superficial resemblance is due to the requirements of their similar adaptive niches. But—and this is extremely important—the marsupial mole remained *genetically* closer to other marsupials like the kangaroo and opossum, with which it shared a relatively recent ancestry, than to its placental "twin" mole. Equally important, the marsupial mole resembled its marsupial kin in the underlying aspects of its anatomy—for example, the marsupials all shared a reproductive physiology quite different from that of the placental mammals. No amount of outward convergence, even among these descendants of a distant common ancestor, would bring their genetic codes (or for that matter, their deeper anatomical traits) any closer to one another—much less bring them to the precise compatibility necessary for reproduction. Once two populations diverge into separate species they become reproductively isolated, and the open-ended nature of DNA coding, together with the action of natural selection and random genetic drift, dictates that the genetic gap between them will only increase. In short, everything we know about evolutionary genetics indicates that parallel evolution will not produce life-forms capable of breeding with one another. Even if we could somehow get past the problem of different genetic codes, *Star Trek*'s references to deep anatomical and physiological differences between Terrans and, say, Vulcans (green blood, different placement of internal organs) or Klingons (multiple redundant organs) would in itself be enough to render viable reproduction completely implausible.

"Just a minute!" the well-versed Trekker may object. "Trek *has* offered explanations for at least some of those humanoid parallels!" True enough, but the "explanations" offered are inadequate, at best, and, at worst, patently unscientific. The first attempt to account for the ubiquity of humans appears in the first-season TOS episode "Return to Tomorrow." Sargon, a pure-thought being, explains that his kind once had humanoid bodies. "It is possible you are our descendants, Captain Kirk. Six thousand centuries ago our vessels were colonizing this galaxy. . . . Perhaps your own legends of an Adam and an Eve were two of our travelers." But the *Enterprise*'s Dr. Anne Mulhall protests, "Our beliefs and studies indicate that life on our planet Earth evolved independently."[4] "That would tend, however, to explain certain elements of Vulcan history," Spock concedes. "In either case, I do not know," admits Sargon. "It was so long ago, and the records of our travels were lost." The humans ignore Sargon's suggestion as if it were of no significance to their scientific mission, and Sargon backs off, apparently unable to tell from Kirk's biology whether this Terran is his own descendant or the product of a completely independent evolution—which leaves us right back where we were before, with the premise that the parallel evolution of identical species is perfectly expectable.

The next attempt to account for humanoid parallels comes soon after the above episode, in "The Paradise Syndrome" of TOS's early third season. Encountering a group of American Indians on a distant planet, Spock decodes the marks on a mysterious high-tech obelisk as the relic of "a super race known as the Preservers," who "passed through the galaxy rescuing primitive cultures which were in danger of extinction, and seeded them, so to speak, on planets where they could live and grow." "I've always wondered," McCoy muses, "why there were so many humanoids scattered through the galaxy." "So have I," Spock replies. "Apparently, the Preservers account for a number of them." However, no one suggests that cutting-edge humanoids like Kirk and Spock are the descendants of endangered "primitive" cultures seeded by the Preservers. Furthermore, unless all these "primitives" were from earth, the process of independent human evolution on different planets remains as unexplained as ever.

The most mythically rich but scientifically challenged explanation of humanoid parallels appears some twenty-seven years into *Star Trek*'s television career, in the late sixth-season TNG story "The Chase." Picard and the *Enterprise* race the ruthless Yridians, Klingons, Cardassians, and Romulans to solve the mystery on which Picard's onetime archeology mentor and father figure, the late Professor Richard Galen, had been working. Upon completing Galen's task of assembling puzzle pieces of ancient DNA from different worlds, the astonished assembly of humanoids watches as the DNA sequence, functioning as a computer program, holographically projects a spokesperson from a long-gone race of humanoids:

> You're wondering who we are . . . why we have done this . . . how it has come that I stand before you, the image of a being from so long ago. Life evolved on my planet before all others in this part of the galaxy. We left our world, explored the stars, and found none like ourselves. Our civilization thrived for ages—but what is the life of one race, compared to the vast stretches of cosmic time? We

knew that one day we would be gone, and nothing of us would survive, so we left you. Our scientists seeded the primordial oceans of many worlds, where life was in its infancy. The seed codes directed your evolution toward a physical form resembling ours: this body you see before you, which is of course shaped as yours is shaped, for you are the end result. The seed codes also contain this message, which is scattered in fragments on many different worlds. It was our hope that you would have to come together in fellowship and companionship to hear this message—and if you can see and hear me, our hope has been fulfilled. You are a monument, not to our greatness, but to our existence. That was our wish: that you too would know life, and would keep alive our memory. There is something of us in each of you, and so, something of you in each other. Remember us.

Here we have nothing less than a full-fledged humanoid creation myth—one that affirms the kinship of assorted antagonists. The Cardassians and Klingons find this message revolting (they were expecting some new source of military power), but the Romulan leader is pensive. Later, when he hails Picard aboard the *Enterprise* to signal his departure, he remarks, "It would seem that we are not completely dissimilar after all, in our hopes, or in our fears." "Yes," Picard responds quietly. "Then perhaps, one day . . ." "One day," echoes Picard, as he cradles Professor Galen's parting gift, a figurine from an ancient and distant culture, which symbolizes the many voices within the one and the one voice within the many.

This "explanation" of humanoid parallels is more than just a footnote to biology as we know it; rather, it overturns the fundamental premises on which twentieth-century biology is based. Human beings are no longer just one among many species, a contingent outcome of our planet's immense biological diversity—they are the final cause and purpose to which evolutionary history was directed. DNA is no longer just an alphabet for transmitting the everchanging outcome of each generation's reproductive success, but a treasure chest in which is hidden a message from the beginning of time, written for our benefit by our creators, a message containing a purpose, and that purpose is—ourselves! The "DNA" terminology is superficially the language of science and of naturalistic explanation; but in this revisioning, DNA replaces the language of Plato's eternal divine essences and Aristotle's teleological final causes as endpoints that draw developmental processes toward them. In the beginning was the word, and the word was DNA.

The VGR episode "Threshold" provides another example of how *Star Trek* represents DNA as a tablet on which the whole of humankind's evolutionary past and future is inscribed. An experimental flight takes

Tom Paris where no one has gone before, to a "transwarp speed" previously theorized to be impossible. He achieves infinite velocity and simultaneously occupies every point in the universe. As it happens, this challenge to physics apparently provokes nature to respond in kind. Paris transforms into a slimy creature who kidnaps Captain Janeway and takes her for a transwarp spin to another planet where the two of them become large salamanderlike beings who mate and produce a spawn of little wigglies before they are rescued and restored to their former selves. The Doctor has an eye-opening explanation for all this: evolution. Their exposure to extreme velocity has evidently accelerated the "natural evolution" of humans, causing Paris and Janeway to "evolve" rapidly into the form our descendants will have millions of years in the future, a form that (according to the Doctor) represents a continuation of present human trends such as brain enlargement and the disappearance of "vestigial organs" (whatever that may mean). Our evolutionary future is written in the strands of our present DNA. The episode sheds little light on why human evolution would take a path so very different from the "pure thought" beings foreseen in other *Trek* episodes. But as a portrayal of evolution as movement along a predetermined track with DNA as the eternal road map, this story is very much in tune with the other *Trek* narratives.

TNG's "Genesis" develops a view of evolution similar to that of "The Chase" and "Threshold" but from the opposite direction: the *Enterprise* crew members are infected with a virus that activates dormant elements in their DNA, causing them to "de-evolve" into more than a thousand different species, each representing some distant ancestral type from their evolutionary past. (We should note here that, since evolution has no definitive direction, the whole concept of "reverse" or "de-" evolution actually makes little scientific sense.) The specific "ancestors" into which the crew members "de-evolve" follow no discernible biological pattern but are clear metaphorical representations of the characters of the individual persons. The bearded, macho Riker degenerates into a hulking ape-man; the crusty Klingon Worf, into a sex-crazed, poison-spitting crustacean; the nervous, obsessive, fantasy-spinning paranoiac Barclay, into a spider; and the newly pregnant Nurse Alyssa Ogawa becomes an anthropoid primate, the mother of us all. In one of the great scenes of *Star Trek*, Deanna Troi is found submerged in her warm bathtub in the form of an amphibian, a characterization that not only draws creatively on her softly defined facial features, but also on her intermediary character as Betazoid-human, breathing the air of two worlds—of telepathy and human speech, empathy and logos. (If this sounds like an overintepretation, try mentally switching Riker's and Troi's—or Barclay's—degenerated forms and consider whether that makes equally good sense.) Whatever one may think of this episode as a story (frankly, we think it's great!), it replays in reverse the same mystified biology seen in "The Chase" and "Threshold." Here, DNA contains a complete archive of the phylogenetic memory of each planet's evolutionary history, with all the genes still arranged in a perfect chronicle wherein all species, even spiders, are points along a unilinear path leading to the human. Interestingly, Worf de-evolves into something quite unearthly, suggesting that his evolutionary legacy is radically unlike the human's, a notion that leads us back into some of the problems discussed above. One final note: the panicked, violent, oversexed, and generally grotesque character of these "de-evolved" species illustrates how far we have "progressed" from our animal past (animals are not nobly portrayed in *Trek*) and why we must strive continually to overcome our regressive elements.

In the episodes described, and throughout all of Trek's post-1960s corpus, DNA is used in a mystical sense, in which these humble replicating proteins take on a cosmic metaphysical role as the keepers of the sacred essence and destiny of a person, race, or species. In VGR's "Distant Origin," *Voyager* encounters lizardlike sentient aliens in the distant Delta Quadrant who share a surprising number of genes with the Terrans; the computer solves the mystery by extrapolating from the genetic codes of certain ancient terrestrial dinosaurs a projection of what their future "evolved" form would have been, thus demonstrating that these aliens are indeed the descendants of earth's ancient saurians. Here again is the idea of a species' evolutionary future as something prophesied and preordained in its DNA.

The myth of DNA as a mystified "essence" is again suggested in TNG's "Up the Long Ladder," in which a genetically deteriorating Terran colony of clones begs Riker and Dr. Pulaski for DNA samples to reinvigorate their gene pool. Although the process would not diminish or inconvenience him in any tangible way, Riker is as morally outraged at the idea as any medieval monk might have been at a demonic succubus who steals his seed during sleep in order to reproduce herself. Picard answers on behalf of the thousand-person crew that no one on the Enterprise would ever consider such a thing, even if this refusal seals the doom of the colony. When the colonists steal cell samples on the sly, Riker and Pulaski kill the incubating clones without compunction, as if they truly were demonic abominations. (As a result, the sex-aversive colonists are obliged to mate with the earthy, whiskey-swilling Irish-in-space who inhabit a nearby Terran colony, thereby spinning a tale of the culturally "primitive"—but that's another story.)

In the end, *Star Trek* gives us a "biology" where scientific terms stand in for the antique metaphysics of teleological predestination and invisible essences—a case of old wine in new bottles. The radical galactic rehabilitation of human destiny that culminates in "The Chase" restores the status of humanity in the cosmos to a level not seen since the Middle

Ages, and arguably not since the pinnacle of Greek philosophy. To the extent that *Trek* functions as a mythos whose task is (among other things) to reaffirm the cosmic centrality of humanity within a naturalistic modernist frame of reference, *Trek*'s strategy generally succeeds, even though it is obliged to break radically with scientific biology in order to do so.

It is not only biology, however, that is involved in the cosmic scheme of "progress," but culture as well. As mentioned earlier, popular evolutionism does not always make a fine distinction between these two. But to the extent that one can examine *Star Trek*'s portrayal of cultural development apart from that of genetic "evolution," *Star Trek* tells a story of destiny and progress in cultural change that reinforces and parallels its concept of biological development.

THE STREAM OF HISTORY

In the episode "A Private Little War," Kirk and McCoy visit the planet Neural, which had been a primitive Eden when Kirk first visited it as a young officer. Now, some thirteen years after that initial contact, Kirk and McCoy are shocked to see Kirk's old friends, the Hill People, being hunted down by flintlock-bearing Villagers. The unexpected appearance of firearms on the planet is explained when Kirk and McCoy discover that the Klingons are arming the Villagers against the Hill People. Kirk reluctantly concludes that he must arm the Hill People just well enough to maintain the "balance of power." In defending this decision to the outraged Doctor McCoy, Kirk refers to the prolonged "twentieth-century brush wars on the Asian continent," which, he claims, proved the desirability of maintaining a balance so that one side (presumably the Communist bloc, represented here by the Klingons) could not achieve the military domination that might have escalated regional struggles into a global holocaust.

"A Private Little War" is transparent in its reference to the Vietnam conflict. The episode was originally aired on February 2, 1968, several months after opinion polls first registered a majority of the American people opposed to the war, and two days into the North Vietnamese Tet Offensive, which marked a turning of the military tide against the United States and its South Vietnamese clients.[5] H. Bruce Franklin argues that this tale upholds the Johnson Administration's rationale for the war.[6] It was only later, Franklin argues, that *Star Trek* took an antiwar stance in its episode "The Omega Glory," the story of a war-exhausted planet where the blonde "Yangs" (Yankees) have degenerated into grunting savages through their mindless, interminable war against the Asiatic-looking "Khoms" (Communists), all in defense of a tattered American flag and their "worship words" (a garbled version of the preamble to the United States Constitution that they no longer understand). Contrary to Franklin's view, Rick Worland's reading of "A Private Little War" emphasizes Kirk's inner doubts about providing the weapons, which Kirk calls "a hundred serpents for the Garden of Eden." For Worland the story portrays the beginnings of doubt about the Vietnam war.[7]

Franklin's and Worland's readings of "A Private Little War" are part of the larger project of mining *Star Trek* for allegories about concurrent political affairs—an endeavor that has led to various graduate dissertations and published essays. It is a worthy undertaking, and not necessarily far-fetched in its methods and conclusions. Certainly it is hard to miss the parallels between, for example, the end of the Cold War and the "détente" between the Klingons and the Federation. One can also find commentary on other social issues, as in the TNG's "The Hunted," which refers indirectly to the plight of returning war veterans in its tale of outcasts who have been unalterably transformed into "supersoldiers" and who are ostracized when their military function is no longer required.

Star Trek's allegorical connections with American political life are important on a number of levels, not the least of which is the contribution to *Trek*'s broader cosmological project. Returning to "A Private Little War," we can see in it some marvelous examples of *Star Trek*'s construction of time, change, and cultural difference in TOS. It is not the appearance of perfect replicas of Davey Crockett–style flintlock rifles that surprises Kirk and Spock, but the timing: the "normal" innovation that "should" have taken about 1200 years has happened in the brief thirteen years since Kirk's first visit, tipping them off that something is amiss. The Klingons, who are no fools, try to cover their tracks by introducing the new technology in small increments—first the flintlocks, then an improved firing mechanism, rifled barrels, and so forth—so that it will resemble the "normal" pattern of change, i.e., the one seen on earth and presumably on other humanoid planets. The apparent triviality of this example is the very thing that makes it such a perfect illustration of *Trek*'s mythos of progress. Even in minute changes in the look and technology of a short-lived form of firearm, it goes almost without saying that a virtually identical sequence of events will occur in parallel fashion across the galaxy.

Pangalactic parallels in cultural evolution are given a "scientific" status in TOS's "Bread and Circuses," when an "earth parallel" society on planet 892-IV is explained by reference to "Hodgkins' Law of Parallel Planet Development," which postulates that "similar planets with similar populations and similar environments will evolve in similar ways."[8] This "law" explains why the people of planet 892-IV possess a technology virtually identical to that of the twentieth-century United States. It is also used to explain the use of American English—an explanation that might possibly help account for the evident monolingualism of other humanoid planets in TOS—that seems to remain in effect until TNG proposes miniaturized "universal translators" to account for our ability to understand alien speech. There are some differences between earth and 892-IV, however. On 892-IV, Rome never fell; hence, slavery and gladiatorial contests coexist with automobiles and television. (Gladiatorial success is measured by television ratings!) Given all these parallels, the *Enterprise* team is only surprised that this "Roman" social system has no insurgent Christians. But the coherence of history is salvaged when it is finally revealed that an oppressed dissident group of "Sun" worshippers are actually Christians, worshippers of the "Son," who are, of course, destined to prevail and to set the society on its normal course of moral progression (that is, once the planet is rid of a renegade Starfleet captain who had been gumming up the works).

Astounding parallels in cultural development appear throughout *The Original Series* as well as *The Next Generation*. "The Omega Glory," with its Yangs and Khoms and its war-torn American flag, contends with "Bread and Circuses" as one of the most ambitious tales of cultural parallelism. In TOS's "All Our Yesterdays," the *Enterprise* team enters a time machine (the "atavachron") on Sarpeidon that takes them into different moments of the planet's history, including a parallel "Ice Age" in which Spock "de-evolves" into a libidinous caveman, and a parallel seventeenth-century England where Kirk is imprisoned for witchcraft. When primitive protohumans attack a landing party in TOS's "The Galileo Seven," science officer Spock has only to glance at one of their spearpoints in order to classify their technology (using terms from North American prehistory) and make a number of deductions about their social organization and behavior.[9] While *The Next Generation* at least acknowledges linguistic diversity and gives the locals some distinctive cultural and racial trimmings, the worlds depicted in such episodes as "Thine Own Self," "Who Watches the Watchers," and "Code of Honor" invite comparisons with specific geographical and temporal counterparts in earth history.

Star Trek did not invent the theory of parallel cultural paths, and neither did contemporary science fiction as a whole. The idea is firmly rooted in late-nineteenth-century theories of unilinear cultural evolution, as promulgated in such widely known works as Lewis H. Morgan's *Ancient Society* (1865), Edward B. Tylor's *Primitive Culture* (1871), and James G. Frazer's *The Golden Bough* (1890). These works share a number of key assumptions: (1) an overarching natural "law" of progress, or improvement, governs both biological and cultural change; (2) cultural "evolution" is simply another term for *progress*; (3) all peoples pass through the same stages and substages of cultural evolution, even though some are farther along than others at a given time; (4) differing rates of progress may be explained by race, environment, historical accident, or some combination of the three; (5) people at a given stage of cultural evolution will resemble others at that stage, even if widely separated from them in time and space; (6) knowing the level or stage of a people's cultural evolution will allow the informed scientist to predict details of their customs, social organization, and ways of thinking; (7) since advanced cultures are objectively better, happier, and more knowledgeable than primitive ones, it is only proper that the advanced cultures do whatever is necessary to control, change, educate, or even replace inferior peoples. This is the anthropology that, understandably, appealed to educated Westerners during the age of colonial expansion. Although contemporary readers may be struck by the patent cultural chauvinism and complacency of this outlook, we can also grant that it embodied a coherent cosmology of human development and a generous mythos of human nature—perhaps more so than any philosophy before or since. In order to believe in unlimited, universal human progress, it is necessary to posit a stable human nature that is good (not fallen or depraved) and common to everyone (not leading peoples down different paths). The essential human "best self," according to the nineteenth-century humanist Matthew Arnold, is "not manifold, and vulgar, and unstable, and contentious, and ever-varying, but one, and noble, and secure, and peaceful, and the same for all mankind."[10]

In varying ways and to varying degrees, Star Trek continues to uphold some aspects of this cosmology. Trek's concept of both biological and cultural change could be likened to rafting down a river of time. It is as though not only Huck and Jim, but all the river's travelers, cannot but pass the same towns, bends, and landmarks in the same order, and even go through the same awakenings, as they move along their journey. Their vessels may have slightly different furnishings, some may travel faster than others, and some may even run aground or get caught in a backwater. But it is the same river for everyone, and we all travel toward the same ocean of human destiny.

There is, however, one very significant exception to Star Trek's adoption of the nineteenth-century mythos of progress. That exception has to do with the supposed right of "superior" cultures to dominate and rule over "primitives." Since the turn of the twentieth century, particularly in America under the leadership of anthropologist Franz Boas and his students, the study of non-Western peoples has taken a turn toward the validation of diverse cultures as coherent, viable lifeways that deserve to be judged by their own standards and respected on their own terms. Accordingly, the theory of unilinear cultural evolution was discredited within the anthropological community (a change that did not greatly reduce its influence on popular thought), while the conception of human universals was considerably broadened (though not necessarily abandoned). The ideal of sympathetic understanding of other cultures found an audience in America largely because the United States possessed few colonies and, by this time, had already dispossessed its native population. Romanticizing cultural difference cost Americans very little, it fit nicely with the ideals of egalitarianism and sympathy for the underdog, and it helped foster a sense of moral superiority over what Americans liked to think of as the elitist, exploitive, and decadent European colonialists. It could be said that our cultural tolerance is by no means universal and that it does not always go very deep, but it does help account for the Prime Directive. In fact, it is precisely because *Trek* supplements its main entrée of nineteenth-century evolutionism with a side dish of twentieth-century cultural relativism that Starfleet captains so often find themselves in a quandary over the Prime Directive.

THE CHANGING FORTUNES OF THE PRIME DIRECTIVE

Starfleet General Order #1, known as The Prime Directive, prohibits "interference in the normal development of any society."[11] The interpretation of the Directive, however, seems to change from one episode to another. Sometimes it absolutely—on pain of death—forbids Starfleet personnel even to reveal themselves to other cultures (TOS's "Bread and Circuses"); at the other extreme, it may be taken as an admonition to persuade, rather than coerce, other groups into desired actions (TNG's "Code of Honor").

Many variables seem to affect the expression of Starfleet's Prime Directive. One of these is the level of the local planet's cultural development. In accordance with the assumption that "primitive" peoples are normally pristine and uninfluenced by contact with others (an image questioned by modern anthropology but still strong in popular culture), Starfleet is especially careful not to reveal itself, or the existence of space travel and other worlds, to people who are not already in contact with outsiders. Such people as those in "Code of Honor," however, are aware of space travel; hence, Picard is allowed to negotiate with them (but not resort to coercion) to acquire a needed vaccine.

The Directive's applicability seems also to vary according to whether the existing situation is "normal" or has been somehow "contaminated" or otherwise diverted from its "natural" course of development. In "The Apple" and other dystopian episodes, Kirk justifies intervention on grounds that the culture is not developing normally. In "A Private Little War," he is able to intervene because the Klingons' previous intervention has already influenced the people's development. When Spock's tricorder shows that there has been no "progress" on Organia ("Errand of Mercy"), Kirk agrees that this "arrested" state is not "right," and he offers to set up schools. These stories rely heavily on the idea that some cultural developments follow correct evolutionary patterns while others do not and that it is up to Starfleet officers to make the distinction. Sometimes the mere fact that a given social arrangement offends Captain Kirk's sense of authentic human growth is enough to justify intervention.[12]

There is a noticeable difference between twenty-third- and twenty-fourth-century Starfleet views (or to use a different frame, 1960s and 1980s American views) on intervention. While Kirk seldom hesitates to destroy false utopias, both Picard and Sisko refuse to tamper with the dystopian colonies they encounter. This is because, as we shall discuss in the next chapter, the later series put less emphasis on a single path of destiny and more on the recognition of diverse, contingent paths of life.

We should also take into account the narrative medium of *Star Trek*'s reality, which requires that such signifiers as the Prime Directive be employed in ways that "work" in the context of a given episode narrative as well as the larger *Trek* mythos. For that reason, the meaning of the Directive may change according to whether the syntax of storytelling requires heroic restraint or heroic intervention. In "The Apple," for example, Kirk's intervention marks the narrative climax; while in "Bread and Circuses," the restraint required by the Directive builds dramatic tension and also helps to contrast Kirk with an earlier, less disciplined Starfleet captain who betrayed his crew to "go native."

The Prime Directive contributes in various ways to the *Star Trek* cosmology. As we shall see, the Directive reinforces the premise that the heroic mission is one of discovery, not power mongering or exploitation—it is Starfleet's way of saying, "We are not imperialists!" But the final importance of the Prime Directive is best understood in light of *Trek*'s mythos of a natural law defining and mandating the normal "evolutionary" path of humanoid development. Definitive humanoids are exemplified by Starfleet and the Federation of Planets and above all, by the crew of the *Enterprise*. As the universe's humans par excellence, the *Enterprise* heroes must recognize and protect the hallowed law of human growth that has brought them so far. That is the real reason for the sacredness of the Prime Directive, and it is also the reason why it is imperative that Mr. Spock's tricorder be able to detect and measure progress.

CHAPTER 9

CODE OF THE WEST

Racial and Cultural Mastery on the Final Frontier

It is perfectly natural for the human mind to resist the assault on it of untreated strangeness; therefore, cultures have always been inclined to impose complete transformations on other cultures, receiving these other cultures not as they are but as, for the benefit of the receiver, they ought to be.

—Edward Said
Orientalism (1978)

In his groundbreaking work *Orientalism*, literary and cultural critic Edward Said contends that "learned and imaginative writings are never free, but are limited in their imagery, assumptions, and intentions" by the language made available to them through the existing cultural milieu. Said goes on to point out that human societies, especially those most advantaged in terms of social power and reach, "have rarely offered the individual anything but imperialism, racism, and ethnocentrism for dealing with "Other" cultures."[1] If Said is essentially correct (and we believe he is), and if the vast majority of *Star Trek*'s writers, fans, and production team are consciously committed to envisioning a world without prejudice or arbitrary privilege (which we also believe to be true), then one might expect the resulting messages in *Trek* to be complex, ambivalent, and subject to a variety of readings.

TRIBAL TRIBULATIONS

The Next Generation's "Code of Honor" was the third episode of the series, and it conveys some of the flavor of both the old *Star Trek* and the new. The *Enterprise D* is in orbit around Ligon II, where its assignment is to negotiate with the "close earth parallel" Ligonians for an organic vaccine needed to combat an epidemic on another planet. Picard, a trained archeologist, is proud of his cosmopolitan understanding of cultures and protocols. He knows that these tribal people are strongly "ritualistic," so he is indulgent of the Ligonian's wish to beam up by using their own transporter. "It's their way," he explains. The Ligonian delegates include the ruler, Lutan, and a contingent of his bodyguards—stoic, turbaned black men in skimpy vests showing plenty of skin, a caricature of Islamic West Africa. The Ligonians barely conceal their shock when Natasha Yar is introduced as the Chief Security Officer of the *Enterprise,* but their disdain turns to curious admiration when one of the Ligonians tries to push past Yar and is summarily thrown to the floor. Troi, speaking of the Ligonians in the third person as though they were not there, advises the Captain not to apologize because "in their view it would weaken us." Picard welcomes them graciously, informs them that they remind him of "an ancient earth culture we all admire," and presents Lutan with a gift. When the Ligonians remark pointedly that the women on their world do not wield authority, Troi responds by coolly comparing Ligonia's present culture with earth's past.

The action shifts into high gear when, after a ceremony in his honor, Lutan seizes Yar and beams instantly to the surface with her. The abduction, Data later explains, has been carried out in strict accordance with the Ligonian code of honor, which he compares to the North American Indian custom of "counting coup," or striking ritual blows against an adversary to gain prestige. Starfleet regulations would permit Picard to rescue Yar, but Lutan makes it clear that he will not consent to turn over the needed vaccine unless the Captain and his officers attend a special ceremony for her release. In private, Troi and Picard muse about "how simple this would all be without the Prime Directive." Picard's mounting frustration over Lutan's defiance provokes an outburst in which he vents his candid opinion of Ligonian culture. "By our standards, the customs here, their 'code of honor,' is the same kind of pompous, strutting charades that endangered our own species a few centuries ago. We evolved out of it because no one tried to impose their own set of . . . I'm sorry, this is becoming a speech." For Picard it is not what the Ligonians *are* but what they might someday become—and the integrity of the "evolutionary" process that will bring them there—that deserves respect.

The Ligonians have "clear and simple ways, deeply rooted in our culture," Lutan explains to his visitors. "Honor is everything." But not honor as Picard knows it, for the devious Lutan has one more trick up his sleeve. During the ceremony, Lutan retracts his promise to release Yar and pledges to make her his "first one," which provokes from Lutan's present wife, Yareena, a challenge of ritual combat to the death. Picard and Troi are allowed to visit Yar in private where, caught off guard by Troi's description of Lutan as "such a basic male image," Yar confides that Lutan's actions "made me feel good," and that "I'm attracted to him." Although Yar is not bound to accept Yareena's challenge, she chooses to do so in the hope that Lutan will relinquish the needed vaccine.

Actually, Lutan's move is part of a wily stratagem: if Yar wins, Lutan will inherit Yareena's land, and if Yareena wins, Lutan has lost nothing. Yar's poison-tipped weapon kills Yareena, but the two combatants are beamed onto the *Enterprise* where Yareena is quickly revived ("This is witchcraft!" Lutan exclaims). Yareena's temporary death dissolves her marital bond to Lutan; she chooses his bodyguard Hagon as her new first husband and (with Yar's slightly hesitant permission) makes Lutan her second, subordinate husband. Since his conditions have been met, Lutan is honor bound to release the vaccine, and the *Enterprise* departs with its mission accomplished. No mention is made of the possibility of the Ligonians' joining the Federation of Planets.

"Code of Honor" illustrates some important characteristics of *Star Trek*'s interplanetary relations. It is significant that *Trek* goes out of its way to avoid outright imperialism—political affiliations and economic transactions require the full and informed consent of all parties. There is, however, a more subtle narrative of privilege and domination at work, one that places the Terran/American/Starfleet culture implicitly at the normative center of "humanness" while marginalizing and condescending to the cultural "Other." Some of the machinations by which this is done are elusive, but we can start with those that are easiest to see in "Code of Honor."

The scriptwriters' intention in this episode may have been a portrayal of Ligonians in the vein of the "proud Africa" image seen in the well-known 1970s television miniseries "Roots." The Ligonians are dignified, independent, and well spoken, and they often chide the Starfleet crew for their ignorance of "civilized" ways. But once one drops a bucket into the well of conventionalized, recognizable media icons of the "tribal," what usually comes up is a collection of ethnocentric images and cultural assumptions about Africa and the "exotic" tribal world in general. In this case, *Star Trek* is no exception.

Some of the racial and cultural stereotypes in "Code of Honor" are so close to the surface that they are hard to miss. There is, for a start, the cunning and treacherous native whose sense of integrity is, to put it kindly, peculiarly culture bound. These turbaned blacks capitalize on popular images of both Africans and Muslim Arabs, with the predictable result that as soon as the Ligonian ruler sees the blonde Yar he wants her for his collection. When asked for her empathic assessment of the

Ligonian delegation, Troi reports that all the Ligonian men are sexually attracted to Yar. This theme of sexuality taps Western images of libidinous Arabs and Africans, their celebrated polygamy, their fabled treatment of women as objects, their legendary attraction to blondes, and their supposed covetousness of whatever the Westerner has.[2] Then there is the gratuitous, out-of-character sexual attraction that Yar confesses for her abductor. This is the same Tasha Yar who, in the preceding episode ("The Naked Now") confided to Data that her tough demeanor conceals a soul scarred by sexual abuse and longing for gentleness. No explanation is given for Yar's bizarre and self-deprecating emotional response to her abduction, other than Troi's characterization of this tall, black chieftain as "such a basic male."

Almost as patently stereotypic as the sexual theme is the Ligonians' irrational attachment to ceremony at the expense of good faith. In a less obvious vein, there is the fact that Data interprets Ligonian behavior by using Plains Indian concepts, as though (à la unilinear evolution) all "tribal" people are pretty much alike. One might ask why Picard chooses to compare the Ligonians with "an ancient earth culture" when the obvious parallel is with West African societies roughly contemporaneous with Lord Nelson's England—a culture that Picard really does admire and that he would not place among the exotica of "ancient" cultures. The "ancient" in Picard's speech may refer more to an assumed developmental stage, or perhaps an evolutionary dead-end status (West Africa has evidently contributed little to Federation culture), than to chronology. Although the Ligonians have transporters, automatic doors, and energy-field technology, they are still primitive at heart: Starfleet medicine comes across as "witchcraft." And Starfleet, despite its stated aim of learning about worlds and peoples, seems more interested in the Ligonians' resources than the Ligonians themselves, whose main value seems to lie in their potential to become more like Picard and company.

"Code of Honor" did not go over well with some viewers who saw these stereotypic images of tribal Africa as thinly veiled racism. In fact, the question of "racism" has been raised often enough by critics of *Star Trek* that it is impossible to ignore it. The concept of race, however, is so emotionally loaded and so slippery in its meanings that it is necessary to unpack the definitions of *race* and *racism* before going on to discuss *Trek*'s handling of human differences.

IS *STAR TREK* RACIST?

Star Trek is often credited with breaking down television's racist stereotypes by depicting the people of various nations, "races," and even planets working in harmony as Starfleet colleagues and equals. Nichelle Nichols's role in TOS as Uhura and George Takei's Sulu may seem peripheral, but they were among the first television characters to portray African Americans or Asians simply as people whose roles were not inherently linked to an ethnic background. As every Trekker knows, the legendary first "interracial" kiss on television was between Uhura and Kirk in TOS's "Plato's Stepchildren." In the three later series, black actors appear in numbers that are (at least) proportional to the black population of America.[3] All the series include a broad diversity of Terran "races," nationalities, and genders, not to mention interplanetary humanoid types, among their central characters; of the nine most important characters in VGR only one (Tom Paris) is a white male Terran.

The Original Series aired episodes whose clear intent was to criticize racism. In "The Cloudminders," Kirk manages to convince the elites of a divided planet that their underclass "Troglytes" are not naturally inferior but are suffering from the noxious effects of their working conditions. In "Balance of Terror," a crewman renounces his prejudice against Vulcans after Spock saves his life. "Let That Be Your Last Battlefield" depicts the unbending mutual hatred between Bele and Lokai, survivors of the two "races" of Cheron whose prolonged conflict has destroyed their planet. The device of representing physical "race" in this episode is unique—Bele is jet black on one side and snow white on the other, while Lokai is the reverse. The strength of this story as a parable (and some would argue, its weakness of sociological insight) lies in its reduction of racial conflict to a trivial preoccupation with color.[4]

Science fiction author and critic Ursula Le Guin finds much to admire in *Star Trek*'s presentation of "alien types, gender difference, handicaps, apparent deformities, all accepted simply as different ways of being human." It is, she says, an example of "what science fiction does best," which is to challenge our prejudices and enhance our "sense of kinship" with those who differ from ourselves.[5] TOS's George Takei puts it more directly when he states that *"Star Trek* is, and has always been, the antithesis of racism."[6] It might therefore come as a surprise that various critics have characterized *Trek* as racist.

Assessing *Star Trek*'s portrayal of "race" is more complicated than it sounds, largely because the term has taken on so many diverse and even contradictory meanings. In the most inclusive sense, "race" refers to a whole species, as in "the human race," which connotes and valorizes the unity of all humanity. In its technical biological meaning, however, "race" refers to local genetic variants within a species.[7] "Race" is also used colloquially to refer to groups of people who are socially categorized as "different" by vaguely defined criteria of nationality, language, religion, or culture (consider, for example, the so-called "Celtic race"). The term "racism," consequently, carries a variety of meanings, including racial essentialism (the belief that peoples' differing behaviors arise from their "racial" genes); race chauvinism (the belief that biological differences justify the supremacy of some groups over others); or ethnocentrism (belief in the superiority of one's own culture). This last meaning, in which "race" is a social category that masquerades as a biological one, is by far the most elusive. It is also, unfortunately, one that haunts most discussions of "race," including some that pretend to be scientific.[8] It is this evasive sense of the term that many commentators on "race" in *Trek* seem to be struggling with.

Another dimension of complexity comes from *Star Trek* itself, which has introduced some convolutions of its own. *Trek* has supplied us with a fantasy universe of other planetary humanoids, thus shifting the traditional universalizing, inclusive meaning of the phrase "human race" to a potentially more parochial one (Terrans only). The biological status of these various humanoids is mightily confusing. Biologically speaking, the Klingons must be members of our species because they can breed with us; yet in the film *The Undiscovered Country*, the Klingons object to the Federation of Planets as a *"Homo sapiens* only club." Does this mean that Klingons are not in our species after all, but that some other humanoid types in the Federation are? In the same film, the Klingons object to the term "human rights," which they see as marginalizing them, even though the term "human" is often used in Trek as a synonym for "humanoid," which according to the *Star Trek Encyclopedia* includes Klingons, Vulcans, Cardassians, and assorted others.[9] It certainly does not help that the Klingons are sometimes referred to as a "species" and sometimes as a "race." Spock, who also passes the official species criterion of reproductive compatibility with Terrans (and is half Terran himself), objects to being called a human. In contrast with *Trek's* sporadic attempts to be consistent in its use of chronology and technical details, its terminology of biological difference contradicts elementary science and is blatantly self-contradictory.

If this were not confusing enough, *Star Trek* scatters contemporary America's "races" somewhat randomly across other worlds; thus we see "black" and "Hispanic" as well as "white"-looking Vulcans, and vaguely Asian Klingons alongside quasi-European ones. At the same time, the "racial" categories that we use are seldom referred to in *Trek*. Native Americans, who are sometimes depicted as racially and culturally distinct even on other planets (TOS's "The Paradise Syndrome," TNG's "Journey's End") are the one significant exception. The Ligonians of TNG's "Code of Honor" are the only all-black alien race, but their physical distinctiveness is never mentioned in the story. America's "races," in short, generally seem to cut across *Trek's* "races." Because of *Trek's* extremely complex depiction of race, commentators on *Trek's* "race" relations risk confusion if they fail to specify whose system of classification they are talking about—the commentator's, America's, or *Trek's*.

Star Trek employs its own "racial" constructs in various ways depending on the narrative contexts in which they are embedded. As mythic narrative, *Trek* does not handle categories and oppositions in quite the same way as formal disquisition does. Rather than erasing ambiguity, myth may play upon it or mediate it in ways that are more poetic and indistinct than we would expect from formal thought. A given identity may be set within different semiotic structures depending on the story-telling context. The meaning of being Vulcan may differ depending on the project of the story in which it appears—for example, whether Mr. Spock is placed in opposition to his full-Vulcan father Sarek, his friend Captain Kirk, the red-blooded human race in general, or the Romulans who differ from Vulcans only by training and habit. Klingonism may be used to signify one thing when Worf is studying the customs of his "own" people so as to fit in with them, and something else when he claims to feel the call of the Klingon warrior in his "blood."

Critical commentators on *Star Trek*, despite their often useful insights, do not always acknowledge the ambiguities already present in our culture's, and in *Trek*'s, deployment of "race." To this bewildering chaos, critics sometimes add their own unstated definitions and assumptions, leaving the reader to sort through some baffling twists and turns. The rewards and pitfalls of analyzing "race" in *Trek* are evident in Leah Van de Berg's engaging analysis of the TNG/DS9 Klingon character Worf as a "signifier of racial, cultural and national differences."[10] Rejecting LeGuin's optimistic assessment of *Trek*'s racial attitudes, Van de Berg maintains that the "pervasive racism and cultural intolerance of our contemporary social world" is expressed through *Trek*'s portrayal of Worf, a Klingon raised by humans, as a "model" of minority assimilation. She cites a scene in TNG's "Redemption" when Worf's fellow Klingons offer him the life of his enemy's adolescent son, whom by Klingon custom he is expected to kill ("It's the Klingon way," they urge). Worf is given the knife, but he lets it fall to the floor, saying, "It is not my way. The boy has done me no harm, and I will not kill him for the crimes of his family." Thus, the episode is said to show a "racist" bias by having Worf recognize the "superiority" of such "Federation values" as compassion. But there is a problem with this argument; for while Vande Berg consistently denounces as "racist" the sort of cultural assimilationism implied in the above story, she also condemns *Trek* as racist because of its alleged racial essentialism. Suppose that Worf had killed the boy—would that not suggest that his Klingon genes had overruled his upbringing and his chosen commitments, and would this not provide a perfect occasion to denounce *Trek* as racially essentialist? *Trek* can't win: if Worf drops the knife, the plot validates assimilation; if he uses it, the story racially essentializes Worf. Either way, *Trek* is racist.

The trouble is that this argument, like many other commentaries on race, is implicitly using more than one definition of "racism." One equates racism with racial essentialism; the other identifies it with ethnocentrism. In fact, these two ideas may contradict one another. True, a chauvinistic racial essentialist would also be ethnocentric (After all, how could an inferior race produce anything but an inferior culture?), but the strident assimilationist cannot logically be an essentialist. To assert that everyone should convert to the ways of a "superior" culture is ethnocentric, but it also assumes that human behavior is not circumscribed by "racial" genes.

Does *Star Trek* purvey racial essentialism? Critic Bill Bolsvert contends that TNG "charts new territory in its obsession with race." "Every social interaction from toilet training to trade negotiations," he argues, "fits onto a template of race essentialism; every species is inscribed with an indelible psychological profile. Bajorans are poetic and mercurial, Romulans cold and cerebral." Bolsvert continues:

> Every individual personality quirk represents a perturbation of the genome, as when Alexander, Worf's quadroon son by a half-breed human, blames his un-Klingonlike bookishness on the fact that he's part human. The problem of foundlings raised by alien families always provokes an inter-galactic incident, requiring Captain Picard to balance the demands of the birth species with the sentimental attitudes of the adoptive parents; inevitably, the former wins out and the child is sent to be with its "own kind."[11]

It is by no means clear which TNG stories would actually fit into Bolsvert's racial essentialist mold, but there are many that clearly violate it. In TNG's "Suddenly Human," the *Enterprise* rescues a Terran child who has been captured and raised by the warlike Talarians; and Picard, recognizing the strength of the boy's enculturation, returns him to his adoptive people. As a boy, Worf made a point of reading everything he could find about Klingon culture, so as not to be entirely ignorant of their ways (hardly necessary if Klingonism were hard-wired into his brain)—and even so, Worf is (as Van de Berg accusingly points out) noticeably different from other Klingons. When forced to choose between Starfleet and a pair of diehard Klingon renegades who try to recruit him to their side, Worf remains loyal to Starfleet (TNG's "Heart of Glory"). Worf's son Alexander has little interest in "Klingon stuff" and his personality is hardly distinguishable from that of the humans among whom he was raised.

Indeed, *Star Trek* has produced countless examples of the power of cultural and personal experience over biological difference. The sharply contrasting Romulans and Vulcans originated as political factions within the same society; hence, the famed unemotionalism of the Vulcans is a cultural trait, a deliberate renunciation of their once-violent ways that must be sustained in each new generation by rigorous training and discipline (in VGR's "Alter Ego," we learn that the Vulcans have a rich vocabulary for the nuances of emotion). DS9's Odo is obsessed with finding others of his shape-shifting species; but when he does, he discovers that he has little in common with them (they are imperialists). On the other hand, there are some examples of racially determined behaviors, as with the Vulcan seven-year sexual cycle and the Betazoid telepathic faculty. In the final analysis, *Trek* seems consciously drawn to the liberal ideals of interethnic goodwill, but its portrayal of "race" appears also to be influenced by our culture's confused categories, by *Trek*'s weird biology, and by the shifting role that "racial" signifiers play in the storytelling process.

So amorphous is the idea of "race" in Euro-American culture that it can be aptly characterized as a "floating signifier."[12] Critic Raymond Williams writes that the term "race" is employed in such a vague social and political sense that "physical, cultural and socio-economic differences are taken up, projected and generalized, and so confused that different kinds of variation are made to stand for or imply each other."[13] The slipperiness with which race has been defined is no accident—it reflects our culture's deep indecision about how to conceptualize human difference. Perhaps American culture is unready to let loose of the concept of "race," with all its attendant confusions, because it is central to our discourse about difference and because cherished arguments from all parts of the political spectrum have been built on it. By the same token, it is difficult to embrace any clear idea of race because to do so might require us to countenance questionable assumptions and muddled arguments, and even to confront the alarming fragility of humanism in a racist society.

Because *Star Trek* has inherited such a polymorphous concept of "race," its attempts to imagine new dimensions of difference have served to amplify the existing conceptual disorder. It is unlikely, given *Trek*'s liberal assumptions, that the tangled representation of race in *Trek* reflects any racist intent. In fact, it is possible that the effect of *Trek*'s complicated repositionings of "race" is to further destabilize it as a concept. *Trek* takes the cultural category of "race," which was mushy to begin with (having been nearly crushed under the load of diverse historical meanings and political agendas), and it playfully inserts it into so many new semiotic structures and contrasts that it virtually pulverizes it. By the time *Trek* finishes working it over, there is so little left of any coherent construct of race that it has become little more than a highly mobile signifier for "difference." Whether it is the conscious intent of *Trek*'s writers to undercut and destabilize "race" as a conceptual category, or whether *Trek* simply reflects the continuing decay of an overworked and moribund idea, is worth pondering, as is the question of whether this destabilization makes the race concept more, or less, harmful.

In any case, the more interesting problem, which actually subsumes most of what critics call "race," is how *Star Trek* places intergroup differences into its master framework of progressive human development. The problem at hand centers upon socially defined and culturally constructed difference, and the question of biological difference is only one dimension of this broader issue.

NOTHING IN PARTICULAR

What if a science fiction fantasy were to represent space explorers, and the interplanetary humanoids they encounter, as culturally Hungarian or Hindu? American viewers might be startled by this seemingly far-fetched premise. We might wonder, almost by reflex, "Why *that*, of all things?" Why a particular *kind* of human, instead of "just" an ordinary human like Captain Kirk, or at least somebody (more or less) American like Sisko, Picard, or Janeway? If so, we would simply be slipping into the same commonsense logic that operates in anthropology texts where human evolution is often pictured (literally) as a parade of successively "evolved" male primates with a European man in the lead (why not an Asian woman?) The Hindu or the female is constructed within our dominant semiotic system as a special case, while the Anglo-American male is simply, generically, human.

Critical social theory suggests that, as Richard Dyer puts it, "white power secures its dominance by not seeming to be anything in particular." Recent scholarship on the social construction of "race" has examined the strategy whereby socially privileged groups are positioned as neutral or "unmarked," in contrast with the Other who is "marked" and differentiated.[14] In a democratic society, hegemony usually avoids the language of direct domination in favor of this subtler process of "normalizing" or "unmarking" of the privileged group. "We," the privileged group, are ordinary. "They" are exotic. We (to continue in this perverse Whitmanesque litany) are center. They are periphery. We are whole and all-encompassing. They are partial and restricted. We have pragmatic common sense. They have customary beliefs. We are cosmopolitan. They are parochial. We see the whole picture (including them). They see only inside their limited frame. We are objective. They are subjective. We use our intelligence freely. They are arbitrarily constrained by culture. We are the understanding observer. They are the object to be understood. We can speak for ourselves. They must be spoken for. We know what is good for us and for them. They know neither. We have a history. They are static. We are rational. They are traditional. Our essence is that of

Figure 1
Schematic of Galactic Normality

unified and unlimited humanity. Theirs is of "their people" only. Now, think of the Klingons. Is there any question where they fit in this scheme of things? Or the Ligonians? Or even the Bajorans?[15]

This "normalization" of the dominant group is entirely consistent with, and even invites, romantic notions about marginalized "exotic" peoples. Just as Native Americans have served as an imagined repository of timeless wisdom, ecological harmony and other objects of white America's collective longing, so can the Klingons or the Bajorans. In our "admiration" and our dabbling in their cultural arts and symbols, we can retrieve some of what "we" presumably gave up to achieve our status as progressive and universal humans (their uncomplicated faith, animal grace, elemental drives, comforting rituals, or whatever), but without any of the fuss of actually being marginalized and limited. From our elevated position, "we" can, with a modicum of effort, know them scientifically and imagine them empathetically, but the process does not work in the other direction. We can play at "being" them, but for them to become us is a serious, disciplined, and irreversible endeavor.

Star Trek's mythic world subtly places "neutral" humanity at the center of the cosmos. Figure 1 illustrates what a schematic of galactic "normality" might look like. Actually, a cone would be a better image, if one adds the vertical dimension of "evolutionary" advancement, which also favors unmarked humanity. The boundaries between the inner/upper and outer/lower circles are fuzzy, and there is room for debate as to precisely where a given "race" or individual might fit. The Klingons, in fact, seem to move outward in this circle between *The Original Series* and

The Next Generation as their religion, rituals, culture, and physical markings become more clearly exotic (this despite the fact that they have made peace with the Federation).

"Unmarked" Terrans are the ones to whose ways all good humanoids gravitate. Worf, for example, becomes progressively more human, but Riker and Picard do not move in the direction of Klingon culture even though they have considerable knowledge of it. When the cultural "fit" between Federation and Maquis crew members on *Voyager* threatens to disrupt the harmony of the ship (VGR's "Learning Curve"), Tuvok tutors the Maquis in Starfleet manners and customs rather than staging a workshop on mutual cultural adjustment. In VGR's "Fair Trade," Neelix meets an old Talaxian friend, only to find that his two years on *Voyager* have made him too scrupulous to engage in the shady dealings that were once his bread and butter—and he manages to convert his friend to these new norms of conduct. Even the android Data aspires to become "human" in the restricted sense (not Klingon, Vulcan, etc.).[16]

David Golumbia offers an insight on this order of privileged neutrality when he observes that, in *Star Trek*, "the more centrally 'white' you are, the greater your abilities and the more your personality is supposed to be able to handle difference and to account for it." The closer to the normative center, he adds, the greater a character's "skill-transfer ability," while those farther from the center are relatively limited in their ability to reach beyond the limits of their special functions or attributes. Even among the "whites" on TNG's *Enterprise*, the women show less of this ability. Crusher is "only the doctor," Yar is "only the security chief," and the empathic counselor Troi is terrified of the role of command to which her rank entitles her.[17]

Even physical markings seem to follow the pattern of marked marginality and neutral centrality. If one were to average out the differences between, for example, the swarthy, robust Klingons and such pallid, androgynous characters as the Bynars (TNG's "11001001") and Talosians (TOS's "The Cage" and "The Menagerie"), the interpolated center would probably not fall far from the "neutral" Caucasoid human ideal. Interestingly, the universal humanoid ancestor depicted in TNG's "The Chase" is still more "unmarked," in a sense, than the white Terran: whiter, nearly genderless, and almost featureless, but closer to the Terran than to such "marked" humanoids as the Cardassians or Klingons.

The normality of the white Terran is echoed in the character and structure of Starfleet. In TOS's first season there is no mention of a "Federation," and no reason to doubt that Starfleet is simply an extension of American sovereignty into space (the "U.S.S." *Enterprise* is designated like a "United States Ship" of the twentieth century). By the second season, Starfleet is linked with the United Federation of Planets, an organization of about 150 worlds founded two centuries earlier. Remarkably, the series' switch from implicit American sovereignty to an interplanetary Federation does not noticeably change the overwhelmingly American character of the enterprise (or the *Enterprise*). And why should it? The center of the Federation turns out to be the "human"; the center of the human is the Terran, and the center of the Terran is the American. Starfleet Headquarters is in San Francisco, and the Federation's official language is "Federation Standard," or American English. Furthermore, the most centrally positioned Americans are those who are most "unmarked." Captain Kirk, the prototypical *Star Trek* hero, is the ultimate "neutral" human: a white Midwestern middle-class male. The pattern eventually becomes relaxed enough to allow for some safe symbols of Federation cosmopolitanism, including the Anglicized Frenchman Jean-Luc Picard, the culturally mainstream African American Benjamin Sisko, and the white American woman Kathryn Janeway.

The film scholar Katrina Boyd suggests a specific connection between the privileging of Terrans and early theories of social progress. In her view, *Star Trek* reflects such evolutionary schema as that of the nineteenth-century sociologist and utopian theorist Auguste Comte, according to whom genuine progress must be practical (manifested in activity, technology), theoretical (science, reason), and moral (feeling). Only those whose development encompasses all three of these aspects are treated in the *Trek* mythos as fully progressive. Women, Boyd suggests, are portrayed as less balanced than men, tending toward feeling at the expense of reason. Similarly, "The Warlike Klingons have an overabundance of feeling; Ferengi tradesmen pursue pointless economic activity; Vulcans struggle with repressed emotions, and so on." Even the godlike but self-indulgent Q fall short in the area of "moral compunction." Only the centrally privileged (i.e., white Anglicized male) humanoids display the three characteristics of advancement in a balanced way.[18]

All this said, however, one can see *Star Trek* as sometimes deliberately undermining the very structures of hegemony and privilege that it elsewhere labors to set up. Spock, arguably the most loved of all *Trek* characters and the one with whom *Trek* creator Gene Roddenberry most closely identified,[19] seems the hardest to fit into the schematic of marginality/centrality offered above. We have noted elsewhere that Spock and his culture seem to offer a counterpoint to some of *Trek*'s dominant messages, calling into question Kirk's patriarchal and individualist doctrines. The puckish Spock darts into and out of "humanity," taking potshots as he goes. He is the composite being, the trickster, the crosser of boundaries. (One could make a similar argument for Data, the Holodoc, or others in the later series.) In the construction of unmarked "white" human normality, as in so many areas of *Trek*'s mythos, simplistic interpretations may miss some of the nuances that leave *Trek* open to more than one reading and help account for its enduring appeal.

The use of out-groups as villains, combined with the seemingly inex-orable tendency to complicate them out of that role, also points to a paradoxical tension in *Star Trek*'s mythos. Although various groups have been introduced to embody evil, the dramatic development of each of these peoples results in the reframing of "good" and "bad" as a matter of contention *within*, not between, "races." In *The Undiscovered Country*, for example, the champions and the enemies of peace are paired off rather neatly within each group (Chancellor Gorkon and his daughter Azetbur vs. General Chang; Spock vs. Lieutenant Valeris; Captain Kirk vs. Admiral Cartwright). The diversity of male/female and white/Asian/black is also folded into the mix, further reinforcing the message that it is not one's category but one's choices that determine character.

SPACE: THE PRIMAL FRONTIER

If an interstellar observer had been watching earth for the past five centuries with the aim of reporting on major human events, the report would surely highlight the swift and unprecedented spread of Western European cultural, economic, political, and linguistic influence to all parts of the globe. The resulting intercultural encounters have presented the West with opportunities for learning from other peoples, for sub-jecting them to brutal and subtle forms of domination, and for using them as vehicles for the imaginative projections of our own dilemmas and concerns. All these things have happened, and all have contributed to transformations of the Western mythos, including the self-congratulatory "progress" paradigm discussed previously. Intercultural encounters challenged old ideas of cultural and social forms as simply given by nature, and they opened realms of social speculation and satire that included such works as Thomas More's *Utopia* and Jonathan Swift's *Gulliver's Travels* (one of Gene Roddenberry's conscious models for Trek), to say nothing of the science fiction genre.[20]

Not every society experienced these confrontations in the same way. Even among the dominant Western societies, differing situations have led to diverse influences on the imagination. Kipling's tales of India are, for example, quite distinct from anything produced in America. England and France's experiences were of an imperialist sort, in which a transient ruling class from the mother country resided as an empowered minority in an exotic setting, among "natives" whose labor and resources were appropriated to benefit the mother country. In North America, trans-planted Europeans established resident populations that gradually dis-placed, contained, or eliminated the native peoples by conquest along a moving "frontier."

It is not hard to find writers who are willing to link *Star Trek* with imperialism in the European colonial sense. Bill Bolsvert is especially biting in his description of TOS as a "saga of empire": "Alien cultures are Kiplingesque caricatures—natives in grass skirts enthralled by squat idols, or harem slaves and gladiators lorded over by an effete aristocracy. The fig-leaf of the Prime Directive scarcely veils Kirk's leering visage as he beholds the galaxy before him: sensual, barbarian, stocked with oriental despots and green-skinned wenches, ripe for non-interference."[21] Bolsvert's observations are not altogether off the mark, but to the extent that there is a difference between the imperial and the frontier versions of the cultural "Other," *Trek* gravitates toward the mythology of the American frontier more than the "white man's burden" of imperial control.

A little more than a century ago, the historian Frederick Jackson Turner introduced his influential "frontier hypothesis," which linked the American character and imagination to the formative influence of the Western frontier.[22] Whatever its value as historical description and explanation (a question still under debate), the frontier hypothesis captures much of the spirit of America's mythology about itself.[23] Americans like to imagine themselves as rugged pioneers, exemplars of anti-authoritarian individualism and resourceful self-reliance. We aspire, at least in our mythic imagination, to be the champions of the underdog, the harbingers of freedom for all, and the nemesis of effete aristocrats, pompous elitists, powerful bosses, and privileged exploiters of all sorts—a leaning that helps explain why the Federation's Prime Directive rules out blatant colonial control.

The apparent contradiction between conquest and human equality is partially erased in the American frontier mythology by imagining the frontier as something unknown, unowned, and of little benefit to humankind until it is turned from a forbidding wilderness into a productive garden.[24] Hence, Native utilization of the land was belittled through the inaccurate representation of Native Americans as nomads whose relation to the land was a transient one and whose utilization of resources was relatively unproductive (this is, of course, the underside of our romantic portrayal of Indians as living "in harmony with nature"). If the land at the frontier belongs to no one, it cannot be stolen. If it serves no one, its "development" by Anglo-Americans is a net gain for humanity.

In keeping with the American fantasy of nonexploitive conquest, the *Enterprise* asks little from, and gives much to, the worlds it encounters. *Star Trek's* "final frontier" is a realm characterized by peoples in need of instruction, protection, or taming; planets in need of settlement; resources in need of employment. In *Trek's* grandest statement of the life-giving character of Federation colonization, the "Genesis" project of *The Wrath of Khan* and *The Search for Spock*, Terran scientists turn utterly lifeless planets into lavish Edens—the ultimate fantasy of nonexploitive "development." The wonders of the frontier do little to illuminate the already well-lit *Enterprise*; rather, the *Enterprise* brings enlightenment and benefit to a dark and underdeveloped universe. Any possible suggestion of exploitive gain is inverted into sacrifice and beneficence.

Star Trek's frontier is a place where order is created from chaos. Eliade has shown that the territory beyond the known or "settled" world is seen traditionally as "chaotic space, peopled by ghosts, demons, foreigners." This "fluid and larval modality of chaos" is brought into the orderly cosmos by a reenactment of the cosmogony—in our case, perhaps, through a ritual return to the American frontier.[25]

The link between popular literary expressions of the frontier myth and the roots of American science fiction is a surprisingly direct one. American historian Gregory M. Pfitzer traces a continuous development from such popular Western novels as Owen Wister's *The Virginian* (1902), to Edgar Rice Burroughs' self-consciously Western-based "John Cartier Martian" series, to Ray Bradbury's science fiction classic *The Martian Chronicles*.[26] *A Princess of Mars*, the first of Burroughs's "Martian" books, begins with the hero fighting Indians in the Wild West and quickly moves to the planet Mars where the hero kills large numbers of red Martians who bear a "startling resemblance" to the "red rascals" he had been obliged to dispatch back home; he is subsequently captured (and admired) by the natives and finally wins the affections of a Martian "princess."[27] If this isn't the exact midpoint between a dime novel Western and TOS's "The Paradise Syndrome," it's only spitting distance away from it.

Robert Jewett and John Shelton Lawrence propose the existence of a special "American Monomyth," in which "a community in a harmonious paradise is threatened by evil: normal institutions fail to contend with this threat: a selfless superhero emerges to renounce temptations and carry out the redemptive task: aided by fate, his decisive victory restores the community to its paradisal condition: the superhero then recedes into obscurity."[28] While Joseph Campbell's global "monomyth" involves a hero's initiatory quest into a "region of supernatural wonder," the myth that Jewett and Lawrence identify is one of redemption by a self-sacrificing "Christ figure." This pattern seems to be drawn from certain Hollywood tales of the Western frontier, where lawlessness and order meet and the restless loner can save society. For Jewett and Lawrence, however, the original *Star Trek* so perfectly illustrates this "monomyth" that they devote the first two chapters of their book to a discussion of it. Although not every reader may be entirely convinced by Jewett and Lawrence's analysis, this "monomythic" formula does seem to be present in some American myths and in some *Star Trek* adventures—particularly if we are willing to stretch it far enough (e.g., to view Kirk's penchant for wrecking paradise as a means of "restoration" to a more authentically "paradisal" condition, or to credit him with the "sexual renunciation" attributed by Jewett and Lawrence to the redemptive hero).

It is not much of a stretch to view Captain Kirk as *Star Trek*'s answer to the classic Western hero: the self-reliant individualist, the noble misfit at the edge of civilization but with wilderness in his blood, between wild and tame, upholding orderly society but never quite containable by it. Even his friendship with Spock can be seen as having its precedents in the literature and legend of the American frontier. We have already noted the parallel that April Selley draws between the Kirk-Spock bond and the intergroup friendships (Huck and Jim, Ishmael and Queequeg, Natty Bumppo and Chingachgook) depicted in American literary romances set at the margins of the civilized realm.[29] A more immediate frontier ancestor for Spock may be seen in *The Adventures of Daniel Boone*, a popular Western series that aired from 1964 to 1970, which features one of television's more dignified portrayals of a Native American in the character of Mingo, Boone's urbane, softspoken, Oxford-educated Indian companion. Mingo, for many viewers the most engaging character of the Boone series, draws on literary, folkloric, and pop-culture precedents, but he also bears an arresting resemblance to the Spock character who joins him on American primetime television.

As in the mythic friendship between the Sumerian hero Gilgamesh and the desert wild-man Enkidu, these difference-bridging bonds may signify a sacred liminal space between the known and the unknown, between wildness and civilization. While the hero is more centrally "us," the companion, who is "from" our imaginary construct of the "out-there" (such as Queegueg, the cannibal from an unnamed distant sea island), is a liaison between worlds—a kind of spirit guide. For Kirk it is Spock, the half-human who works at being a Vulcan; for Picard the android Data who bridges earth/space and human/machine; for Sisko the symbiont Dax who bridges the dichotomies of humanoid/nonhumanoid and old-male-buddy/young-female-colleague. Only in Chakotay do we find a Terran (and a person of unambiguously opposite sex) as the hero's companion; but for Janeway and *Voyager* it is the earth and sexual companionship that are "out there" at the end of the quest. Chakotay, the virile but ambiguously celibate Native American, might be interpreted as the bridge to those worlds. When the companion is marked in the same direction as the imagined "Other" realm that the hero confronts, it allows the hero to bridge the gap on a personal level, to embrace and imbibe the otherness and become empowered by its special mysteries, and to link with the "humanity" at the core of the "Other"—all without compromising his/her own privileged centrality.

INDIANS IN SPACE

Just as the frontier, both literal and metaphorical, is the favored setting of American mythology, the Native American is our premier model of the mythic Other. Although Burroughs' hero in *A Princess of Mars* may have been the first to encounter "Indians" in space, he was not the last. Native Americans seem to be the only Terrans not to have assimilated to Anglo-American ways in the next few centuries. TOS, TNG and VGR have each spun fantasies of Native American culture in an extraterrestrial setting.

"The Paradise Syndrome," which aired in TOS's first season, is a story as much in the tradition of the Western as of science fiction. Arriving to warn the people of an unnamed planet about an approaching asteroid, the *Enterprise* team makes two surprising discoveries: a high-tech obelisk covered with runic markings and a village of Indians assessed by Spock (at a glance) as a "mixture of the most advanced and peaceful tribes— Navajo, Mohican, and Delaware." Having decided that the natives, though "advanced" by Indian standards, are too primitive to appreciate their predicament, the team is about to beam up when Kirk unexpectedly falls through a trap door and is imprisoned in the mysterious obelisk. Spock and McCoy have no choice but to leave him behind while they attempt to blast the asteroid off its collision course with the planet. Unfortunately, they not only fail to do so, but they damage the *Enterprise*'s warp drive during the attempt. With two months' journey before them and the asteroid following close behind, they set course again for the planet. During the long journey, Spock deciphers the inscriptions on the obelisk to learn that the Indians had been rescued from earth and taken to this distant planet by a philanthropic race called the Preservers, who took it upon themselves to rescue such people from extinction by relocating them on new planets.

Meanwhile Kirk, whose memory has been erased by the obelisk, wanders outside and is taken in by the natives who assume that he must be a god. The old chief, who speaks the stilted, broken English for which movie Indians are famous, appoints this stranger "Kirok" as medicine chief of the tribe, an office that carries with it the privilege of marrying his daughter Miramanee, the standard Alluring Indian Princess. Kirok is deliriously happy in this "peaceful, uncomplicated" world, proclaiming to the heavens that he has "found paradise." His bliss is momentarily interrupted by the obligatory knife-flashing struggle with Miramanee's discarded fiancé—which Kirk easily wins although he refuses to kill the vanquished warrior. But paradise, as we already know, is not for Kirk. The asteroid draws near, the skies darken, and Kirok is expected to save the day by entering the obelisk (actually an asteroid-deflector thoughtfully installed by the Preservers, which the Indians have unfortunately forgotten how to operate). The tribe turns angry when Kirk is unable to unlock the obelisk; and Miramanee, carrying Kirk's unborn child, is lethally injured in their attack. But the *Enterprise* saves the planet and Kirk, after Miramanee's tearful death scene, is restored to his rightful place of command.

The Indian village is described from the beginning as a carefree "Shangri-La," and McCoy warns Kirk about the "Tahiti syndrome" of longing for release from the cares and responsibilities of a complex world. But Kirk is fated to be a leader wherever he goes, so he naturally rises to an exalted position among the primitives. Before long he is planning irrigation systems and teaching the people to make oil lamps and to preserve food for times of famine—none of which, apparently, the Indians could think of without help. Kirk clearly does not fit into this culture, which is so inert that even the experience of being relocated on another planet (or being thrown together with tribes from thousands of miles away) has made no noticeable impression on them. As elsewhere in *Trek*, the condition of "paradise" and the inability to change and grow are but two sides of the same coin, and this is a life that Kirk and other culturally advanced people might fantasize about but would never really choose.

TNG's "Journey's End" involves a colony of Native Americans who have fled to the planet Dorvan V to avoid cultural assimilation. As luck would have it, their planet has been ceded by treaty to the Cardassians, and Picard has been ordered, over his objections, to oversee the removal of the Indians "by whatever means necessary." In justifying this policy, Starfleet points out that these Indians are "a nomadic group" (therefore, being relocated shouldn't be a big deal for them), and besides, they were warned not to settle so near the Cardassians.

An aside: either the scriptwriters are making some subtle historical allusions here, or they have stumbled into some unintended ironies. "Removal" was the term used for a particularly cruel episode in American history that began in the 1830s, during which nearly all Native Americans residing east of the Mississippi were "removed" to the West by any means that the U.S. Army deemed necessary, including forced death marches with extremely high casualty rates. The misleading characterization of Native Americans as nomads (in fact, all the tribes in question were sedentary farmers) was falsely employed at the time, and throughout American history, to justify their dispossession. The "nomad" premise is especially ridiculous in "Journey's End," since the people are clearly modeled on the Pueblo Indians, whose architecture is among the most durable on earth!

To *Star Trek*'s credit, these Native Americans almost manage to avoid the stilted speech of Hollywood Indians, and their culture is depicted as "rooted in the past but not limited to the past," as shown in their adoption of Klingon and Vulcan visages for some of their ceremonial spirits. They have a clear sense of historical movement but manage to reconcile this historical sense with a continuing separate identity. They are articulate political realists and at the same time are confident in their own assessment of what is good for them. All this is such a refreshing change from the images of Indians seen elsewhere that it compensates in part for the somewhat patronizing portrayal of Indian spirituality (predictable babble about vision quests, the sacredness of everything, talking to the mountains). One might cringe a bit at Picard's overinsistence that he "respects" the "cultural beliefs" of the Indians, especially since, when a crew member asks whether he himself believes any of it, he unhesitantly responds, "Of course not." It is also somewhat troubling that the dilemma of a people is largely overshadowed by Wesley Crusher's New Age journey (via Indian culture) into a spirit realm, guided by the mysterious other-dimensional being, the Traveler,[30] who has taken the identity of an Indian medicine man. Wesley's spiritual journey away from Starfleet and into a new plane of existence, which turns out to be the primary referent of the title, smacks of the New Age appropriation of Indian spirituality that many contemporary Native Americans find particularly annoying.

The episode ends with the Indians agreeing to take their chances with Cardassian rule (portending a political future as precarious as their past). Picard is relieved of the burden of "removing" them, thus wiping away the "stain of blood" left by one of Picard's ancestors who, seven centuries earlier, had helped brutalize the Pueblo people. Not only does the outcome relieve Picard's immediate dilemma and his inherited guilt, but the assurance that Native American peoples and cultures are, after all, alive and well somewhere in the twenty-fourth century may help do the same for white America.

Voyager's Commander Chakotay is the only example of a *Star Trek* regular to be portrayed as a Native American, and the only Terran *Trek* hero to come equipped with a distinctive culture or religion (unless one counts Scotty's affection for whiskey as "culture"). Chakotay, who is descended from the "Rubber Tree People" of Central America, has the usual accouterments of Native American spirituality, including a medicine bundle, an animal spirit guide, and a fondness for vision quests. As with many contemporary New Agers, Captain Janeway seems more interested in Chakotay's spiritual beliefs than in any other religious tradition (most of the *Voyager*'s crew seem about as religionless as those of the original *Enterprise*).

The story of Chakotay's people is told in the episode "Tattoo." While exploring a jungle planet in the Delta quadrant, Chakotay unexpectedly runs across the sacred design that his people refer to as a "Chamuzi." The encounter with this sign, and later with the hostile natives, touches off a series of flashbacks to Chakotay's youth when his urban-Indian father had dragged the reluctant lad into the jungle for a tense reunion with the Rubber Tree People. As it becomes increasingly clear that the people of this remote Delta Quadrant world share his religion, Chakotay reconstructs enough from his earlier encounter to make peaceful contact with the elusive but powerful aliens.

The true background of Chakotay's people, and apparently of all Native Americans, is then revealed. The aliens are his people's legendary "wise ones," who visited earth some 45,000 years ago and chose a particularly eco-sensitive group to become their "Inheritors." Through the miracle of "genetic bonding," they infused the Inheritors with a special reverence for life and a spirit of adventure that led them to colonize the New World and to accomplish great things there. On a later trip, the Wise Ones were unable to locate any of the Inheritors, which explains their hostility toward these earth-usurping Starfleet visitors. Chakotay finally manages to convince them that non–Native Americans have changed for the better. The absolution of whites from guilt over the fate of Native Americans is replayed again here, but it offers less comfort than did the other Indian tales. For the first time, we learn that Native Americans are genetically endowed with a special wisdom that, at least in the eyes of the Wise Ones, makes them superior to those who callously extinguished native cultures as they pillaged the earth.

This comparison of *Star Trek*'s "Indian" episodes leaves us off at a good vantage point from which to size up *Trek*'s messages about the cultural Other. To begin with, one can say that even the most ethnocentric of these portrayals, "The Paradise Syndrome," does not partake of vulgar race hatred or ill will; if anything, it is a patronizing picture of a people who are noble but who are, alas, going nowhere fast. It is not hard to detect a change from the condescending, romantic ethnocentrism of the 1960s to the 1990s' apotheosis of Native Americans as otherworldly genetic Inheritors of superior extraterrestrial wisdom. But while outright ethnocentrism has diminished, or at least changed its face, there is a different prejudice about otherness that remains strong in all these episodes and that may be the elusive culprit that accounts for the recurrent perception of *Trek* as "racist." It is a prejudice that is much harder to nail down, since it is as often employed by "noble savage" romantics as by crude racists, and it is one of the main subjects of Said's critique in *Orientalism*, with which we opened this chapter.

The prejudice to which we refer is "cultural essentialism," or the belief in deep, unchanging traits that segregate cultures into natural units that ought not "contaminate" one another. Cultural essentialism mystifies culture into a deterministic force by overlooking the complexities of change and diversity within each culture and by emphasizing the exotic and presumably inscrutable character of the cultural Other. Essentialism plays down the role of human agents as active, creative critics and interpreters of their own cultures (or rather, it claims these abilities only for ourselves—the "unmarked" progressive culture). It underestimates the historical dynamism and the openness of "exotic" cultures by envisioning them as isolated, static, and lacking a history, while at the same time lavishing the observer's own culture with plenty of credit in all these areas. In a culturally essentialist universe, one central culture has the "mainstream" qualities of changeability and historicity, while all others are destined either to remain pristinely "authentic" or to assimilate to "us."

Star Trek often falls into cultural essentialism not because it is especially conservative but because some version or other of this essentialism is pervasive in American thought, whether conservative or liberal. Yet, as in other aspects of its mythos, *Trek* sets up a dialogue between the authoritative voice of mainstream Americanism and the boundary-crossing tricksters who beckon us beyond self-satisfied complacency. Spock, in his tolerant and unjudgmental philosophy of IDIC, or "infinite diversity in infinite combinations" (a "philosophy" that is never elaborated in *Trek*, and which we are left to imagine on our own), and Data, in his childlike wonder at all things, serve a special function for Trekkers, pointing beyond the commanding wisdom of the captains, toward the mission of discovery that brought us aboard in the first place.

The later series deal with cultural discord in an increasingly nonessentialist way. The meanings of cultures are contested from within, as people like the Klingons grapple with changing circumstances and divergent possibilities for self-definition. The Klingons are a people on the cusp of great change, and interpretations of Klingon tradition are openly contested by Worf and others. The same is true of other formerly nonintrospective peoples including the Cardassians and the Bajorans. Where the liberalism of a decade or two ago still took for granted a cosmos with mainstream humanity at the center and others arranged around it in reassuringly stable, bounded and knowable domains, the nineties has ushered in a "postmodern" perspective that decenters this comfortable universe.

CHAPTER 10

DECENTERED COSMOS

Trekking Through Postmodernism

In the postmodern worldview, narrative has lost its sacred power. The semiotic significance of this loss is profound, for by rejecting the traditional narratives of the West, the postmodern myth has rejected the centering structures that have long given meaning to human history. At the postmodern center there is only a void.

—Jack Solomon
The Signs of Our Times (1988)

"Postmodernism," the buzz term of 1980s and 1990s intellectual circles, is an appropriately impossible word. The English word "modern" comes from a Latin root meaning what is in fashion, "just now," the latest thing. Does postmodern, then, mean "after the latest"? "Postmodern" begins to make a bit more sense, however, if we consider the specific historical meaning of "modern" that was touched upon in Chapter 8. In that sense, "modernism" refers, roughly, to the confident rational humanist outlook of the past few centuries, according to which human beings can rely on their powers of observation and reason to progress in their understanding and control of an orderly, objectively knowable world. The modernist cosmos differs from the medieval one that subordinated human understanding to divine revelation and otherworldly salvation, and also from the Renaissance's emphasis on the superiority of ancient Greek and Roman civilization. Modernism has a built-in narrative structure that hinges on a belief in progress as the natural tendency of all things, the redemptive power of human understanding, the accumulation of objective knowledge about the world, and the existence of a common human nature that bridges human difference and allows us to make universally valid assessments on questions of goodness, beauty, and truth. To be sure, the modernism of the 1990s is not identical to that of the 1790s, but they share a mythos of the unity of humankind and the universal benefit of advancement in human knowledge.

Postmodernism is not so much a clean break with the past as it is a fruition of the seeds of doubt that have sprouted within modernism itself. In the arts, in philosophy, and even in science there has been an increasing recognition that "truth" is relative to one's frame of reference. The question arises: Are there any limits to this relativity, and if so, how and where shall we find them? We keep drawing lines in the sand, only to retreat and retrench. Postmodern philosophy raises the possibility that this process of retreat either has no end or that it ends only with an arbitrary choice of commitments (the reduction of truth to partisanship). Dostoyevsky warned that it would come to this.

Various social and historical developments have served to undercut modernist optimism. Disappointment with the utopian promises of capitalism, communism, fascism and other "-isms" has bred a distrust of all grand narratives of human redemption. A succession of wars in our century, the Holocaust, the threat of nuclear annihilation, and the environmental ravages wrought by industrial development have given cause to doubt whether our so-called advancements are truly beneficial. The breakdown of the colonial international order has been accompanied by an outspoken intercultural dialogue in which the foundational ideas of Western humanism have come under attack as self-serving and ethnocentric. Even the liberalism of mainstream social science has, as we have noted, acquiesced in the essentializing of other cultures and in reinforcing the privileged centrality of the Western intellectual elite.

It is not quite true that we have entered a postmodern "era," for the modernist outlook is still central. Postmodernism is an apparition that haunts modernist dreams, a nagging worry that any coherent narrative we might try to live by is, in the end, fallible and mortal. Like an angel of death, the postmodern critique has an unyielding presence that demands recognition, but it is more a negation than a positive form of existence. Despite reactionary efforts to make postmodernism disappear, our only real alternatives may be to use postmodernism in the service of a broader and more durable humanism or to give up on humanism altogether. Much is at stake. Ignoring the quandary is futile; best to confront it straight on and to deal with it by using whatever resources are available, including the construction of new mythic narratives that reconcile the core of humanism with the postmodern critiques.

DARK VISIONS

While the *Star Trek* of the 1960s depicted an almost defiantly untroubled modernist cosmology, *Trek* in the 1980s—and especially in the 1990s—ventures into postmodernism like Orpheus descending into the underworld, endeavoring to pluck living hopes from the dusky regions of despair. The project of *Trek* in the 1980s and 1990s has been neither an affirmation of modernism nor of postmodernism but an attempt at a mythic mediation of the two. The portrayal of postmodern doubt in *Trek* becomes the setting for a myth of redemption that is retold, in small and large ways, throughout the *Trek* narratives of the last decade.

As Jack Solomon observes, narrative has lost its "sacred power" to frame everyday events in cosmological terms. The postmodern outlook rejects "centering structures" and recognizes only a "carnival of arresting images and seductive surfaces." Attention is redirected from "reality" to an endless stream of representations, imitations, and parodies. Heroes are replaced by celebrities, understood as concocted facades. In radically postmodern art forms, sensual, enigmatic, and often disturbing images are juxtaposed in a restless and seemingly random collage contrived to defy narrative coherence or closure of meaning.[1] The 1994 film *Pulp Fiction* destabilizes narrative by bending linear time into an endless loop, where the action at the end of the film converges with that of the beginning (but from someone else's point of view). Futurist fantasies like *Blade Runner*, *Terminator*, and *12 Monkeys* depict anarchic futures set amid the wreckage of the modernist dream, where bands of brigands rule and cruel tyrants hide behind cynical, mocking charades. Reluctant heroes survive by maintaining a mask of irony, hostility, or callous indifference, and if they do opt for heroism they may find that their world no longer accommodates it. Constant doubts are raised as to who or what is real, for people and things can (almost) be depended on not to be what they seem. Endings are left unresolved; no outcome is stable; there is no happy, or even unhappy, "ever after." Alienation has been raised to an art form.

The 1988 feature film *Star Trek V: The Final Frontier* literally depicts the discovery of meaninglessness at the center of the cosmos. The charismatic religious visionary Sybok hijacks the *Enterprise* to travel to the center of the Galaxy, seeking the place where, according to mythologies, God holds the answers to eternal questions. When Sybok arrives there with Spock, McCoy, and Kirk, the setting changes unexpectedly from that of a biblical wilderness to a dark place enclosed by rib-shaped stones—a hybrid image of Stonehenge and the whale's belly—where a cruel superbeing menaces them. The being ultimately takes the form of an evil-twin Sybok, and Sybok sacrifices his own life in combat with it so that the others may escape. At the center of this universe, where God and ultimate meaning are supposed to reside, there is only an impostor who takes the form of our darkest self.

The DS9 series began in 1993 and overlapped with the last two years of TNG. The look and feel of the two series is, however, quite different. TNG was the second and last series to be directly influenced by *Star Trek* creator Gene Roddenberry prior to his death. While TNG often touches on postmodern themes, it retains the basic character of the first series— an active mission of discovery carried out by a harmonious fellowship of diverse comrades on the bright, orderly bridge of a sleek starship. DS9, by contrast, takes a leap into the postmodern universe.

The viewers' introduction to the DS9 world is a holodeck illusion: Benjamin and Jake Sisko appear in a bucolic earth setting where, as Jake fishes, they discuss Benjamin's new assignment. The station is a former slave-labor mining facility once called Terok Nor (evoking "terror," "noir"=night) used by the Nazi-like Cardassians during their occupation of nearby Bajor. When Jake and Benjamin leave the serenity of the holodeck, we see a space station wantonly trashed by the departing Cardassians. Smoking debris and wrecked machinery are strewn everywhere in this nightmare parody of inner-city deterioration. The architecture is one of drudgery, domination, and surveillance. Huge toothed gears, reminiscent of those in Charlie Chaplin's dystopian *Modern Times*, serve as doors.

Resentment, suspicion, and cynicism abound. The Bajoran representative, Major Kira Nerys, is a surly ex-terrorist who predicts the rapid demise of the Bajoran provisional government and the early departure of Federation representatives. The only crew member who seems enthusiastic about DS9 is the brash young Doctor Julian Bashir, who proclaims his excitement at being on the "frontier" in a "remote wilderness." Major Kira, for whom this "wilderness" is home, counters with acid sarcasm about friendly "natives." Constable Odo, who kept order during the Cardassian regime, has stayed on as the Chief of Security. A shape-shifter who usually assumes a near-human appearance for convenience's sake, Odo is a foundling who has been forced, as he resentfully puts it, to pass himself off as a humanoid. His first words to his new commanding officer are "Who the hell are you?" Sisko, striving for a modicum of control, blackmails the lecherous Ferengi profiteer Quark into remaining on the station as Morale Officer, despite Quark's protest that when provisional governments fail, people like him are "lined up and shot." Since Quark's "establishment" is not bound by Starfleet codes, it quickly becomes a boisterous frontier saloon and virtual-reality brothel with a permanent swarm of barflies. The cheerily diabolical Gul Dukat, DS9's former Cardassian warden, later drops in to taunt Sisko for a while and to point out ominously that this is still a Cardassian neighborhood.

The premier episode serves notice that *Deep Space Nine* will be a different sort of *Star Trek* series. It presents, both literally and figuratively, a darker visage. The DS9 station is a postcolonial place, an abandoned concentration camp with an ominous look, in a rough neighborhood where cultural diversity has its menacing side, where it is not easy to tell right from wrong, and where transients do things our heroes would rather not know about. It is more reminiscent of multiethnic postcolonial London or Paris, where far-flung empires have come home to roost, than of Kipling's India or Lord Nelson's Royal Navy. Here, the "frontier" talks back, and the "native" is prepared to resist anything resembling a colonial presence. Commander Sisko is only nominally in control, more like the concierge of a dingy multiethnic hotel than the skipper of a British man-of-war. Even the opening credits give a different sense of things: instead of a starship zooming purposefully through space, we see a splendid rock, perhaps a comet, tumbling entropically toward nothing in particular, while the space station awaits nearby—skeletal, hollow, receptive, embracing empty space within its emaciated arms.

For the first few seasons, Commander Sisko is stuck in the passive and poorly armed space station over which he has only limited jurisdiction. Although they guard an entrance to an unexplored Gamma Quadrant of the galaxy, Starfleet seldom ventures there. Even after it's been cleaned up, DS9 is a dark, uncentered place with nothing corresponding to the *Enterprise*'s clean, bright, all-seeing bridge. Starship bridges are ceremonial precincts, with their central axes and captains' thrones oriented toward the viewscreens, and their clear portals of entry with the whoosh of sliding doors trumpeting each entry and exit. DS9's Operations room, "ops," is more a cloistered chamber for the station's inner dialogues and soliloquies than a commanding citadel casting its subordinating gaze over the surrounding stars. The 1994 discontinuation of *The Next Generation* allowed DS9 to occupy some of the dramatic space formerly claimed by that series, and DS9 acquires a spaceship called the *Defiant*, commanded by the newly promoted Captain Sisko. The name suits its commander well, for despite his growing freedom, Sisko's mood often remains one of brooding defiance in a world that seldom shows him the automatic respect and deference accorded Kirk and Picard.

DS9's human drama mediates the traditionally optimistic message and the 1990s postmodern style. Two differences from the earlier series are especially apparent: first, DS9 portrays more conflict among the crew than did the earlier series. Roddenberry's taboo on interpersonal conflict in *Star Trek* is no longer a direct factor, and the premises of incomplete jurisdiction over the station, as well as a politically divided crew, lend themselves more easily to an element of conflict. There is also conflict at the level of individual personalities; for example, Chief Engineer Miles O'Brien at first finds Doctor Bashir intolerably annoying. These conflicts, however, mask a deep if unspoken camaraderie. When the going gets tough, even the devious Quark shows his loyalty; the misfit Odo chooses his friends over his own "race"; Bashir and O'Brien "bond"; the hardened terrorist Kira Nerys carries and bears a baby for the dutiful wife of Chief Engineer Miles O'Brien while stoically suppressing her romantic feelings for the Chief.

Furthermore, DS9's stories are a departure from the patently mythic philosophical tales so frequently seen in the other three series. The plots tend to emphasize action, political intrigue, interpersonal strife, romantic liaisons, and conflicting personal loyalties. While this difference may have something to do with the initial need to differentiate DS9 from the ongoing TNG series, it is also a bow to the postmodern outlook and its concern for conflict, power, and moral malaise. Major Kira, for example, is an unregenerate ex-guerrilla, but her changing circumstances have given her enough distance to see that one person's freedom fighter is another person's homicidal terrorist, and she is troubled by this. Her inner conflict is more mundane than, say, Spock's Manichean struggle between human feeling and Vulcan reason. The preoccupation with worldly conflict is not necessarily an abandonment of the mythic project but a way of linking DS9's mythic role to the 1990s conception of human problems. All that said, DS9 still does, in some of its episodes, venture into deep metaphors and ambitious mythmaking in the classic *Star Trek* style, as our numerous episode references illustrate.

Star Trek Voyager, which began after the end of TNG and continues concurrently with DS9, combines elements of the other series. More even than the original *Enterprise*, and certainly more than the *Enterprise D*, *Voyager* is footloose and fancy free. Gone are the encumbrances of Federation bureaucracy, alliances, protracted wars, treaties, diplomacy, family ties, and the other entanglements of a complex interplanetary society. Once again, we see our heroes on the well-lit bridge of a state-of-the-art Starship, blasting blithely into the heart of the unknown. But *Voyager*'s mission, like DS9's, is a reactive one. The heroes have been hurled a lifetime's journey from home—and for the most frivolous of purposes (to be tested and found wanting as genetic material for some goofball superbeing's flubbed attempt at reproduction). They have been dumped in a rough part of the galaxy where no one seems to like them. Although the *Star Trek* mission of exploration occasionally diverts the *Voyager* crew, their overriding goal is a return to the status quo ante. They have no real plan for accomplishing this, aside from the unpromising strategy of plodding toward earth at a rate too slow to get them there during their lifetimes. The crew, like that of DS9, consists of former enemies and strangers thrown together by circumstance. But as with DS9, these significant departures from *The Original Series'* confident modernist mythos are merely the new obstacles against which humanity proves itself. Friendship, community, human decency, reason, and idealism triumph even in these trying circumstances. Like DS9, *Voyager* has modified and adapted, rather than abandoned, its project of validating the human quest.

WORLDS OF CONTINGENCY

We have seen that the nineteenth century's grand scheme of universal evolution, progress, and destiny, which continues in the "popular evolutionist" assumptions of mainstream humanism, is clearly reflected in Gene Roddenberry's original *Star Trek*. There is little room for randomness or plural pathways in this view; everything has its place in the orderly movement toward a higher state. It was also noted, however, that scientific evolutionary biology harbors a more radical way of thinking, one that implies an opportunistic and unpredictable process of change leading to an endless diversity of legitimate possibilities. Contemporary evolutionary theory emphasizes the element of accident, or "contingency," and it suggests that evolution would produce quite different outcomes if key events were to occur slightly differently.[2] In other branches of science there has also been a great deal of attention paid to the randomness of certain kinds of events, to "chaos" theory, and to phenomena in which tiny variances in causation lead to widely divergent outcomes. Perhaps the universe is not so neat, nor so predestined, as earlier generations of scientists once assumed. According to the more current view, there is nothing preordained about the way nature is; it could just as easily have been otherwise.

Cultural anthropology has done the same in its own domain by documenting the variety of human "realities" in different human cultures, each the result of historical contingency. Had a certain battle or migration occurred differently, our culture—and with it our notions of what is "normal"—might be utterly different. There is nothing special about our culture's way of looking at the world, except that it happens to be ours. This postmodern turn toward "cultural relativism" was long in forming, but it has surfaced dramatically in American culture in the post-Vietnam decades, leading to bitter debates over the durability and universality of Western cultural precepts. *Star Trek*'s message and its historical timing place it directly over the major fault lines of these tectonic cultural displacements, and *Trek* is confronted with the challenge of keeping the humanist faith in the less-than-hospitable context of a postmodern world.

Because TOS was predicated on universal progress along an orderly path, Captain Kirk could in good conscience violate the Prime Directive whenever a society was discovered that did not seem to be on the "normal" track of "evolution." As we have suggested, the greater seriousness with which the Prime Directive is taken in the three later series is more than just a twenty-fourth-century policy adjustment: it expresses our culture's growing appreciation of diversity. The Prime Directive is more strongly enforced for the same reason that *The Next Generation* introduces the concept of miniaturized "universal translators" to account for the apparent ubiquity of English, for the same reason that the "cultural parallels" of the later series are seldom so far-fetched as those in such TOS episodes as "Bread and Circuses," and for the same reason that the 1993 TNG episode "The Chase" finally offers a comprehensive, if strained, explanation for humanoid similarities. The driving force behind all these changes is the fact that a single, universal evolutionary sequence in cultural or biological development can no longer be taken so easily for granted. Instead, there is a greater awareness of the contingency of the universe and the legitimate possibility of diverse evolutionary paths. Of course, the actual depiction of evolutionary diversity remains limited—not only are there few nonintelligent animal forms seen, but humanoids continue to prevail among intelligent beings, while sentient nonhumanoid creatures (as in TNG's "Encounter at Farpoint" or VGR's "The Cloud") remain almost as rare as the rocklike "Horta" in TOS's "Devil in the Dark." In principle, however, major concessions have been made to the idea that we live in a universe of infinite possibilities.

The theme of contingency is apparent in *Star Trek*'s handling of moral relativism—the idea that value judgments are relative to their cultural setting. Here again, *Trek*'s development follows a definite pattern. Despite Spock's philosophy of "infinite diversity in infinite combinations" (IDIC) and his tolerance of un-American ways, social arrangements that Captain Kirk finds distasteful are subject to intervention. By the twenty-fourth century, such intervention is no longer considered appropriate. Genetically engineered collectives, matriarchies, and greedy merchant societies are "respected" and sheltered from interference. In TNG's "Symbiosis," Picard and his crew encounter two neighboring planets, one of which is inhabited by sufferers of a strange "disease" for which the other planet supplies a medicinal "cure" at exploitive prices. When the *Enterprise* scientists discover that the "medicine" is actually a narcotic to which the unsuspecting sufferers are addicted, Picard honors the Prime Directive and refrains from informing the addicts of their situation; however, he also declines to aid them in rehabilitating their merchant fleet, thus ending the drug trade and, presumably, causing the truth to emerge on its own.

DS9 tangles with cultural relativism in such episodes as "Captive Pursuit," when the reptilian-skinned Gamma Quadrant humanoid Tosk takes refuge on the station and befriends O'Brien while his ship is being repaired. Although Tosk is sworn to silence about his mysterious mission, the truth comes to light when a band of humanoid "hunters" board DS9 in search of their "prey." Tosk has been bred for the hunt, and he can imagine no fate better than to elude the hunters and eventually to die nobly at their hands. There is a tense confrontation between the hunters and Commander Sisko, during which the hunters defend the hunt as right and normal, both from their perspective and Tosk's. Sisko cannot refute another culture's logic, and besides, the Prime Directive requires that he not interfere. He does, however, allow O'Brien the opening he needs to pull off a daring rescue in which Tosk escapes in his ship and everyone, including the hunters, is pleased with the resulting continuation of the hunt (everyone except Sisko, who is obliged to go through the motions of reprimanding O'Brien).

Voyager is in an even worse position than DS9 to go around pontificating about right and wrong for other worlds, and *Voyager*'s Captain Janeway has no inclination to do so. In "The Chute," Kim and Paris are wrongly convicted of terrorism and cast into a hellish prison whose inmates slit throats for unappetizing bricks of nutrient substance. In order to survive and plan their escape, Harry and Tom must do what the other prisoners could not: resist the influence of aggression-inducing neural implants, rely on their friendship, and keep their wits. Janeway, meanwhile, traces down the real terrorist/freedom fighters, an earnest young man and his fourteen-year-old sister. Janeway refuses to discuss the justice of the resistance cause but threatens to turn in the two young captives unless they lead her to the prison. She is not only indifferent to the other inmates, but kills several during Harry and Tom's rescue. In this story, those who have no compassion, dignity, or moral sense at all (the other prisoners), as well as those who use their righteous moral judgments to justify extremism (the young terrorists), are inferior to those who refrain from grand moralizing but remain true to themselves and their personal commitments.

These episodes not only illustrate the way *Star Trek* of the 1990s backs away from moral and ethical abstractions, but they also show how standards of conduct are displaced from universal rules of right and wrong to matters of personal commitment and integrity. O'Brien may object to the idea of the "hunt," but in the end his helping Tosk is an expression of personal loyalty. The theme of personal integrity permeates all the *Trek* series, but in the *Trek* of the 1980s and 1990s it increasingly comes to fill a vacuum left by the decline of absolute moral imperatives. *Trek*'s narrative strategy, by which the potentially conflicting demands of personal integrity are portrayed as serendipitously harmonizing to produce outcomes that just happen (more or less) to satisfy our traditional ideas of justice and decency, is a good example of mythic reconciliation. Although the possibility is raised that things may not turn out well, the episodes' outcomes continually reassure us that people of integrity will, even without moral absolutes, somehow find it in themselves to do what is right for all the deserving parties. It is an extraordinarily hopeful view of the triumph of humane values in an uncentered cosmos, and a prime example of the ability of myth to achieve its own sort of reconciliation where none seems philosophically possible.

THROUGH THE LOOKING GLASS

Few things could be more upsetting to our idea of an orderly cosmos than the notion of divergent coexisting universes. *Star Trek*'s earliest depictions of parallel realities tend to answer this challenge with a reaffirmation of cosmic order. In TOS's "The Alternative Factor," the *Enterprise* encounters a corridor between two universes represented by two versions of the same character, Lazarus. From what little is revealed about the alternative universe, it seems to be an antimatter copy of our own. The two universes are not "supposed" to come into contact, not only because of the violent reaction of matter and antimatter, but also because, as in the case of the Lazarus from "our" universe, knowledge of the other universe can drive a person to insanity. At the end of the episode, the two universes are safely separated from one another while the good and evil Lazaruses remain locked in eternal combat in a sealed-off corridor between the two. Far from being random, these two universes are so parallel as to reinforce the idea that the familiar order of things is necessary and preordained.

In TOS's "Mirror, Mirror," Kirk, Scotty, McCoy, and Uhura encounter a disturbance while beaming aboard the *Enterprise* and find themselves in an alternate universe where the Federation is a ruthless imperial force and Spock, Checkov, and Sulu are fascist thugs. This upside-down universe confirms rather than denies the recognized order of things, just as Satan and his backward recitation of the Mass indirectly confirm the right order of God and Church in traditional Christianity. The mirror Spock, however, shows some redeeming "parallel" traits, and he seems to consider seriously Kirk's argument that, in view of the self-defeating nature of this alternate universe, it is both logical and necessary that it evolve in a direction convergent with Kirk's own world.

This theme of modernist optimism and orderly destiny takes a new direction, however, when the same mirror universe is encountered in the twenty-fourth century. In DS9's "Crossover," Kira and Bashir enter the mirror universe, where they learn that Spock had converted the Federation to his teachings of peace (inspired by his contact with "our" Kirk), with the unintended result that the Federation has been conquered and Terrans enslaved. In "Through the Looking Glass" and "Shattered Mirror," Sisko is abducted into this universe by the mirror O'Brien, who has taken Kira and Bashir's advice and is involved in a rebellion against the tyrants. Captain Sisko succeeds in his task of persuading the scientist Jennifer Sisko, who in this universe did not die at Wolf 359 but became an accomplished scientist estranged from the ruthless alternate-Sisko, to stop working for the evil empire and join the Terran rebellion. Later, Jennifer is killed by the cruel, libertine mirror-universe Kira Nerys, the Intendent of Terok Nor (the DS9 station, but in this universe still an imperial outpost). The DS9 representation of the mirror universe conveys something quite different from the optimistic message of "Mirror, Mirror." While DS9's mirror humans sometimes strive to emulate the example of the "real" universe, their universe remains stubbornly out of balance.

Roughly contemporaneous with the DS9 mirror-universe stories is the last-season TNG episode "Parallels," one of the few alternate-universe stories that comes close to presenting infinitely diverse and equally valid realities. After encountering a space disturbance while on a solo shuttle flight, Worf begins to slip back and forth between alternate universes. Although parallel characters exist in each reality, none of these is a systematic reflection of our universe (as in "Mirror, Mirror" and "The Alternative Factor"); they are just . . . well . . . different. In one universe, Picard has died in an earlier encounter with the Borg, Riker is Captain, and Worf is married to Troi (Worf's comic "take" on this unexpected development ranks among *Star Trek*'s great moments). Data and La Forge explain that, according to some theories, every possible universe exists simultaneously in different quantum dimensions. At the climax of the episode, the opening between quantum universes spills thousands of Enterprises into the same region of time and space. The crew finds the *Enterprise* with Worf's original quantum signature and sends him back to it, which causes the rupture to be sealed—but not before we learn that in some universes things are going so badly with the Borg that one *Enterprise* causes itself to be destroyed rather than return. On the other hand, Worf seems impressed with some of the alternatives he has seen, and he invites Troi to join him for dinner. Having been "lost" among alternate universes, Worf now seems to have "found" himself with more direction and potential than before; radically chaotic contingency is once again resolved in a humanizing narrative of growth.

CHUANG TSU'S BUTTERFLY

"Last night I dreamed that I was a butterfly," mused the Chinese sage Chuang Tsu, who then posed the question, "How do I know today that I am not a butterfly dreaming I'm a man?" The Western tradition, by and large, has seldom had much use for foundational challenges to "reality." However, the relativity of perspectives has become such a commonplace idea in the late twentieth century that we now consider these questions worth pondering. Who is to say that quarks and black holes are real, while guardian spirit visions are not? Isn't all "proof" ultimately guided by cultural and personal assumptions about what counts as evidence and what doesn't? Certain elements of contemporary culture—copying, genetic cloning, virtual reality, "recovered" memory—only help to blur traditional distinctions between what is real and what is not. This radical problematization of "reality" is reflected in today's popular culture fantasies—and especially in science fiction, which has always been in the business of stretching notions of reality.

There is a recurrent genre of *Star Trek* stories that might aptly be called "reality plays" (the postmodern counterpart of the medieval morality plays), in which everything hinges on the question of what is real. Of the more than 500 *Trek* episodes to date, a substantial portion (easily one fourth) revolve around the problem of distinguishing reality from illusion or deception. Reality plays appear in TOS, where Kirk and others face convincing illusions such as the monsters and seductresses of "The Cage," an Old West shootout in "Spectre of the Gun," Halloween-like visages adopted by aliens in "Catspaw," and apparitions unwittingly conjured from the crew's own fantasies on a recreational planet in "Shore Leave." While these sensory phenomena seem real enough to the *Enterprise* crew (and, of course, to the television viewer), the heroes are able to penetrate the illusion, and each episode ends with a clear sorting out between how things seemed and how they really were.

The reality-play genre is developed with increasing complexity in the later series, culminating in some of *Star Trek*'s most artful tales. In TNG's "Frame of Mind," Riker slips back and forth between one reality, where he is on the *Enterprise* acting out the role of an abused mental patient in a play, and another reality, in which he is a patient in a mental hospital on Tilonius IV, whose doctors are trying to cure him of his illusions of being a Starfleet officer. Before the episode is over, Riker is responding to "treatment" and rejecting his "hallucinations" of the *Enterprise.* The Tilonians have, in effect, convinced Riker that he is a butterfly dreaming he's a man. The viewer is led through so many layers of illusion that, even when Riker seems to be back on the *Enterprise*, one does not know for sure. A similar hall-of-mirrors story is told in VGR's "Projections." The Holographic Doctor is activated only to find himself alone on the ship. As various characters mysteriously reappear, they give him conflicting explanations of the situation, and each version calls upon him to take a different action to save the ship. As in "Frame of Mind," the story seems at one point to have reached its end with a return to the familiar frame of reference, only to take a surprising turn that reveals the false ending to be another illusion.

Reality plays like "Frame of Mind" and "Projections" are mystery stories, of a sort. They present a dizzying kaleidoscope of conflicting realities, only to resolve everything in the end with a plausible explanation that divides the illusory from the real. Sometimes, however, the line between reality and illusion is not so easy to draw. In TNG's "Night Terrors," *Enterprise* crew members have nightmares and hallucinations that seem utterly deranged; but when properly interpreted, these visions turn out to be residual echoes of actual experiences. The interpretation of their hallucinations leads the crew to the realization that they are being abducted and experimented upon by some particularly nasty insectlike aliens. Similarly, TNG's "Phantasms" has Data experiencing hallucinations so disturbing that at one point he is compelled to attack Troi with a knife. These images, which depict Troi as a cake being eaten by her shipmates and Crusher sucking out Riker's brains through a straw, strike Data as symbolic. He gets nowhere in a holographic session with Sigmund Freud, who concludes that Data hates his father and wants to possess his mother ("I do not have a mother," Data protests. "Don't interrupt," snaps Freud). But when Data pools his own insights with those of his comrades, they surmise that the ship and crew are being consumed by invisible parasites that Data has unconsciously detected.

The theme of dreams and hallucinatory images as indirect but informative representations of reality is, of course, an ancient idea (consider, for example, the biblical story of Joseph interpretating the Pharaoh's dreams). The dream-as-reality motif is revisited in "The Thaw," when *Voyager* encounters a planet whose few remaining inhabitants have survived a natural disaster by being placed in a protective state of suspended animation, or "stasis," linked neurally to one another and to a central computer. Because the people have not come out of stasis as they were programmed to do, Kim and Torres "plug in" and enter their dreamworld to find out what the trouble is. They learn that the survival fears of the people have, with the help of the computer, become manifested as grotesque mimes and acrobats led by a demonic clown who holds the humans (including Kim and Torres) captive. These beings, generated by a combination of human fear and computer intelligence, have acquired self-awareness and prove willing to execute anyone who threatens to resist or escape. Janeway fights illusion with illusion by offering herself as a hostage to replace the others, but sending in a holographic image instead. In "Night Terrors," "Phantasms," and "The Thaw," the phenomena that the heroes encounter are, however bizarre, representations through which the actual truth can be apprehended; reality is a prize to be won through heroic feats of discernment.

The futuristic technologies of copying, cloning, and holographic imaging allow for some special twists in the "reality play" theme. In DS9's "Whispers" and TNG's "Rightful Heir," Miles O'Brien and the ancient Klingon Kahless the Unforgettable are replicated as clones who imagine themselves to be the originals.[3] The holodecks and holosuites of the later series, of course, specialize in the production of "artificial reality." One of the most imaginative uses of the holodeck in a reality play occurs in

TNG's "Emergence," when an evolving life-form on the ship draws upon the crew's memories and thoughts stored in the holodeck memory banks to find metaphors—the *Orient Express*, cowboys, and gangsters—with which to organize its thoughts (we shall return to this story in the final chapter). What we see is not exactly false; it is an unconventional representation of reality that offers metaphorical clues about what is going on and how to deal with it. The same can be said for VGR's "Heroes and Demons," in which the Holographic Doctor must enter a potentially lethal holographic "Beowulf" program and confront an antagonistic life-form manifested as the monster Grendel, in order to gain information needed to mollify the creature and rescue three of his shipmates.

One of *Star Trek*'s most engaging holodeck tales runs through TNG's "Elementary Dear Data" and "Ship in a Bottle." In the first of these episodes, Data and La Forge program the holodeck computer to pose a suitable challenge for Data's Sherlock Holmes impersonation. Unfortunately, La Forge gives the instruction to create a villain capable of outwitting Data (not Holmes), and the computer dutifully creates a self-aware Dr. Moriarty who is capable of taking control of the holodeck computer on his own. Although he is holding the ship's doctor, Katherine Pulaski, as a hostage, Moriarty has already grown beyond the villainous character that he was programmed to be, and he willingly allows Picard to place his program in computer storage (a classic example of *Trek*'s optimism—the more tangibly human Moriarty becomes, the less evil). Four years later, both in our time and in the story line, Lieutenant Barclay accidentally lets the genie out of the bottle. Irate that Picard has made no progress in getting him into the real world, Moriarty, to everyone's amazement, simply walks off the holodeck. He then threatens to take over the ship unless he and his holographic lover are given their freedom. Picard complies and gives them a shuttlecraft to explore the galaxy. In the episode's conclusion, however, it is revealed that neither Moriarty nor anyone else who had entered the holodeck had ever left it. Moriarty and his virtual lady friend have actually been placed in a small desktop computer unit with enough stored information to allow them the illusion of a lifetime of adventure and exploration. In a moment of philosophical reflection reminiscent of Chuang Tsu, Picard points out that the *Enterprise* crew has no way of knowing that they are not living a similarly illusory existence in a box on the table of some other being (which, in a sense, they are).

Although "Ship in a Bottle" goes far in problematizing reality, it stops short of wiping away the distinction between illusion and real life. Virtual reality may be okay for virtual beings, but it's not enough for redblooded humanity. In all, *Star Trek*'s message is that determined humans, through strength of character and will, can finally penetrate even the most seamless illusions and restore themselves to an authentically "real" plane of existence. In the 1994 feature film *Generations*, Picard ventures into a euphoric illusory world called the Nexus into which Kirk had disappeared during a mysterious space accident in the previous century when he was presumed killed. So irresistibly pleasurable is the Nexus that the mad scientist Tolian Soran plans to destroy the entire Veridian solar system just to reenter it. Once inside the Nexus, Picard must resist the charming illusions of a longed-for family and lost loved ones, and he has to persuade Kirk to leave his idyllic mountain cabin, his lover, his dog, and his horse. Kirk returns with Picard to the real world just in time to stop Soran, but he is mortally wounded in the process, thus giving his life not just to save a faraway solar system but, more important, to affirm his absolute commitment to a genuine existence. This tale is reminiscent of *Trek*'s beginnings, as Kirk and Picard replay Captain Pike's choice of harsh reality over pleasant illusion in the original 1965 pilot, "The Cage."

The later series and feature films bow to postmodernism by problematizing reality in a far more radical way than did *The Original Series*, when the difference between reality and nonreality was always made absolutely clear by the end of each episode. Yet, far from embarking on a ruthless postmodern deconstruction of reality, the latter-day *Star Trek* uses problematic realities as yet another challenge against which human heroism can, and invariably does, prove itself.

GUARDIANS OF FOREVER

Immanuel Kant, the great eighteenth-century philosopher of mind, speculated that time and causality are *a priori* principles of human thought—in other words, they are not derived from sensory experience but are ordering devices that the human mind employs to organize experience in a coherent way. In the metaphor of modern computing, one might say that these are part of our system software, without which we cannot process any data. If that is so, then any attempt to tamper with our operative concepts of time and cause-effect relations might make thinking, at least in the ordinary way, rather difficult. For the same reasons, toying with concepts of causation and temporal sequence may also have a way of opening up intriguing, and often paradoxical, new spaces for the play of human fantasy. Suppose, for example, that it were possible for a person to travel "back" to a previous point in time and take some action that would disrupt the chain of events that led to the existence of the time traveler. In that case, the time traveler could not exist in the later time, and therefore could not have traveled back to commit the action that erased her existence, so the traveler does exist after all, in which case she could have traveled back . . . and so on.[4] Merely to imagine time travel is to enter a realm of paradox where the usual structures of logic do not easily apply. Like many science fiction tales going back at least to H. G. Wells's 1895 novel *The Time Machine*, *Star Trek* makes use of time travel as a convention for discussing the contingency or necessity of the world as we know it.

So prevalent is the time-travel theme in *Star Trek* that the 1996 *Star Trek Chronology* has a special appendix for alternate time lines, which discusses twenty-eight such time lines involving thirty-four episodes.[5] The "time" theme is such a commonplace in *Star Trek* that by DS9's 1996–97 season Starfleet has established *Dragnet*-style time cops, who interrogate Sisko after his encounter with the original *Enterprise* in DS9's "Trials and Tribble-ations." In VGR's "Future's End, Parts 1 and 2," *Voyager* encounters deadlier twenty-ninth-century Starfleet time-enforcers who are bent on destroying *Voyager* in order to prevent a harmful time disruption. Early in this story, Janeway confesses her impatience with these ubiquitous time anomalies: "Future is past, past is future—it all gives me a headache!"

Of all *Star Trek*'s time-travel sagas, none is more legendary among Trekkers than TOS's "The City on the Edge of Forever." After accidentally being injected with a powerful psychotropic drug, the delirious Doctor McCoy beams to a nearby planet where he leaps through a time portal (the Guardian of Forever) left by a long-dead civilization. Kirk and Spock, following close behind, notice that the *Enterprise* disappears shortly after McCoy makes his jump through time—evidence that McCoy does something in the past that wipes away the events leading to the *Enterprise*'s voyage. Trying their best to enter at the same time and place as McCoy, Kirk and Spock land in the United States in the year 1930, preceding McCoy by about a week. While waiting for McCoy to appear, Kirk meets and falls in love with Edith Keeler, a visionary social reformer. Meanwhile Spock, having constructed a monitoring device to scan historical events, links Keeler to the corruption of the time line. In the version of history that leads to space exploration and the *Enterprise*, Edith Keeler is hit by an automobile in 1930. In the other time line, Keeler does not die but goes on to establish an influential peace movement that delays America's entry into World War II long enough to allow the Germans to develop the atomic bomb and win the war. This turn of history apparently prevents the progress of humankind that makes space exploration possible. Spock therefore informs Kirk that, if history is to be restored to its proper course, Keeler must die "as she was meant to." When the critical moment comes, grief-stricken Kirk blocks McCoy's attempt to save Keeler's life. History is set on its progressive course, massive human suffering and millions of needless deaths are prevented, and the trio emerges from the time portal to find the *Enterprise* waiting for them. For this human gain to be possible, the love of Kirk's life, an innocent idealist who foresaw the moral and technological progress that was to come, was fated to die.

The reason for discussing time paradoxes in this chapter on postmodernism is not that time travel stories are specifically postmodern or even particularly new to science fiction writing but because they illustrate the use of certain contemporary popular narratives to challenge what we normally take for granted as real. If followed through to their logical extreme, in such postmodern fantasies as the film *12 Monkeys*, time paradoxes can deconstruct reality to the point of erasing all stable points of reference. *Star Trek*, however, does not use time paradoxes in this way. *Trek*'s time anomalies, as with its other problematizations of reality, are posed as tests of human character in which humanity always emerges triumphant. Although it might logically be expected that all time lines would be equally valid and mutually exclusive, and that an alteration in the time line should alter its participants' memories and their ideas of how things ought to be, this does not happen in *Trek*. Even when the history that produced their memories is wiped away, Kirk and Spock in "City on the Edge of Forever" retain a sense of their "own" time line and their conviction that it is "the" proper and correct one that is "meant" to be (meant by whom or what, we might well ask). And sure enough, as it turns out, all time lines are not equal: alternate time lines almost always seem decidedly inferior to "normal" ones. This privileging of the "native" time line over all others, and the heroes' ability to remember it even when sucked into alternate time lines, are central features of *Star Trek*'s time paradoxes. When Harry Kim wakes up to find himself safely home in San Francisco with a lovely fiancée and a respected position in Starfleet, he knows without question that this reality is "not how it's supposed to be," and he spares no effort to find his way to the time line that places him back aboard *Voyager* ("Non Sequitur"). In TNG's "Yesterday's *Enterprise*," the clairvoyant Guinan tells Captain Picard that their current reality does not "feel right" and that the *Enterprise* is "not supposed to be here." Picard takes the cue and discovers—of course—a temporal disruption.

One more time story will serve to illustrate the myth of human redemption that emerges from these potentially disorienting fractures of time and causality. In "All Good Things," the last episode of TNG's seven-year run, Picard finds himself inexplicably flipping about between three points in time: one in the calendar year 2370, the "normal" time of the series' chronology; one in 2364 at the beginning of his tour of duty on the *Enterprise*; and one in approximately 2395, after he has retired to tend the family vineyard in France. Only Picard can tell that he is darting randomly from one time to another, and this knowledge, of course, causes him to behave strangely from the perspective of his companions in any one time. The matter is further complicated by the fact that the Picard of the year 2395 is suffering from a degenerative brain disease (an affliction of the "temporal" lobes, appropriately enough) that might explain all this as a delusional state—a possibility that everyone in that time is well aware of but politely avoids mentioning.

Picard's determination is unshakable. He is deeply concerned about a dangerous "temporal anomaly" in space that he has observed in both 2364 and 2370, and in 2395 he insists that his old friends La Forge, Crusher,[6] Riker, and Worf help him make a daring voyage into the neutral zone to investigate the disturbance. The urgency of the quest has by now achieved grand proportions, for Q has appeared to Picard to explain that the Continuum has pronounced a death sentence on humankind, that the anomaly will play a part in the erasure of humanity, and that Picard himself is fated to be the agent of this doom. The prospects are dimmed when Picard fails at first to discover the temporal anomaly in 2395. Q lends a helping hand by transporting Picard to the earth of three and a half billion years ago—a dark, sulfurous underworld where the anomaly is enormous enough to disrupt the origins of life in the primordial ooze. Picard pieces together these bits of information and concludes that the anomaly grows backward in "antitime," and that he actually brings it into existence by the very act of searching for it in 2395. He also realizes that he can prevent its growth only by simultaneously deciding in all three time lines to desist from projecting the tachyon beams used to probe the anomaly. But these actions are not sufficient. Picard must enter the anomaly and form a warp shell to collapse it, even though this means sacrificing himself, his friends, and his ship in all three time lines. Picard faces the ultimate leap of faith: he and all that he loves must die three times to redeem humankind from the godlike Continuum's judgment of doom.

The redemption is more than a reprieve—it is meant by the Continuum, or at least by Q, as a revelation. "We wanted to see if you had the ability to expand your mind and your horizons," Q explains, "and for one brief moment you did. For that one fraction of a second you were open to options you had never considered. That is the exploration that awaits you—not mapping stars and studying nebulae, but charting the unknown possibilities of existence." What Q may have meant by this, we are left to guess. But Picard, perhaps inspired by the invitation to expand his horizons, takes the unorthodox step of revealing to his comrades their fates as he had witnessed them in the future: the marriage and subsequent estrangement of himself and Doctor Crusher; the enmity that develops between Worf and Riker following Troi's (unexplained) death; Picard's own debilitating mental disease; and the dispersal of the fellowship of the *Enterprise*. Is this a forbidden "pollution" of the time line, or is it a second chance? The disconcertingly accidental or "contingent" course of history becomes, as played out in the conclusion of this story, a source of hope and renewal, a reinstatement of the open-endedness of existence, and an opportunity to alter the patterns of destiny. As the usually formal Picard joins his comrades, for the first time in their seven years together, in their customary poker game, he remarks, "I should have done this years ago." "You were always welcome," says Troi warmly. Dealing the cards, Picard announces, "The sky's the limit."

CHAPTER 11

PHOENIX RISING

Reclaiming Humanism

Trojus, Anchises' son,
The descent of Avernus is easy.
All night long, all day,
The doors of dark Hades stand open.
But to retrace the path,
To come up to the sweet air of heaven,
That is labor indeed.

—Virgil
The Aeneid (19 B.C.)

The 1996 feature film *Star Trek: First Contact* ventures deeper into the postmodern underworld than any other *Star Trek* production to date; yet at its core it is *Trek*'s most ambitious tale of human redemption. The story is set in the year 2373, when the Federation of Planets faces its most electrifying threat—an all-out Borg assault on planet Earth. As the fleet assembles, Picard and the *Enterprise* are sent far away from the action. Starfleet Command, knowing that Picard had once been "assimilated" by the Borg and forced to preside over the Federation's defeat at Wolf 359, is taking no chances. When news of the battle indicates another defeat, however, Picard and his officers defy orders and speed toward the fray. Although Picard's intuitions enable him to destroy the Borg cube, an escape vessel emerges and the *Enterprise* pursues it through a time vortex to emerge on Earth. It is April 4, 2063, a decade after global war has decimated the Earth's population and just one day before Zefram Cochrane is fated to make the first faster-than-light spaceflight, which will initiate contact with other worlds and usher in an unprecedented era of human advancement. The Borg have chosen this vulnerable time to conquer the planet.

Arriving shortly after the Borg have blasted Cochrane's remote Montana settlement, the *Enterprise* crew finds Cochrane in a drunken stupor. Meanwhile, Data and Picard encounter Cochrane's injured associate, Lily Sloane, in the missile silo that houses their spaceship. Picard suddenly senses that something is amiss on the *Enterprise*, and he beams aboard with Data and Lily to find that the Borg, who must have transported when the *Enterprise* destroyed their escape vessel, are assimilating the ship deck by deck. The bewildered Lily escapes from Dr. Crusher and threatens Picard with his own phaser until she realizes she has little choice but to believe his story. They are pursued by Borg drones (assimilated *Enterprise* crew members) into a holodeck "gangster" simulation, where Picard guns them down and (literally) extracts information from their innards while Lily looks on in horror.

As Riker, La Forge, and others help the reluctant Zefram Cochrane prepare for the flight, Picard and his team battle the Borg. Data is abducted and awakes in the company of the Borg Queen, whom we first see as a pallid organic head, upper torso, and wiggly spine being lowered into a mechanical body. While the Queen woos Data, Picard, believing Data beyond help, angrily ignores the advice of his officers to abandon ship, electing instead to fight the Borg aboard the *Enterprise*. When Lily tells Picard that vengefulness has clouded his judgment, Picard dismisses her arguments with an eloquent speech about retreating no further. But when she compares him with "Captain Ahab," he experiences a sudden illumination and orders the crew to safety. Picard himself stays behind, having sensed that Data is alive and not yet "assimilated." He enters the dank belly of main engineering, now a steaming jungle festooned with vinelike Borg tubing, where he confronts the Borg Queen. Picard becomes aware that this is not their first meeting and that she had tried to recruit him as her "equal" during his earlier abduction (TNG's "Best of Both Worlds"). He offers himself in Data's place, but too late—Data has apparently accepted her affections.

At that moment, Cochrane's ship, the *Phoenix*, is rising from the ashes of its ruined world. As Cochrane, Riker, and La Forge approach warp speed and the Queen orders Data to fire on their rickety ship, Data unexpectedly smashes the plasma coolant container, melting the Queen and destroying all the Borg on the *Enterprise* (as well as the organic parts with which the Queen had endowed Data). Their momentous flight completed, Cochrane and his people are visited by the Vulcans, who had been passing through the solar system and are surprised to find humans advanced enough to merit their attention. Human progress is back on course, and the *Enterprise* returns to its own time.

DESCENT INTO HELL

First Contact carries its postmodernism on its sleeve, if not in its heart. Even before the *Enterprise E* is commandeered by the Borg, it is a gloomy ship compared with its predecessors. People on the bridge, attired now in gray uniforms, catch fleeting patches of light against a shadowy background of dusky furnishings. The bridge's interior space is visually confining and lacks a clear central axis. The frame lists as though the cosmos were out of kilter, and shots are close-cropped so that the floors, ceilings, or other stable points of reference are seldom visible. Wherever the Borg take over, the ship is shrouded in a sodden gray fog pierced occasionally by weapons fire, flashlights, and the Borg's facially mounted lasers. Scenes of Earth, too, are mostly at night, or in gray weather, or underground (in *The Original Series*, by contrast, it seems that night seldom falls anywhere).

Vision, light, and the eye are recurrent metaphorical subjects in *First Contact*. The eye is, of course, an active organ of power, vision, observation, discernment. But it is also a portal to the human interior, the most delicate place on the surface of the body, and a place where, according to folk tradition, evil can readily enter. The eye may be a convincing source of misinformation and a seat of illusion. The film begins with a spectacular pull-back from a close shot of Picard's eye to his Borg face and accoutrements, his alcove, and finally the immense Borg "hive" with its thousands of inhabitants—as if we are drawing all this out of Picard's mind through his eye. We then see the eye in profile, about to be penetrated by a mechanical tool, perhaps to install the machine prosthesis that replaces one eye of these organic-mechanical cyborg beings. As the eyeball begins to give way under the pressure of the drill point, Picard wakes from his nightmare. He stares into his mirror with horror as a Borg servo erupts from his face. His eyes snap open once again and he is truly awakened, this time to the call of Starfleet command.

Picard's eye-piercing nightmare is more metaphorical than literal— when he was previously assimilated into the Borg he did not actually receive the usual cameralike eye implant, perhaps because he was chosen as a spokesperson to impress other humanoids with such Borg slogans as "resistance is futile." The Borg eye reduces everything to a mechanical simplicity—the opposite of the "naked eyeball" with which Emerson impartially welcomed all that nature presents.[1] The Borg have no openness of vision but see only what the collective mind of the hive counts, for some instrumental purpose, as worth seeing. Picard and others pass unnoticed among the Borg even in the hive, except when the humans are deemed a threat or an object for assimilation. The world as seen through the Borg eye is a flow of distorted, two-dimensional black and white images. Geordi La Forge, on the other hand, no longer has his

familiar visor prosthesis; in its place are bright blue eye implants that
are as mechanical in their way as those of the Borg, but through which
he looks on the world with characteristic compassion. It is not the fact
of being mechanical or organic that is important, but the meaning given
these elements in relation to others. The Borg Queen, in her attempts to
seduce Data into becoming her counterpart, not only gives Data an organic flesh implant on his arm and the left side of his face and torso,
but she also gives him an organic eye through which, ironically, he is
expected to see the same dehumanized world the organic beings with
cyborg implants do.

In his criticism of *The Next Generation*, Bill Bolsvert argues that despite
their superficial opposition, "on a deeper level the Borg *are* the Federation—without the euphemisms." Putting aside Bolsvert's unabating hostility toward *Star Trek*, there is merit in his observation that the Borg are
the sinister reflection of the Federation, and indirectly, of America. Every
personal or collective character might be viewed as having a dark side,
which represents the very evils to which its virtues make it vulnerable—
its peculiar potential for righteous self-deception. In Jungian psychology,
the confrontation with our darkest latent possibilities allows us to master
them rather than be seduced or driven by them. The projection of a
person's dark side onto another character is, as discussed earlier, a common literary device. Thus, it may not be unreasonable to see in TNG
and *First Contact* a systematic, deliberate portrayal of the Borg as the
doppelganger or shadow of the Federation, a reading that might explain
why Picard calls the Borg "our most evil enemy."

Originating in the Delta Quadrant, the Borg embarked eons ago upon
the project of "assimilating" the humanoid populations of the worlds
that they encountered. Their stated aim is to improve the quality of life
in the galaxy by freeing humanoids from the limitations of their individual organic existence and bringing them closer to the "perfection" of the
hive. As the Borg Queen explains to Data, "We, too, are on a quest to
better ourselves, evolving toward a state of perfection." Given that every
society defines the quality of life according to its own standards, how
can one judge that the Borg's claim is any less valid than that of any
other expanding political entity, including the Federation? Is the program of the Borg so very different from that of the American "melting
pot," or on a broader scale, the European expansion that fostered the
Westernized version of "earth" culture that later becomes the dominant
culture of the Federation of Planets? The Borg's promise to incorporate
each culture's distinctiveness rings hollow, but is the distinctiveness of
Navaho or Zulu culture truly preserved in the Federation culture of the
twenty-fourth century? Are the Borg, with their interdependence of the
organic and the mechanical/cybernetic, so different from Starfleet personnel? Picard himself, with his artificial heart, is a cyborg, as is La

Forge. What is the difference, really? While the rank-and-file Borg lack passion or a sense of self, no one could accuse the Borg Queen of those particular deficiencies.

Having supplied the Federation with an evil twin, how does the mythos of *Star Trek* valorize the Federation and contrast it with its dark shadow? One obvious difference is that membership in the Federation is voluntary. Furthermore, the claims of the Borg are so patently dishonest that American society, and the Federation, come across well by comparison. Their talk of retaining distinctiveness is not even a pious fiction—it is an outright lie, since all indications are that each Borg is like every other across the galaxy. As Data puts it to the Queen, "You do not evolve, you conquer." Because the Borg are constructed in large part as a parallel to our own society (and our collective alter ego, the Federation), the obvious hypocrisy of Borg claims seems to vindicate us by comparison.

On a more symbolic level, *Star Trek* employs the logic of mythic narrative to set the Federation apart from its evil twin. Semiotically speaking, the Borg are imbued with the culturally familiar signifiers of ugliness, horror, and loss of control. They combine the traits of partially mechanized cadaverous zombies, enslaved people, and destructive social insects complete with drones, a queen, and a hive. Their invasive, flesh-wounding machine parts evince everything frightening and distasteful in technology. In the imagery of absorption and merger, we are presented with a mystified corporate organization that is as anonymous as it is absolute: you are owned but you don't quite know by whom. But it is in the actual story lines that the differences are most dramatically worked out: there are in *First Contact* two interrelated tales of human redemption, each of which highlights the quintessential humanizing traits that are central to the *Trek* cosmology. These narratives center on two very different champions of humankind: Zefram Cochrane and Jean-Luc Picard.

The broad historical narrative of human redemption in *First Contact* has to do with the rise of twenty-first-century humankind as represented by Zefram Cochrane and the flight of the *Phoenix*. In previous *Star Trek* lore, the all-important transition between the flawed world of the twentieth century and the socially progressive world of *Trek* times was the subject of differing accounts. *The Original Series* suggests at times that Earth had managed to avoid global destruction; but by the time of TNG, *Trek*'s account of history refers to a nuclear holocaust in the mid–twenty-first century.[2] The difference is important, for the first possibility implies that humanity is already on the right track, while the second suggests that things are going to get much worse before humankind changes its ways. It is the difference between smooth progress and the degeneration into a cleansing apocalypse. *First Contact* is a myth about the redemptive transition from fallen to risen humanity, or from postmodernist nihilism to a recuperated humanism.

Zefram Cochrane, despite his pecuniary motives and his debauched life, is visionary enough to believe that a nuclear missile, an instrument of destruction brought forth by misguided twentieth-century ideologies, can become the "Phoenix" that takes humankind into a bright new realm. The achievement of faster-than-light speed not only is a practical requirement for exploring other solar systems, but it also bursts the bonds imposed by traditional physics. In Western thought, speed has become a metaphor for progress, and light signifies not only mental "illumination" but also energy, power, and hope. The flight of the Phoenix (in Egyptian and Greek myth, a bird whose rebirth from its ashes symbolized the beginning of a new era) has in this case a thoroughly magical effect on human history. For reasons that are scarcely explained, this technological breakthrough is the harbinger of an unprecedented era of human progress. It initiates "first contact" with the Vulcans, which in turn helps bring about a new age of reason. Because people realize that "they are not alone" in the universe, they are inspired to eliminate poverty, war, disease, greed, and prejudice within the span of less than fifty years.

A parallel narrative of redemption in *First Contact* centers on Picard himself, his struggle with the Borg and their Queen, and his deliverance at the hands of two very different savior figures: Lily Sloane and Data. Picard's confidence, and his prior history (shared with other *Star Trek* captains) of always being right, lulls the viewer into a complacency from which both Picard and the audience will want rescuing. When Starfleet Command reveals a lack of faith in Picard, every red-blooded Trekker naturally shares his indignation. We follow Picard as he shoots down assimilated crew members with the conviction that he is "doing them a favor." We hardly falter when he calls Worf a coward for suggesting that they destroy the *Enterprise* and the Borg with it. Has the Captain ever been fundamentally wrong? When Lily Sloane steams into the Captain's ready room and accuses Picard of being obsessed with vengeance, we may listen with sympathy to his pious response, "In my century we don't succumb to revenge. We have a more evolved sensibility."

"Bullshit," Sloane replies, asking where his evolved sensibilities were when he emptied his tommy-gun into the assimilated Ensign Lynch during the holodeck encounter. "You're as possessed now as you were when the Borg possessed you." "I don't have *time* for this," Picard snaps, and Sloane retorts, "Oh, hey, sorry. Didn't mean to interrupt your little quest. Captain Ahab has to hunt his whale." Lily's comparison so enrages Picard that he smashes his phaser rifle into the display case containing models and mementos of *Enterprise* starships. Recovering his composure, Picard declares that "the line must be drawn here—this far and no further! I will make them pay for what they've done!" "You broke your little ships," Sloane observes quietly. As she starts to leave, her insight finally catches hold of Picard. It is the turning point in his self-understanding and in the fate of humanity. "Ahab spent years hunting the white whale that crippled him—a quest for vengeance," he broods. "And in the end, the whale destroyed him—and his ship." A humbled Picard gives the order to evacuate the *Enterprise* and begin the destruct sequence.

Picard cannot find his own way because his habitual posture of genteel discernment and confident command has become his blinder. It takes the insight of an African American woman and an outsider to the cultural and institutional hierarchy in which Picard is so steeped to show him the meaning of the parable of *Moby Dick*. After Lily Sloane saves Picard through insight, Data, another marginalized "outsider," saves him through sacrifice.

Convinced that Data is alive and unassimilated, Picard makes his way to the chamber of the Borg Queen. As he confronts her there, the full meaning of his obsession becomes clear. She is the terrible witch queen of folklore: sexually aggressive, insatiable, megalomaniacal—a usurper and abuser of power rather than one in whose hands power naturally rests. Just as she has seduced Data, so she once violated Picard sexually—in spirit, and perhaps in flesh—in her attempts to recruit him as her mate. But like Satan, she needs one who gives himself willingly, and this he would not do. For that reason, the Queen is as vengeful against Picard as he is toward her. The difference is that, like all *Star Trek* "supermen," she is ultimately alone and asocial, and she therefore cannot gain insight into her obsession. Even more fatally for her, she lacks all sense of sacrificial love, or any way to understand and anticipate it. Picard offers himself in Data's place; but only moments later, it is Data who sacrifices his treasured flesh by releasing the plasma coolant. As Picard pulls himself up the snakelike Borg tubing and out of the lethal cauldron, Data drags the Borg Queen down into the hell from which only his android half will return.

CAN *MOBY DICK* SAVE THE WORLD?

The cultural redemption portrayed in *First Contact* is from an imagined state of post-holocaust despair to a recuperated humanism, and one of its pivotal points is the recognition of the enduring message in a literary classic. Of course, the classic in question need not always lead to such a humane understanding—the reader may recall that Khan's spiteful dying words were also from Melville's Ahab: "To the last I grapple with thee; from hell's heart I stab at thee; for hate's sake I spit my last breath at thee."[3] Khan wields literature as the sword of unexamined belief in his superiority over others, while Picard uses it to bring himself down from his mightily righteous seclusion and back into the common human enterprise. The story thus suggests that the insights of a true literary classic can, when approached with humility rather than arrogance, stand above the vicissitudes of time and culture as a beacon to illuminate the human condition. This premise is given an additional poignance by the fact that it is Picard, for all his erudition and gentility, who is the "savage" in need of tutoring, and the marginalized, powerless Lily Sloane who leads him back to humanity.

The decade preceding this 1996 film was characterized by a bitter public debate, not only on university campuses but in popular writings and even political speeches, over the ideal of an enduring canon of great thinkers and classic literary works. One of the opening salvoes of this canon war was conservative scholar Alan Bloom's bestselling 1987 jeremiad *The Closing of the American Mind*.[4] Bloom, and others after him, argued that the cultural equality promoted by feminists, minority scholars, multiculturalists, and other radicals has ruined American education by undermining reverence for the truly great ideas and thinkers of Western civilization. Whatever one may think of Bloom's arguments,[5] he was basically correct in his assertion that social science and humanities scholarship has increasingly questioned the superiority of Western culture and its recognized "great" thinkers.

The debate over the "great books" canon is the iceberg tip of a deeper dialogue about cultural hierarchy. Critics of the traditional canon point out that the West, having gained military and economic power through its worldwide colonial adventures, lost no time in making the convenient discovery that its tastes in religion, literature, philosophy, art, family life, and the rest, are objectively superior to anything found in other cultures. This remarkable coincidence, the critics suggest, smacks of the ubiquitous cultural chauvinism known as *ethnocentrism* (or more specifically, in this case, *Eurocentrism*). By contrast, the egalitarian cultural critics argue that no standards of truth, beauty, or goodness can be "objective" because all of them are ultimately social constructs that reflect the background and interests of whoever is making the judgment.

THE POSTMODERN FLIGHT FROM HUMANISM

Postmodern social critics are often suspicious of humanism, in part because their social constructionist perspective makes them wary of the notion of "humanity" as a general frame of reference or a set of essential attributes. Roland Barthes, in his critique of the acclaimed 1950s photographic exhibit "The Great Family of Man," identified an insidious "traditional humanist" message in the exhibit—i.e., that "in scratching the history of men a little, the relativity of their institutions or the superficial diversity of their skins . . . one very quickly reaches the solid rock of universal human nature.''[6] This is, of course, exactly the thing about the liberal humanist message that irks racists as well. Barthes, however, is lodging his complaint not against equality but against the privilege that he believes this liberal humanist view surreptitiously awards to Western ''bourgeois'' culture by assuming that (1) the underlying patterns of human nature are not much different from those of the Euro-American middle class, and (2) that the same capitalist social order that produced the existing structures of domination will successfully lead us into a harmonious utopian future. In short, Barthes's critique of ''bourgeois'' humanism is rooted in the broader radical critique of liberalism: that it tries to project onto a liberating future the same comfortable social furnishings that have provided the mainstay of the old order.

The film studies scholar Katrina Boyd, quoting with approval Barthes's complaint against ''Family of Man'' humanism, criticizes TNG for promoting what she calls an ''essentialist view of human nature'' that fails to take account of the role played by European domination in fostering the prevailing liberal humanist ideas.[7] Boyd writes with insight about some of *Star Trek*'s essentializing tendencies, in which the Western ideals of progress, individualism, and rationality are given cosmic status. But while much of Boyd's criticism seems persuasive, it is reasonable to ask whether Boyd herself is essentializing the liberal humanist viewpoint that she wishes to criticize. According to Boyd's argument, *Trek* is guilty of harboring a ''view of human nature that favors consent and harmony rather than recognizing the inevitability of difference''—a position that, in Boyd's thinking, is part of the repressive and outdated ''nineteenth-century utopian'' mode of thought. In developing her argument, Boyd lumps together a variety of views—utopian theories, patriarchy, colonialism, Matthew Arnold's oft-quoted 1869 essay in defense of great Western literature as the reflection of universal human virtues,[8] and the late-twentieth-century liberalism of *Trek*—as though they were all of one piece. One could quibble with certain details (for example, her summary of nineteenth-century utopian thought),[9] but our main quarrel is with Boyd's strategy of grouping together such a variety of perspectives into an unwieldy entity that she then characterizes, with her ''nineteenth century'' label, as an attempt to ''recuperate'' an archaic ideology. By this argument, the ideas of consent, harmony, shared humanity, and liberal humanism in general are linked to anachronistic forces of oppression.

There is much to be gained from the postmodern critique of ''essentializing'' statements on human nature. Too often these have functioned as hegemonic devices that ''naturalize'' society and culture in a way that serves privileged interests. Contrary to the view implied in some postmodern criticism, however, it does not follow that every claim on behalf of ''humanity'' must necessarily be hegemonic.

RECLAIMING THE DREAM

Humanism is, to put it as plainly as possible, a faith in and commitment to shared humanity. Antihumanists of the political right have seen humanism as a ploy by which the weak and inferior attempt to bring down their betters. Antihumanists of the left view humanism as a Trojan horse used by the socially privileged to smuggle in definitions of humanity that favor their interests. What these various antihumanists agree upon, however, is that, contrary to the humanist ideal, people are fundamentally different and divided from one another—that the so-called "brotherhood of man" (or whatever nongendered phrase we may substitute for it) is a sham. There is no denying that, historically, humanity has indeed been divided and that partisan interests have been pursued under the banner of humanism. All this, however, leaves unanswered such questions as whether humanity is *absolutely* divided and whether humanism can ever be anything more than self-serving legerdemain.

The "old left" of classic Marxism had an answer: although the so-called humanism of the past had been a tool of class interest, "objective" (i.e., Marxist) understandings of the human condition are valid beyond the narrow interests of any social class. The Revolution will usher in an age when class conflict will no longer obstruct our view of common humanity—an age conducive to the full and unbiased development of humane understanding. With the fall of classic Marxism and the rise of postmodern social criticism, however, this optimistic scenario seems quaint.

Postmodern cultural criticism is ingenious (and very usefully so) in exposing the political and hegemonic interests behind any point of view or line of inquiry. In this capacity it has much to teach us, and we have only begun to explore its potential. But can this mode of criticism also serve as a positive point of reference? If not, and if postmodern criticism merely "deconstructs" the potential truth claims of every viewpoint including its own, we may all be in trouble.

Is it possible to build a satisfactory world view upon a postmodernist critical foundation? The prominent philosopher Richard Rorty seems to have made an earnest attempt to do so. Rorty rejects "foundationalist" claims that attribute any objective merit to one point of view over another. Rorty describes himself as a "liberal ironist." By "liberal" he means that he believes cruelty to be the worst thing we can do, and by "ironist" he means that he holds his liberal convictions even though they have no particular validity compared with any viewpoint—that he is a liberal only because social forces have made him one. An ironist, it seems, could give a young person no particular reason to devote his or her life to, say, feeding hungry children instead of exterminating them (other than the fact that liberals prefer the former and that this preference has some popular support). Rorty himself admits that only "intellectuals" are capable of being ironists in his sense; and if one reads his critics, it becomes clear that not all intellectuals are on board either. This seems to leave at least 99% of humanity without much to go on.[10] Even if it were philosophically irrefutable, this viewpoint is so austere as to offer neither comfort nor effective practical orientation.

Faced with this dilemma, our choices are not many. We could, of course, denounce human self-guidance and return to divine revelation. Or we could—which amounts to almost the same thing—follow the urgings of the cultural conservatives who seek a return to the golden age when credentialed humanists knew what true humanity was: what literature was worth reading, what music worth hearing, what ideas worth thinking, and what voices worth listening to. Stick with the eternals, the best that has been thought and said by our species, and leave the study of lower culture to the anthropologists. There is much to be said against such a quest, not the least of which is that those good old days never existed—rather, the canon of Worthy Ideas has always been bitterly contested.[11] Even if an elite Western consensus had existed, only the most determined nostalgist could overlook the abuses against humanity that have been committed in the name of sociocultural hierarchies, nor can they ignore the global political changes that have rendered these hierarchies untenable. Pine as they may, cultural conservatives cannot take us back to an Eden of ethnocentric innocence.

Yet another option is to concede to the relativistic or "ironist" position and try to live with its inadequacies. In addition to the psychological deficits noted above, however, this option has some practical drawbacks. If we assume that there are no authentic points of common reference to help bridge the gaps between individuals or cultures, then there can be no such thing as honest persuasion. Deprived of the possibility of legitimate dialogue influenced by impartial criteria of evidence, practical reason, or common goals, we can only deal with human diversity in one of two ways: indifference or domination. Either we agree not to care what one another thinks or does, or we settle our differences through coercion. Whether or not hard-line relativism is, as it claims, a form of "realism," it may fail the test of humane usefulness.

Turning to the mythic realm of discourse, which primarily occupies us here, we may note that postmodernism doesn't merely shy away from the mythic construction of a cosmos—it directly renounces it. Eliade's description of a profane, noncosmological universe applies above all to the postmodern world: "No true orientation is now possible, for the fixed point no longer enjoys a unique ontological status; it appears and disappears in accordance with the needs of the day."[12] *Star Trek*'s project, in the face of this chaos, is one of establishing a "fixed point" of orientation for the cosmos, and that point is the starship or station that carries its center with it in the otherwise decentered universe. This is the center to which adventurers always return—the *axis mundi*, the paragon of the questing spirit, the germinal point of psychic growth that defines the human.

THE HUMANIST ENTERPRISE

There is a middle path between the sterile wastes of anything-goes relativism and elitist cultural chauvinism: a quest for human kindredness that leads *through*—not around—our ever-expanding appreciation of diversity. It may be something like this that Barthes actually had in mind when he criticized the too-easy "traditional humanism" of the "family of man." For Barthes, "progressive" humanism requires that we take the trouble of listening to other voices before we decree what is or is not human. This is no easy task, nor is it one that we can ever finish and have done with. If we embrace humanism as an open-ended, process-oriented perspective, then it could be defined as a belief—a faith, perhaps—that as human beings we can, through an open and humble process of self-insight and dialogue, clarify and construct useful points of reference that will partially and provisionally bridge human differences.

Insofar as it denies this hope, dogmatic postmodern antihumanism is essentialist and authoritarian. It prematurely dictates the outcome of a process of human self-exploration that is only beginning. The idea of honoring diverse cultures as fully legitimate expressions of humanity is, for all intents and purposes, a recent invention—and since the genuine exploration of human diversity is still in its infancy, it would be rash to leap to the conclusion that we cannot find common ground with other people. To deny on theoretical grounds that an earnest dialogue could produce any common points of reference is to allow the savants of the West to overrule the intercultural self-explorations of humankind, which is the very thing that postmodern criticism has rightly taught us to avoid.

By viewing cultural differences as absolute and final, hard-line postmodernism may also be relying on an outdated view of culture. Contemporary social science has, for good reasons, moved away from cultural essentialism toward a greater appreciation of the fluidity of cultural processes. Better data and more sophisticated analytical frameworks suggest that cultures have never been static. They have always been subject to internal questioning and renegotiation; they have always had permeable boundaries through which intercultural influences continually flow. As the arena and intensity of interaction expand, so do the scope and reach of change. Such processes can, at worst, lead to the exaggeration and exploitation of difference—but they can also lead to the building of a shared conception of humanity. The question of whether this "common humanity" is something we discover or something we construct might be debated endlessly. In either case, pragmatically speaking, we bring it into consciousness only through the act of searching for it.

Stubborn philosophical questions will remain. How does one guard against privileging one's own familiar norms as definitively "human"? How fast can the human dialogue move without imposing hasty, ethnocentric conclusions? How is it possible to be open to genuine, deep-seated otherness? How far can we—or should we—attempt to go in establishing a common humanity? These issues may occupy us for a very long time to come. However, it is useful to bear in mind that mythology addresses such questions on narrative, not philosophical, terrain. Myth does not argue or prove; rather, it exemplifies the reconciliations that are elusive in philosophy and in life. To critique mythic mediations as though they were philosophical arguments, empirical predictions, or policy proposals is, as Marilynne Robinson put it, to "grumble about the apple and the snake."[13]

Good myth often makes for poor theory. Having Moby Dick save the world through the agency of an African American nuclear holocaust survivor is, by the standards of rigorous philosophy or social theory, a facile contrivance. So is the notion of a ravaged planet eradicating its most recalcitrant social problems overnight simply because its horizons have been broadened by contact with extraterrestrials. These are parables, morality plays, illustrations of hope, idealizations of our "unrealized possibilities." In order to have force, they must speak to a cultural world with which we wish to identify, even as they stretch our imagination.

Perhaps the ultimately liberating feature of *Star Trek*'s mythos is its emphasis on the growth of understanding. Gene Roddenberry's belief in humanity's potential for self-transcendence, and his conviction that we are "an adolescent species" that is only "a quarter formed," may be his most durable contribution to the ethos of *Trek*.[14] In TOS's "Let That Be Your Last Battlefield," Spock pleads with Bele to abandon his essentializing prejudices about his enemy Lokai's race, arguing that "change is the essential process of all existence." Throughout *Trek* are cautionary examples—from the dystopias of TOS to Picard's avenging righteousness—of the dangers of unexamined belief. At just those climactic moments when Kirk waxes most eloquent on the subject of "human" values, Spock gently suggests that humanity still has much to learn. Spock, too, is involved in self-examination and self-transcendence; in *The Motion Picture*, *The Voyage Home*, and *The Undiscovered Country*, Spock entertains doubts about his trademark devotion to pure logic. In *The Wrath of Khan*, Kirk learns the truth of Spock's Vulcan creed, "The needs of the many outweigh the needs of the few," but in the sequel, *The Search for Spock*, Spock is brought to the realization that Kirk's claim that "The needs of the one outweigh the needs of the many" is equally valid. The truth, in each case, is in the dialogue—the interplay of difference. Consensus, wherever it leads to totalizing, smothering, unexamined "truth," is the enemy.

Star Trek's heroes never stand taller than when they are challenged and humbled. *The Undiscovered Country* is ultimately a story about the overcoming of historically formed prejudices, as exemplified in Kirk's outgrowing his own hatred of the Klingons. In *First Contact*, Picard becomes more heroic when humbled by Lily Sloane. In TNG's "All Good Things," the summation of the series' seven-year run, Picard must accept the tutorship of his nemesis Q, who obliges him to reconsider his knowledge of everything from time and causality to camaraderie and destiny. *Trek*'s real quest, as Q points out, is not primarily one of space exploration but of becoming open to possibilities yet unimagined.

The premise of being a galactic student rather than a mentor not only is a quality of the heroic character, but it is also built into the dramatic structure of *Deep Space Nine* and *Voyager*. DS9 is located on the periphery of the Federation world, not only geographically but politically and culturally. Domination over the "other" is not a realistic possibility. The station hovers near the threshold of an unexplored world, more to keep the portal open than to push through it as glorious pioneers of the frontier. In *Voyager* the removal from the human/Starfleet center is even more dramatic, and the heroes are, at best, tolerated guests in a realm where they do not belong and on which they have no claim. In its own way, *Voyager*'s mythology must tread the same delicate line between human integrity and openness to otherness that each of the previous series did. The terms on which the mythic reconciliation of humanity and otherness is achieved may change, but the centrality of the process does not.

In our earlier discussions of gender, sexuality, evolution, colonialism, and cultural difference, we suggested that *Star Trek* often strives to reassure us of the cosmic centrality of humanity and to reinforce a faith in human worth and progress—sometimes in ways that reinforce hegemonic ideologies. Is it possible that *Trek* can do this, and at the same time portray a humanizing process based on openness and self-transcendence? Perhaps this is not, as Spock might say, entirely logical. Myth, however, excels at bringing together paradoxically related elements. Writer Marilynne Robinson comments on the ability of myth to bridge paradox and contradiction, speculating that "the attraction of the mind to myth comes from a sense that experience really is more complex than we can articulate by any ordinary means, or more than momentarily, emblematically. We know from physics that contrary things can be true at the same time, and we seem also to know this intuitively. I would suggest that the power of myth lies in the fact that it arrests ambivalences."[15]

If we view *Star Trek* as part of a project of enlarging our sense of the human and of promoting a humanism worthy of the name, we must recognize that it is a project that will always fall short of its own ideals. The new must be framed in terms that are appealing and creditable within the mentality of the familiar. Yet, the idea of such a project gives a viewpoint for understanding *Trek* and for celebrating and criticizing its achievements in terms of its own goals. Looking back over thirty years of change, it might be said that the project is moving in an appropriate direction. The early *Trek* was often a liberating and broadening influence within its social context; but to place Kirk's speeches in the mouth of Picard or Sisko would, in many cases, produce a startling disjuncture. This is not simply a matter of changing fashion or "political correctness" but of an expansion of our sympathies and an enlargement of what we are able to grasp. To the extent that the project of a continually deepening humanism is successful, the dialogue of *Trek* in the 1990s may someday seem as dated as that of the 1960s often does now. Or at least, to believe so is to express our faith in a humane reading of *Trek*.

In *The Undiscovered Country*, Spock converses with a precocious (but as it turns out, treacherously reactionary) young Vulcan officer, Lieutenant Valeris. She queries Spock about a print, apparently a Chagall, that hangs in his quarters.

Valeris: I do not understand this representation.

Spock: It is a depiction from ancient Earth mythology—the expulsion from paradise.

Valeris: Why keep it in your quarters?

Spock: As a reminder to me that all things end.

Valeris: It is of endings that I wish to speak. Sir, I wish to speak to you as a kindred intellect. Do you not recognize that a turning point has been reached in the affairs of the Federation?

Spock: History is replete with turning points, Lieutenant. You must have faith.

Valeris: Faith?

Spock: That the Universe will unfold as it should.

Valeris: But is that logical? Surely we must . . .

Spock: Logic, logic, logic. Logic is the *beginning* of wisdom, Valeris—not the end.

FAR BEYOND THE STARS

Can faith, a futurist vision, and the storyteller's art combine to bring about self-transcendence? Can a myth be both inside a culture, repro-

ducing it, and outside the culture, surpassing and perhaps even transforming it?

In posing such questions as these, we come full circle to the place
where we began our explorations—to the question of whether myth is
an agent of human growth or a handmaiden of the status quo. And,
having traveled the length and breadth of the *Star Trek* universe, we
bring to this homecoming a more complex sense of American mythology
and its diverse possibilities.

Deep Space Nine's story "Far Beyond the Stars," which aired in 1998,
is *Star Trek*'s own reflection on its three decades of mythmaking. This
unprecedentedly self-referential tale weaves together such perennial *Trek*
themes as race, gender, utopia, faith, the reality problem, and the power
of stories. The narrative goes about its task of self-reflection by collapsing
the boundaries between writer and text, present and future, real and
imaginal, audience and stage.

The episode begins when Captain Sisko, despondent over Starfleet's
latest setback at the hands of the imperialist Dominion, is seized by unexplained hallucinations. His visions transport him to Harlem of the early
1950s, where he experiences life as Benny Russell, an African American
science fiction writer. The frame-breaking nature of the episode is signaled by the casting of DS9's regular actor as Benny's friends, colleagues
and tormenters, and by the characters' occasional oblique references to
their DS9 counterparts. For the first time ever, *Star Trek*'s black actors
portray characters who exist in the explicit context of African-American
social history.[16] Five of the fifteen readily identifiable actors from the
regular DS9 cast are black, and all five play African American characters.
The numbers in themselves say something about the racial heterogeneity
of the DS9 cast, but as the episode title suggests, the story aims to take
us beyond the phenomenon of casting and "stars." For the first time,
Trek directly explores the racial politics of twentieth century American
culture. It is as though the characters on the movie screen are able to
peer back into the projection booth, and beyond, to illuminate the social
milieu that produced them.

The story centers on a team of writers who work for a second-echelon
science fiction magazine, *Incredible Tales*. Already the viewer may feel a
slippage between frames of reference, since it was the medium of mid-
twentieth century science fiction writing that did, in the "real" world,
lead to the creation of *Star Trek*. The episode's characters are, in a sense,
writing themselves into existence. And they are, at the same time, im-
proving upon themselves, since most members of the writing team are
rather limited and unheroic compared to their twenty-fourth century
counterparts (Dax's alter ego is a gum-snapping secretary, and O'Brien's
is an inarticulate bumbler). The historical situation that frames this tale
of self-creation is the stifling cultural atmosphere of the McCarthy era.

The writing staff must cater to popular prejudice by, among other things, concealing the fact that Benny Russell is a "Negro" and that another of the writers is a woman.

Benny's writing career takes a fateful turn when an image from the staff illustrator inspires Benny to write a story about the Deep Space Nine station and its commander, Benjamin Sisko. The staff editor, Douglas, rejects this story of a black man in command of a space station, arguing that such a premise is "not believeable" even for readers of *Incredible Tales*. "And men from Mars are?" one of Benny's colleagues counters indignantly. The editor maintains that commercial popular culture can only reflect prevailing social opinion and should not aspire to change the world.

Douglas is not the only one who defines science fiction as escapist entertainment, or who dismisses Benny's vision as irrelevant to the real world. Few of Benny's black friends, it seems, share his optimism about the transformative potential of science fiction. Jimmy, played by Cirroc Lofton (DS9's Jake Sisko) is a cynical young hustler who scoffs at the stories about "white people livin' on the moon." When Benny tries to tell him about Captain Sisko, Jimmy replies scornfully, "Today or a hundred years from now, it don't make no difference—as far as they're concerned, we'll always be niggers." Benny's lover Cassie (Penny Johnson, DS9's Kasidy Yates) treats Benny's writing as a diversion, and she sets her own sights on the more realistic goal of owning a small restaurant. Willie (Michael Dorn, DS9's Worf), has found his niche as a baseball celebrity whose macho self-absorption helps him endure the humiliations of racial prejudice. These diverse representations of mid-century African American life are complicated by the inclusion of yet another black character, a mysteriously clairvoyant streetcorner preacher (Brook Peters, Benjamin's father Joseph in DS9) who urges Brother Benny to "write those words," and "show them the glory of what is to come."

Benny keeps writing amid his own fears that he is somehow "becoming this Captain Sisko." Eventually, his editor allows the first DS9 story to be published, on the condition that it is framed not as a "real" future but as a dream on the part of someone with little hope—perhaps a Negro, but Benny's hopes are soon crushed by social realities. The publisher has an entire issue of the magazine destroyed rather than permit the circulation of a story with a Negro protagonist. Jimmy is murdered, and Benny is savagely beaten by the police. Benny finally suffers a mental breakdown, raving that the future he has created is real, and that no force can destroy the power of the human imagination.

Suddenly we are back on DS9, where Benjamin Sisko has awakened from his mysterious coma. We are reminded that, like Chuang Tsu's butterfly, Ben Sisko was dreaming of Benny Russell who in turn was imagining Ben Sisko. Captain Sisko finds this all quite perplexing, and he confides to his father his vexation over the possibility that DS9 is only a fictional illusion—a figment of some writer's imagination. "For all we know," the Captain muses, "somewhere beyond all those distant stars, Benny Russell is dreaming of us."

This is the sort of thing that ought to make the viewer squirm, since we know that Sisko has got it just about right, and that he is indeed the invention of twentieth century writers who are imagining each word he speaks. For us, of course, the question is not whether Benjamin Sisko is fictional. The question is, rather, whether the capacity to imagine this non-racist future is merely a sign of our ability to deny social realities and soothe ourselves with comforting escapist fantasies—or whether it is, on the contrary, a step toward transcending our historical limitations. The kind of hall-of-mirrors disruption of perceptual frames that we see in "Far Beyond the Stars" occurs often in *Star Trek*, but here it serves a more ambitious moral purpose. It explores the inherent paradox of any cultural mythos transcending the ideological structures from which it emerged—the mythic projections of one social order sowing the seeds of another, radically different one.

Star Trek's humanist cosmos is, like any other mythic world, held together by faith. Central to *Trek*'s faith is a belief in the liberating power of the imagination—of the ability to perceive our limitations, and thereby to move beyond them toward a more inclusive awareness. Perhaps it is this faith toward which Benny's spirit guide, the streetcorner preacher, beckons. It is also he who suggests that the question of culture and hegemony can be answered only with a paradox: that we exist as both the creators and as the creations of our narratives. As Benny is being taken away, he asks the preacher,

Who am I?
Don't you know?
Tell me.
You are the Dreamer, and the Dream.

CHAPTER 12

PROSPERO'S WAND

Owning the Mythic Legacy

Our revels now are ended. These our actors,
As I foretold you, were all spirits, and
Are melted into air, into thin air:
And, like the baseless fabric of this vision,
The cloud-capp'd towers, the gorgeous palaces,
The solemn temples, the great globe itself,
Yea, all which it inherit, shall dissolve,
And, like this insubstantial pageant faded,
Leave not a rack behind. We are such stuff
As dreams are made on, and our little life
Is rounded with a sleep.

—Shakespeare
The Tempest (ca. 1612)

Insofar as humans are deprived of preexisting supernatural will or heavenly essences, they are faced with the possibility that they do not so much *discover* meaning and order in the world as *create* it by constructing narratives into which they can place the disconnected data of their lives. Hence, finding or making a bountiful story may acquire a renewed significance in human affairs.

When Lily Sloane alludes to Captain Ahab, she tosses Picard the lifeline that redeems humanity. Picard catches the narrative thread that allows him to place his own overreaching righteous vengeance into the context of a larger human drama as represented in Melville's *Moby Dick*. Picard recites, as if in a trance: "He piled upon the whale's white hump the sum of all the rage and hate felt by his whole race.... If his chest had been a cannon, he would've shot his heart upon it."[1] That Lily admittedly never read Melville is beside the point, for she understands the kernel of the story that eluded the erudite Picard, and she can connect it to their circumstances. Her insight helps Picard find the thread that leads him out of the labyrinth of self-absorption and back to his friends, his ship, and his mission. Without Lily's ability to find the meaning in a story, the human race might not have been saved.

Stories are depicted as a source of both adventurous peril and heroic empowerment in the *Star Trek* universe. We began with a retelling of such episodes as "Masks," in which the hero's quest involves entering and taking creative control of a realm spun from the "baseless fabric" of myths and stories. *Trek*'s heroes reappropriate narratives and rework them toward their own creative and humane ends. Cultural legacy, which all too often seems to confront us as a static, formidable realm guarded by "literate" gatekeepers, is here portrayed as a treasury subject to boundless reappropriation, revisioning, and reframing.

THE DREAMWORLDS OF *TREK*

Star Trek not only tells stories that are mythic in character, but it also dips freely into the ancient well of narrative resources. The revisioning of narrative materials is a common device of mythology, folklore, and even formal literature, but rarely is it done in such a conspicuous and self-conscious way, drawing the audience's attention so explicitly to the use of preexisting narrative. Since *Trek* writers show no lack of aptitude for original invention, it is reasonable to inquire why this sort of textual recycling should play such an important and highly visible role in *Trek*. Before turning to that question, however, it might be useful to glance at the overall landscape of textual borrowings and reworkings in *Trek*.

Star Trek enters a diverse range of imaginative worlds from Greco-Roman myth and Judeo-Christian scripture, to European folklore, to twentieth-century cinema and genre fiction. Biblical references abound in *Trek*'s character names, places, and episode titles: Genesis, Eden, Paradise, the Apple, the Devil, Armageddon, Methuselah, Adam, Babel, Lazarus, and so on. Equally common are terms from Greek and Roman mythology, such as Adonais, Elaan of Troyius (Helen of Troy), Vulcan, Romulus, Remus, Kronos, and the like. The TOS episode "Is There in Truth No Beauty?" shows how classical language can be more than window dressing and can become part of the idiom and meaning of a story. This TOS episode contains in its title a general reference to an issue that preoccupied Plato and other Greek philosophers, and the names of its main characters (Miranda, Kollos the Medusan) draw a complex relation between classical references and the interplay of narrative themes in the story.[2]

In addition to Greco-Roman allusions, elements of traditional European folk legend, lore, and spiritualism also appear in a number of *Star Trek* episodes. In VGR's "Heroes and Demons," the Doctor becomes Beowulf in a holographic battle with a deadly Grendel. In TNG's "Q-Pid," Picard and his officers are obliged to play the parts of Robin Hood and his Merry Men (the occasion for Worf's deadpan gem: "I am *not* a merry man"). DS9's "If Wishes Were Horses" features aliens who embody the crew members' fantasies in order to study their reactions, and O'Brien's personal apparition is a leprechaunish Rumplestiltskin. TOS's "Catspaw" uses witches, black cats, and other elements of occult lore.

Holodecks, time travel, parallel planetary cultures, and altered consciousness allow *Star Trek* episodes to operate within the settings of classic literature and genre fiction. American gangster and detective worlds are featured in TOS's "A Piece of the Action," in Picard's Dixon Hill[3] holodeck detective fantasies (TNG's "The Big Good-Bye," "Manhunt," "Clues"), and elsewhere. The world of Arthur Conan Doyle's Sherlock Holmes provides the setting for Data's holodeck adventures in TNG's "Elementary Dear Data" and "Ship in a Bottle."[4] The American Western genre also appears, as in TOS's "Spectre of the Gun" and TNG's "A Fistful of Datas." Other fiction genre settings borrowed for *Trek* fantasies include Doctor Bashir's spy-thriller fantasy in DS9's "Our Man Bashir." *Trek* makes at least one tongue-in-cheek foray into its own genre of science fiction in DS9's "Little Green Men," when Quark and two other Ferengi land at Roswell, New Mexico in 1947; the Ferengi's universal translators are malfunctioning, which contributes to their somewhat comical fit with the prevailing image of aliens in that era's science-fiction fantasies.

Star Trek reserves an especially hallowed place for the narrative worlds of William Shakespeare. The alert fan can find abundant Shakespearean references—for example, in such episode titles as "All Our Yesterdays," "Dagger of the Mind," or "Thine Own Self,"[5] and in numerous unidentified brief quotations and phrases (our favorite is Data's inebriated rendering of Shylock's line, "If you prick me, do I not . . . leak?"—followed by a slapstick pratfall [TNG's "Naked Now"]).[6] Scenes from Shakespeare are performed in at least four *Trek* episodes (TOS's "Catspaw" and "Conscience of the King"; TNG's "The Defector" and "Emergence"). *The Globe Illustrated Shakespeare* is prominently visible, under protective glass, among the spare furnishings of the Captain's ready room ("Hide and Q").[7]

Why is *Star Trek*'s world so suffused with references to Shakespeare? That is the question to which the spring 1995 issue of *Extrapolation*, a journal of science fiction criticism, is devoted.[8] Many of the contributing authors agree that Shakespeare serves as a "symbol of high culture" and that it is used in *Trek* and elsewhere to establish "elitist" and "repressive" messages with regard to, for example, gender issues.[9] Much attention is given to the prolific Shakespeare quoting depicted in *The Undiscovered Country* (whose very title, by the way, is taken from a *Hamlet* soliloquy). In this connection, one author makes the rather novel argument that the Klingons' close familiarity with Shakespeare is consistent with a frequently encountered theme of Shakespeare quoting as a mark of "personal villainy" in the minds of rank-and-file Americans who associate Shakespeare with the high-handed cultural elitism of their schooling.[10] Conspicuously absent from these essays, however, is any recognition that the television viewer might be able to appreciate these revisioned and reframed snippets of Shakespeare in a thoughtful way.[11] The critics implicitly dismiss Picard's claim that Shakespeare provides moving insights into the human condition (TNG's "The Defector"). The *Extrapolation* contributors do put forth fruitful observations, some of which are discussed elsewhere in this book, but it is interesting that these critics give little credence to the possibility that the reasons for *Trek*'s use of Shakespeare might be similar to the reasons for its recycling of Westerns and detective stories—that is, a genuine appreciation of these fantasy worlds for their imaginative merits, or the intrinsic pleasure of their creative reappropriation.

We can now revisit the question of why *Star Trek* engages in such a very conspicuous process of recycling and revisioning of classical, folk, and literary texts. There may be many reasons for this practice, aside from the obvious consideration that it is easier to borrow than to invent. One does not have to be a Jungian to grant that there is usually something special about the narrative elements that are chosen for revisioning; that they have stood the test of memorability because they resonate, if not with a universal human condition, at least with some broadly shared sensibilities. Furthermore, the placing of familiar elements into unexpected contexts creates a dissonance that resolves into an unexpected new "fit," a frame-shifting device that makes for a good joke or a playful dramatic refiguration. To these general reasons for textual revisioning may be added some that are more specific to *Trek*. The practice of incorporating past fantasy worlds into future ones conveys the message that cultural heritage is, or can be, empowering rather than oppressive. By showing its characters as producers and consumers of fantasy as well as actors within it, *Trek* situates itself and its viewers as heirs and guardians of age-old storytelling traditions. In short, *Trek* validates and exemplifies the notion of a populist, democratic reappropriation of textual resources. Rather than being felt as a smothering weight upon us, the patrimony of literature and traditional narrative becomes a fertile soil from which endless new forms may grow and, in turn, be decomposed to nourish still others.

DEATH BY INTERROGATION

Our discussions of gender, utopia, race, and cultural hierarchy in *Star Trek* have sometimes involved critical "interrogations" of the *Trek* mythos. The choice of the term "interrogation" by some postmodern critical theorists, however, has ominous overtones that are not altogether unwarranted, calling forth images of the rubber hose, the back room, the bare lightbulb. An interrogation bent on producing incriminating testimony is, as we all know, liable to torture the life out of its subject in return for some notoriously unreliable evidence.

In recent scholarship on gender and sexuality in *Star Trek*, for example, it is virtually a forgone conclusion that rigorous analysis will reveal a dreary landscape of patriarchal oppression, punctuated perhaps by eruptions of homophobia and/or homoeroticism. Consider, for example, Sarah Projansky's analysis of TNG's "The Child." The episode begins with Deanna Troi's being impregnated in her sleep by an incorporeal life-form. Ignoring the warnings of the hypermacho security officer Worf, she opts to keep the child, who passes through gestation and childhood within a few days. Troi loves the alien child as her own, but the child leaves the ship when he realizes that he is causing danger to the crew. Projansky's argument hinges on her contention that Troi's choice shows that she is "consumed by her body" and that her body "speaks for her." Troi is not only reduced to a reproductive "body," but the body "loses the right to choose because it makes the wrong choice" since it "speaks against the greater social good" by endangering the ship. Thus, the story "naturalizes the Federation's superiority over both women and other species" and affirms *Trek*'s "neocolonialist narrative" of "paternalistic militarism."[12] Projansky's reading of the episode is difficult to reconcile with our own perception that the story valorizes Troi's choice. Certainly the text supports more than one reading.

Jay Goulding, in a book that takes TOS to task for its justification of American capitalism and militarism, mixes plausible arguments with others that appear to misread the *Trek* texts. Goulding's analysis of TOS's "The Cloudminders," for example, contends that the episode rationalizes and preserves the exploitive class division between Troglyte miners and aristocratic Strato-dwellers, when in fact the episode ends with a clear condemnation of the class system and an understanding that it will immediately be dismantled.[13]

Similarly, there is an element of arbitrariness in the way in which "race" is sometimes read in characters and plot elements. One critic cites Worf under the heading of "racist" depictions of African Americans, because under the heavy Klingon makeup is the African American actor Michael Dorn.[14] Another says that Data's representation of African

Americans is "certainly central" to his dramatic function, arguing that his exaggerated whiteness gives him a "marked" status that inverts (and thus represents) the nonwhite and especially the African American.[15] While each of these authors has worthwhile observations to offer, the fact that the African American can be read in such different signifiers raises the question of how far one can stretch an analytic frame before it begins to show signs of strain.

Critics determined to reveal a consistent political ideology in *Star Trek* may run into the problem that plagued the debate over whether TOS's "A Private Little War" was a brief for or against American involvement in Vietnam.[16] While it is true that *Trek* operates within a language of taken-for-granted structures and premises that are worth ferreting out, it tends to favor open-endedness over ideological closure, ambivalence over dogma, raising questions over resolving them, dialectical exploration over didactic exposition. And *Trek*'s mythic explorations are not restricted to the social level—they also address questions of personality and character, as well as experiences that take place within the self.

MASKED PERSONAE

Analysts who insist on reading all visible icons of human difference in terms of race, gender, and class hegemony may overlook other, equally cogent influences on *Star Trek*'s narrative forms. A consideration of *Trek*'s appropriation of the tradition of dramatic masks, for example, illustrates the relevance of historical form and artistic function as factors that complement and interact with the social and poltical functions of narrative.

Masks were used not only in the "high" theater of ancient Greece but also in the earthier folk rituals and dramas known today from pottery decorations that show masked comics, tricksters and ribald clowns with bulging bellies and enormous fake phalluses. Masked figures continued in the religious and secular drama of medieval Europe, although the sparse written accounts favor the religious allegories sanctioned by the Church. A well-documented tradition of secular theater called *commedia dell'arte* thrived in Renaissance Italy, and this form of drama quickly spread to become a dominant art form in both urban and rural settings throughout Europe until well into the eighteenth century. *Commedia dell'arte* and its offshoots, like earlier folk theater, employed a predictable set of characters, often representing particular cities or locales. Most of these were masked: the pompous intellectual *Dottore* (Doctor); the lecherous, controlling old man *Pantalone* (Pantaloon) with his hooked nose and bulging phallus; the swaggering but cowardly mustachioed Spanish *Capitano* dressed always in black; and various zannis, or comical servants. The English harlequin, with his black half-mask, his patchwork costume, and his "slapstick" wand, whose loud slapping noise signaled magical transformations, was derived from Arlequino, one of the zanni ("zany") figures of *commedia dell'arte*. Shakespeare, Molière, and other playwrights borrowed freely from characterizations and situations developed by this form of drama.

The use of the theatrical mask as such was in decline by the nineteenth century—or rather, it was evolving in new directions, including England's "Punch and Judy" puppet shows and the forerunners of modern clowns, which were also classified into named types. Today's circus clowns are derived from the masked characters of *commedia dell'arte* and, more distantly, from mask traditions going back at least to Greek times. Mime (from the Greek *mimesis*, or "imitation") and pantomime ("imitator of all things," a sort of one-man show in Greek times) also made their way from Classical through Medieval and Renaissance types into the forms that we know today, and they also exhibit an evolution from mask to standardized makeup as their signifying visage. But the story does not stop there. Such vaudeville masters and film pioneers as Charlie Chaplin, Buster Keaton, and Stan Laurel inherited the arts of the nineteenth-century pantomime and clown, and they in turn became the idols and mentors of generations of stage, film, and television actors. TNG actor Brent Spiner (Data) explicitly acknowledges his debt to these early masters.[17]

The early cinema also inherited another ancient storytelling tradition, that of magic and horror. Around the turn of the century, the professional magician George Mèliés saw the potential of the new medium for producing feats of illusion, and he became one of the first commercial filmmakers, turning out a large number of widely shown films of magical tricks (as well as the first science fiction film, *A Trip to the Moon* [1902]). The ability of film to show what "real life" could not was also recognized by Thomas Edison, whose silent *Frankenstein* was one of the earliest story-films ever produced (and, of course, the forerunner of innumerable sequels). The many horror films of the early cinema (*Phantom of the Opera, Frankenstein, The Mummy, Dracula*) not only drew on European folkloric traditions but also gave renewed vitality to traditions of the theatrical mask.

This overview of the legacy of dramatic masks illustrates that, contrary to what commonsense intuition might suggest, there is actually a long dramatic tradition that links such modern television characters as Spock, Data, Worf and others to the complex evolution of masked personae, both on the general and, in some respects, the specific levels. Quark and Neelix, both jester figures, are sometimes seen wearing Harlequin's diamond-patterned suit (which began as the patchwork clothing of a servant zanni). Worf resembles, in name as well as character and appearance, the wolf-man of folklore and cinema—and more distantly the ritual animal-human mask figure seen in Greek paintings and even pre-historic cave art. Spock's pointed ears, while not quite like anything in *commedia dell'arte*, have their precedent in folk images of elves and fair-ies,[18] as well as the images of Pan and the Satyrs depicted in Greco-Roman and Renaissance painting. Data's mime character is part of a theatrical tradition reaching back to ancient Greece, and it is no accident that he is a tireless imitator, or mimic, of all things human. When Picard tutors Data on his acting method, he counsels Data against mimicking others' techniques—in effect, not to be such a mime—but the advice is hard for Data to follow, given his characteristic inclination toward mi-mesis.[19]

It is not simply the outward form and evolution of the theatrical mask that is of interest here, however, but also the dramatic function of mask characters in the storytelling process. In ancient Greek drama, as in the dramas and rituals of various cultures, masks have been used to repre-sent a stock set of traits attributed to well-known archetypal characters, or to general categories of beings represented by a masked figure. Masks may represent deities or sacred animals, but they may also signify a constellation of abstract human character traits that is understood in ad-vance by the audience, and the interplay of such masked characters tells a story that, at one level, has to do with the interplay of personality traits that are manifested in a more elusive form in day-to-day situations. The reduction of complex human diversity to simplified masks contributes to narrative in several ways. For one, it allows a degree of abstraction that facilitates the narrative play of oppositions and mediations that myth is about. Masks also provide a sort of narrative shorthand: the Vulcan ears, the Ferengi lobes, or the furrowed Klingon brow instantly signify a set of traits, struggles, contradictions, and dramatic functions associated with a type, even though the audience has never encountered that particular individual before, allowing the story to go farther and faster than it could if a detailed exposition were necessary.

Of course, this kind of shorthand, when set in a context of social dom-ination and applied to actual human individuals or groups, can easily lead to the vicious abstractions of racism, sexism, class prejudice, and ethnocentrism, and in that sense the mask character, by its very essence, treads perilous ground. The Ferengi character Quark, for example, bears an unsettling resemblance to the crafty, avaricious Jew of European anti-Semitic lore; yet the Quark character also has features of the Harlequin and other zanni-jester figures who may serve as unexpected sources of insight or benevolence. To view the use of mask characters as a phenom-enon simply motivated by, and representative of, these malevolent racial stereotypes gives too little credit to the complexities of the human imag-ination.

SORCERERS' APPRENTICES

Magic and sorcery play a prominent role in *Star Trek*, especially if one grants that transformations, transportations, and other miraculous feats of *Trek* science sometimes have little relationship to known technology, nor a very plausible basis in theoretical physics[20] but bear a strong resemblance to the techniques of shamans and sorcerers in various folk traditions, to say nothing of magician-entertainers. When Tuvok teaches Kes to make water boil with her gaze (VGR's "Cold Fire"), or when Odo changes himself into a hawk and soars around the DS9 station ("The Begotten"), we are closer to the realm of ancient sorcery than the scientific-rational world to which *Trek* is nominally so committed. The magiclike technology of *Trek* is, to be sure, "officially" presumed to be operating by natural laws, even though the explanations may sometimes be framed in scientifically questionable terms or opaque technobabble. Of course, magic and its resulting spectacles make for good entertainment—no less now than they ever did. Magic also provides ways of moving the plot and action that could not be accomplished as easily if the stories adhered to mundane physical limitations. However, the significance of magic and its relation to science in *Trek* goes far beyond parlor tricks or plot expediency. In the narrative world of *Trek* and science fiction, science is magic that has been reframed in secular, democratic terms.

In his 1895 study *The Golden Bough*, the pioneering anthropologist James Frazer showed that magic and science have much in common, since both are seen by their respective believers as the automatic and impersonal operation of cause and effect, morally neutral in itself and having little to do with deities. Thus, magic and science are, according to Frazer, more like one another than either is like religion. As a literary device, magic may be used as a metaphor for science, and in Renaissance literature the distinction between the two is often blurred. Marlowe's *Doctor Faustus* and Shakespeare's *Tempest* treat magic, with its arcane special language and formulae, almost as a subset of science or "the learned arts."

Of course, from a modern perspective there are various criteria that can be used to distinguish magic from science. In principle, science produces hypotheses that can be experimentally tested, while magic relies on faith to explain away its failures. Magic, Frazer demonstrated, assumes certain underlying notions of causality that science does not recognize, such as the principle of imitation (causing something to happen by mimicking the desired effect, such as pouring water on the ground to make it rain), or contagion (manipulating the unseen link between things formerly in contact—for example, using a lock of someone's hair to cast a spell upon them). Although the Western scientific worldview does not generally recognize these as laws of nature, they appear to be basic associative principles of human thought. This brings us to a deeper aspect of magic: the primacy of the word.

Western images of the archetypal magician (Merlin, for example) may not always call to mind Frazer's imitative and contagious principles, but they do evoke the power of *logos*, the word. In this way, Merlin's magic is both like and unlike science. Each relies on disciplined effort, learning, books, and the power of special language. But Merlin's learning is esoteric and looks backward to ancient lore. Science, on the other hand, is exoteric, democratized, teachable to everyone, forward looking, repudiating even its own established lore in its search for the innovative. Merlin's secret words have power in and of themselves; the power of words in a scientific age lies in their ability to reach out to others. Merlin represents the esoteric, supernatural powers of a Golden Age, while science represents the democratized, naturalized, utopian future.

In the context of science fiction, however, science and magic may at times merge. If Isaac Newton could witness some of the technology taken for granted today, much of it would seem as close to magic as to any science recognizable to him. Similarly, the apparent fusion of the two in futurist fantasy can be defended by reference to our own state of scientific ignorance compared with what might be known in the twenty-third and twenty-fourth centuries. *Star Trek* is able, by working imaginatively within its basic premises, to have its magic and its science too. It can coalesce traditional aspects of the mythic-fantastic into the naturalistic-empirical and can assimilate some of Western culture's oldest narrative lore with some of its most futuristic and "scientific" imaginings. How Merlin-like Picard seems when his ritualized incantation "Engage" causes his ship to vanish in a flash of light! Science fiction excels in bringing about a mediation between the exhilarating wonders of magic and the democratic accessibility of science—the reconciliation of the fantastic with the worldly, and the democratic with the arcane.

MYTH AND MAGIC ON THE *ORIENT EXPRESS*

"Emergence," one of the mythically richest TNG stories, opens on the holodeck with Data acting the role of Prospero in the final act of Shakespeare's *Tempest*, where Prospero says that

> graves, at my command,
> Have wak'd their sleepers; op'd, and let them forth
> By my so potent art. But this rough magic
> I here abjure; and, when I have requir'd
> Some heavenly music—which even now I do—

To work mine end upon their senses that
This airy charm is for, I'll break my staff,
Bury it certain fathoms in the earth,
And, deeper than did ever plummet sound,
I'll . . .

". . . drown my book," the passage should conclude, but Data pauses when he notices Picard's inattentiveness. Sensing that his performance is missing something, Data inquires about the meaning of Prospero's speech, and Picard responds:

Shakespeare was witnessing the end of the Renaissance and the birth of the modern era, and Prospero finds himself in a world where his powers are no longer needed, so we see him here about to perform one final creative act before giving up his art forever. . . . [B]ut there is a certain expectancy, a hopefulness about the future. You see, Shakespeare enjoyed mixing opposites, the past and the future, hope and despair . . . [The shriek of a steam whistle is heard, and a shaft of light flickers in the blackness] Data—what is it?

What it is, in fact, is a steam locomotive hurtling toward them through the night. Their command to the holodeck computer to "end program" is futile, and Picard, pushed from harm's way by Data at the last instant, is lucky to escape with a few scrapes. Once outside the holodeck, Data informs Picard that the train that nearly killed them is the *Orient Express* from one of Doctor Crusher's holodeck programs. "But what is it doing on Prospero's Island?" Picard demands to know. What, indeed?

A locomotive or other loud machine bursting suddenly into an idyllic pastoral landscape is the guiding image of Leo Marx's *Machine in the Garden*, a wonderfully astute treatment of America's ambivalent mythos of progress and the pastoral ideal. The image, Marx points out, is repeated throughout Anglo-American literature since the 1840s, appearing in the works of Hawthorne, Thoreau, Emerson, Whitman, Melville, Twain, and many others.[21] Following his opening discussion of the intruding-machine image, Marx's second chapter, "Shakespeare's American Fable," is an extended analysis of *The Tempest* as Shakespeare's meditation on the themes of wilderness, civilization, utopia, and the "arts" of magic/technology.

Given Picard's explanation of Prospero's plight in a modern world where his magic no longer has a place, one might suppose that the train represents the juggernaut of soulless, alienating technology. Not so: this Orient Express is a fantasy train in more ways than one. When the crew members are unable to end the holodeck program, they begin to suspect

that the mysterious holodeck activity is connected with the fact that the
Enterprise is "growing" new circuitry and that the ship had spontane-
ously changed course and speed to protect itself from a dangerous space
anomaly. Upon reentering the holodeck's Orient Express, the crew members encounter an inscrutable collage of images drawn from different
holodeck programs, including an armored knight cutting out paper dolls,
an Old West gunslinger, a worried engineer, and an irate conductor who
threatens to put them off the train. It begins to dawn on them that the
Enterprise is developing a "self-determining intelligence" and that the
holodeck is "a focal point where all the ideas and instincts of this emerging intelligence are first expressed in some form." As Troi observes, "The
holodeck was full of metaphoric imagery, like it was having some kind
of daydream. It may not make literal sense, but symbolically it probably
does have some kind of logic to it. . . . It's as though this emergent intelligence is like an infant, acting on impulse, trying to figure itself out
as it goes. The only source of experience it can draw on is ours, through
our holodeck programs."

"Emergence" is one of the last episodes of *The Next Generation* series,
and there is more than a hint that the writers are having some fun with
self-referential images, some of which may be too obscure for the average
viewer to catch. In a divertissement from the main plot development, a
gangster (played by Patrick Stewart's longtime stand-in) has to get a
golden brick to Keystone City. Why? "It's where everything begins." He
gets off the train and inserts the brick into a wall: "Layin' the foundation," he explains. This may or may not be a reference to Hollywood's
Keystone Studios, the training ground of such film greats as Charlie
Chaplin and the source of Paramount Studios' most talented artists during the studio's own formative years.[22] In a tale like "Emergence," with
its nested frames of dramatic reference, it would not be out of character
for the narrative to step one frame farther back and salute *Trek*'s own
fantasy legacy. This is, after all, theater about theater.

As the plot unfolds, the *Enterprise* officers decide to help the emerging
intelligence get the energy source that it needs; but since the holodeck
now controls the ship, the crew can only do so by entering into the
"daydream" of the ship and playing roles within its metaphoric fantasies. The effort is successful: the alien entity, having reached a mature
physical form, is finally able to strike off on its own, leaving the crew
members to control their own ship and dream their own dreams. The
episode's final scene returns to the opening Shakespeare motif, as Data
invites the Captain to his performance of a scene from *The Tempest* in
which Miranda has her first contact with people from the outside world.
"O brave new world that has such people in't," ruminates Picard. Then
Data, thoughtful, returns to the subject of the alien being. "You took a
risk," he points out. "The object may be dangerous." Picard responds:

"The intelligence that was formed on the *Enterprise* didn't just come out of the ship's systems. It came from us, from our mission records, personal logs, holodeck programs—our fantasies. Now, if our experiences with the Enterprise have been honorable, can't we trust that the sum of those experiences will be the same?"

Picard's statement gives a fitting closure to this fantasy about the uses of fantasy, and an answer of sorts to the question raised by the machine-in-the-garden image. The story asserts the inherent role of mythic metaphors and fantasies in complex thought—even for an exotic alien intelligence. The machine age need not alienate us from this cognitive function—it merely provides a new venue and new symbols. Even the machine itself thinks narratively, using mythic daydreams to "figure itself out." Narrative and metaphor are thus essential elements of intelligent life, necessary for fully developed self-awareness. Furthermore, the democratization of these narratives can only be a benign and humane influence.

Picard's speech clarifies an essential shift from the old esoteric mythic and magical lore of Merlin and Prospero. The emerging intelligence draws on the democratized, collective images of the crew, and that is why it can be trusted. The shift depicted here is away from passive obeisance to a sacred, mystified, esoteric, backward-looking lore—and to an active, self-aware, democratic, forward-looking, and forever open-ended mythic narrative. Prospero's magic wand or staff, the symbol of his esoteric special powers, may indeed be broken, but it is not necessary to "drown the book," (the pledge of Prospero that Data stopped just short of saying); rather, it can be opened for all to write upon. This story is, in short, about the humanization and the democratization of the magical and mythic arts.

This is essentially what Prospero says of his own magic when he steps out of his narrative frame and addresses his audience at the close of *The Tempest*. Having used his arts of enchantment to achieve many of his purposes—summoning the usurpers to his island and using a magical play-within-a-play to bring them to a more humane understanding—he frees his "airie spirit" and forswears his magic. He must now appeal to the audience, placing in their hands—or rather, in their powers of imagination—the final task of sending him back to Naples where he can enjoy the rewards of his success:

> Now my charms are all o'erthrown,
> And what strength I have's mine own—
> Which is most faint: now, 'tis true,
> I must be here confin'd by you,
> Or sent to Naples. Let me not,
> Since I have my dukedom got,

And pardon'd the deceiver, dwell
In this bare island by your spell;
But release me from my bands
With the help of your good hands.
Gentle breath of yours my sails
Must fill, or else my project fails,
Which was to please.

With these words, Prospero (or rather, Shakespeare) relinquishes his "art to enchant," and he empowers the members of his audience to bring the story to their chosen conclusion. This ending is a reminder that the world of fantasy exists only through the indulgence of the audience, in whose hands rests the power of ultimate creativity—the power to make of a story what they will. Likewise, the stories told here are only a passing moment in the ongoing conversation, reinterpretation, and fresh creation that surrounds *Star Trek*. The book of *Trek* is not, and has never been, any conjurer's sole property.

NOTES

CHAPTER ONE

1. Michael Logan, "Endless Voyage: Celebrating *Star Trek*'s 30th Anniversary," *TV Guide*, August 24, 1996, 13–14; Logan also cites the less known *Star Trek: The Animated Series* (1993–94).

2. Michael Jindra, "Star Trek as a Religious Phenomenon," *Sociology of Religion*, 55, no. 1 (Spring 1994), 27.

3. Michael Wolff, Kelly Maloni, Ben Greenman, Kristen Miller, and Jeff Hearn, *Net Trek: Your Guide to Trek Life in Cyberspace* (New York: Michael Wolff, 1995).

4. Cassandra Amesley, "How to Watch Star Trek," *Cultural Studies*, 323–39.

5. For an extended treatment of the *Trek* fan subculture and its activities, see Camille Bacon-Smith, *Enterprising Women: Television Fandom and the Creation of Popular Myth* (Philadelphia: University of Pennsylvania Press, 1992); Henry Jenkins, "*Star Trek* Rerun, Reread, Rewritten: Fan Writing as Textual Poaching," *Critical Studies in Mass Communication* 5, no. 2 (1988): 85–107; Constance Penley, "Feminism, Psychoanalysis, and the Study of Popular Culture," in Lawrence Grossberg, Cary Nelson, and Paula Treichler, eds., *Cultural Studies* (New York: Routledge, 1992), 479–500.

6. Logan, "Endless Voyage," 14.

7. "The Captains: Kate Mulgrew." *TV Guide*, August 24, 1996, 18.

8. Keith Basso, *Wisdom Sits in Places: Landscape and Language Among the Western Apache* (Albuquerque: University of New Mexico Press, 1996).

9. The terms *myth*, *mythos*, and *mythology* are used somewhat interchangeably here, although the latter two tend to connote a whole body of interrelated narratives, while the first suggests either a particular narrative, or the general phenomenon of myth. *Story* and *narrative* are also used interchangeably, in an

even broader sense that includes myths along with literature, history, and various other narrative forms.

10. "Hearing Silence: Western Myth Reconsidered," in Kurt Brown, ed., *The True Subject: Writers on Life and Craft* (Saint Paul: Graywolf Press, 1993), 35–151.

11. Mircea Eliade, *The Sacred and the Profane: The Nature of Religion* (New York: Harcourt, Brace, and World, 1959), 23, 34.

12. Ovid, *The Metamorphoses*, Book 1, as quoted in Carl Sagan, *Cosmos* (New York: Ballantine Books, 1985), 223.

13. Alan Dundes, *Sacred Narrative: Readings in the Theory of Myth* (Berkeley, University of California Press, 1984).

14. Mircea Eliade, *Cosmos and History: The Myth of the Eternal Return* (New York, Harper and Row, 1959).

15. "Lucy" is the nickname of a three-million-year-old fossil specimen of *Australopithecus afarensis*, regarded by most paleoanthropologists as a human ancestor. Spider Grandmother is a benefactor of humanity in Pueblo Indian mythology.

16. The latter is the premise of Ursula K. Le Guin's *The Left Hand of Darkness* (New York: Ace Books, 1969). For the idea of science fiction as thought experiment, we are indebted to Le Guin's *The Language of the Night: Essays on Fantasy and Science Fiction* (New York: Putnam, 1979).

17. Larry Nemecek, *Star Trek: The Next Generation Companion*, rev. ed. (New York: Pocket Books, 1995), 30.

18. Ibid.; Yvonne Fern, *Gene Roddenberry: The Last Conversation*, rev. ed. (New York: Pocket Books, 1996); David Alexander, *Star Trek Creator: The Authorized Biography of Gene Roddenberry* (New York: Roc Books, 1994).

19. Lawrence M. Krauss, in *The Physics of Star Trek* (New York: Harper Collins, 1995), xvi, puts it this way: "Based on an informal survey I carried out while walking around my university campus the other day, the number of people in the United States who would not recognize the phrase, 'Beam me up, Scotty,' is roughly equivalent to the number of people who have never heard of ketchup."

20. Raphael Patai, *Myth and Modern Man* (Englewood Cliffs, NJ: Prentice-Hall, 1972), 35.

21. Ibid., 11.

22. William G. Doty, *Mythography: The Study of Myths and Rituals* (Tuscaloosa: University of Alabama Press, 1986), 25; Patai, *Myth and Modern Man*, 15–16.

23. In six one-hour videotapes, hosted by Bill Moyers (New York: Mystic Fire Video, c. 1988); see also the companion book, *The Power of Myth* (New York: Doubleday, 1988).

24. *The Hero with a Thousand Faces* (New York: Meridian Books, 1956), 30.

25. In Claude Levi-Strauss, *Structural Anthropology*, vol. 1, trans. Claire Jacabson and B. G. Shoepf (New York: Basic Books, 1963).

26. Claude Levi-Strauss, *Introduction to a Science of Myth*, vols. 1–4, trans. John Weightman and Doreen Weightman (New York: Harper and Row, 1969–1981). Specific titles and dates are *The Raw and the Cooked* (1969), *From Honey to Ashes* (1973), *The Origin of Table Manners* (1978), and *The Naked Man* (1981).

27. Levi-Strauss, *Structural Anthropology*.

28. Roland Barthes, *Mythologies* (New York: Hill and Wang, 1972).

29. See, for example, Karin Blair's Jungian work *Meaning in "Star Trek"* (Cham-

bersburg, PA: Anima Books, 1977) and the structuralist analyses of William Blake Tyrell's "*Star Trek* as Myth and Television as Mythmaker," *Journal of Popular Culture* 10, no. 4 (1977), pp. 711–719; and Peter B. Claus, "A Structuralist Appreciation of *Star Trek*," in Johnetta B. Cole, *Anthropology for the Eighties* (New York: Macmillan, 1982), 417–429.

30. Various examples will be cited in later chapters; an excellent cross-section of this genre is to be found in Taylor Harrison, Sarah Projansky, Kent A. Ono, and Elyce Rae Helford, eds., *Enterprise Zones: Critical Positions on "Star Trek"* (Boulder, CO: Westview Press, 1996).

CHAPTER TWO

1. A typically male deception, perhaps: according to standard reference works on mythology, Apollo's mother was the goddess Leto or Latona, a daughter of the Titans.

2. Allan Asherman, *The Star Trek Compendium* (New York: Pocket Books, 1989), 73; James Blish's adaptation of the story for *Star Trek: The Classic Episodes 2* (New York: Bantam, 1991) also ends with McCoy's announcement that Palamas is pregnant, and the doctor's musings on delivering a baby god.

3. Fyodor Dostoyevsky, *The Brothers Karamazov* (New York: Signet Classic, 1957); the "vaudeville of devils" remark is from a letter quoted in the foreword of this edition by Manuel Komroff (xiii).

4. Joseph Campbell, *The Hero with a Thousand Faces* (New York: Meridian Books, 1956), 77–90; 245–246.

5. We treat "The Cage" as TOS's pilot episode because it was Roddenberry's chosen vehicle to present his concept of the series, and the only one he wrote for the express purpose of serving as its pilot (see Asherman, *Star Trek Compendium*). If one considers the network's pick, "Where No Man Has Gone Before," as the pilot episode, the pattern we describe here applies to it as well.

6. In "The Cage," these words are spoken to Pike about Vina; in the broadcast episode "The Menagerie," which uses the same footage in a new context, they are addressed to Kirk in reference to Vina and Pike.

7. David Alexander, *Star Trek Creator: The Authorized Biography of Gene Roddenberry* (New York: Penguin, 1994), 37, 157. See also Yvonne Fern, *Gene Roddenberry: The Last Conversation*, rev. ed. (New York: Pocket Books, 1996).

8. See Alexander, *Star Trek Creator*, 422, 423, 568; Fern, 118–119.

9. This reticence is the rule, unless one counts the film, *The Final Frontier* a "false god" tale discussed later in this chapter.

10. Betsy Caprio, *Good News in Modern Images* (Kansas City: Sheed Andrews and McMeel, 1978).

11. Similar themes are broached again in DS9's "Fascination" and VGR's "Persistence of Vision."

12. One crew member becomes temporarily hysterical but recovers to perform beyond the call of duty.

13. Another writer's contrary interpretation of "The Child" is discussed in Chapter 12.

14. Michael Okuda, Denise Okuda, and Debbie Mirek, *The "Star Trek" Encyclopedia: A Reference Guide to the Future* (New York: Pocket Books, 1994), 265.

15. Dostoyevsky, *The Brothers Kamarazov*, 251.

16. William Kilpatrick, *Why Johnny Can't Tell Right From Wrong: Moral Illiteracy and the Case for Character Education* (New York: Simon and Schuster, 1992).

CHAPTER THREE

1. This characterization of Inuit tales is based on Jon Wagner's unpublished graduate research at the Indiana University Folklore Institute, involving content analysis of over a hundred folktales gathered from numerous sources, particularly Knud Rasmussen's *Report of the Fifth Thule Expedition, 1921–1924* (Copenhagen: Gyldendalske Boghandel, Nordis Rorlag, 1928).

2. Adams's remarks on the machine are quoted and discussed in Jack Solomon, *The Signs of Our Time: The Secret Meanings of Everyday Life* (New York: Harper Perennial, 1988), Chapter 11.

3. Julien Offray de La Mettrie, *L'Homme Machine* [*Man a Machine*], 1748.

4. Mary Wollstoncraft Shelley, *Frankenstein; or, The Modern Prometheus*, 1816.

5. See Chapter 10 for a discussion of the Moriarty saga.

CHAPTER FOUR

1. See, for example, Alexis de Tocqueville's *Democracy in America* (1835) and Robert N. Bellah et al., *Habits of the Heart* (Berkley and Los Angeles: University of California Press, 1985).

2. See, for example, Jan Brunvand, *The Vanishing Hitchhiker: American Urban Legends and Their Meanings* (New York: Norton, 1981).

3. The examples given in this chapter are meant to be illustrative rather than comprehensive, since the cited themes can be seen in literally dozens of episodes across the four series.

4. *A Psychoanalytic Study of the Double in Literature* (Detroit: Wayne State University Press, 1970), 2.

5. Bruno Bettelheim, *The Uses of Enchantment: The Meaning and Importance of Fairy Tales* (New York: Knopf, 1976).

6. "Aion: Phenomenology of the Self," in Joseph Campbell, ed., *The Portable Jung* (New York: Viking Press, 1971), 145.

7. In addition to TOS's "Mirror, Mirror," the mirror universe is featured in DS9's "Crossover," "Through the Looking Glass," and "Shattered Mirror."

8. Plato, *Phaedrus*, 245A ff.

9. A detailed analysis of these two films can be found in Lane Roth, "Death and Rebirth in *Star Trek II: The Wrath of Khan*," *Extrapolation* 28, No. 2 (1987): 150–166.

10. This is, at least by some readings, the premise of *Star Trek*'s transporter technology (for a detailed discussion of its implications, see Lawrence M. Krauss, *The Physics of Star Trek* [New York: Basic Books, 1995], Chap.5).

11. William Butler Yeats, "Sailing to Byzantium," in *The Collected Poems of W.B. Yeats* (New York: Macmillan, 1956), 191–92.

CHAPTER FIVE

1. William Shatner, *Star Trek Memories* (New York: HarperCollins, 1993), 65.

2. Roddenberry's personal ambivalence about gender liberation probably influenced the tone of the series as well. Although he later characterized himself as a "feminist," he admitted to an interviewer that his wife Majel Barrett (who, prior to their marriage, had been cast as Number One in "The Cage") had helped him become more aware of sexist attitudes that he had taken for granted during the 1960s. See David Alexander "Gene Roddenberry, Writer, Producer, Philosopher, Humanist," *The Humanist* (March–April 1991), 29–30, 38.

3. Shatner, *Star Trek Memories*, 212–214.

4. Mary Dutta, "Very Bad Poetry, Captain: Shakespeare in *Star Trek*," *Extrapolation* 35 (Spring 1995): 38–45.

5. Simone de Beauvoir, *The Second Sex* (New York, Knopf, 1952).

6. The toothed vagina motif as an expression of female sexual predation occurs in various folkloric traditions, including the Zuni Indians' "Toothed Vagina Woman" (Ruth Benedict, *Zuni Mythology* [New York: Columbia University Press, 1935]).

7. For example, "Turnabout Intruder," "The Conscience of the King," "The Cage," "Where No Man Has Gone Before."

8. Rand's discontinuation had to do with a combination of personal reasons on the part of the actress Grace Lee Whitney and various story line considerations, but Whitney later appears—rather inconspicuously—as Janice Rand in several of the feature films.

9. Clyde Wilcox, "To Boldly Go Where Others Have Gone Before: Cultural Change and the Old and New *Star Treks*," *Extrapolation* 33, no. 1 (1992): 88–100.

10. For an extended analysis of Troi's "eroticized garb," see Amelie Hastie, "A Fabricated Space: Assimilating the Individual on *Star Trek: The Next Generation*," in Taylor Harrison et al., ed., *Enterprise Zones*, 115–136.

11. There are some notable exceptions: for example, the first season TNG episode "Justice"; in some of the DS9 scenes of Quark's saloon, and the costuming of "7 of 9" in VGR's "The Gift."

12. Victoria Korzeniowska, "Engaging with Gender: *Star Trek's* 'Next Generation,'" *Journal of Gender Studies* 5, no. 1 (March 1996): 19–25; Lynne Joyrich, "Feminist Enterprise? *Star Trek: The Next Generation* and the Occupation of Femininity," *Cinema Journal* 35, no. 2 (Winter 1996): 61–84.

13. Joyrich, "Feminist Enterprise?" 64.

14. Korzeniowska, "Engaging with Gender," 21; Joyrich, "Feminist Enterprise?" 75.

15. Barrett is the *Enterprise's* computer voice in TNG and in most TOS episodes.

16. John Hiscock, "Space Girls to Spice Up 'Prudish' *Star Trek*," Fantasy League Online Website (www.fantasyleagueonline.co.uk), September 16, 1997.

17. Ibid.; it is unclear whether Hiscock is quoting the character Janeway or the actor Kate Mulgrew. Since he quotes VGR creator Rick Berman and co-executive producer Brannon Braga in the same piece, he may also have interviewed Mulgrew.

18. Ibid.

CHAPTER SIX

1. Yvonne Fern, *Gene Roddenberry: The Last Conversation* (New York: Pocket Books, 1996), 110.

2. Rosabeth Moss Kanter, *Commitment and Community: Communes and Utopias in Sociological Perspective* (Cambridge: Harvard University Press, 1972).

3. Ovid, *The Metamorphoses*, translated by Horace Gregory (New York: Mentor, 1958), 281.

4. Rhonda V. Wilcox, "Shifting Roles and Synthetic Women in *Star Trek: The Next Generation*," *Studies in Popular Culture* 13, no. 2 (1991): 53–65.

5. Emily Hegarty, "Some Suspect of Ill: Shakespeare's Sonnets and 'The Perfect Mate,' " *Extrapolation* 36, no. 1 (1995): 55–64.

6. Hegarty, "Some Suspect of Ill," 60. See also Lynn Joyrich, "Feminist Enterprise: *Star Trek: The Next Generation* and the Occupation of Femininity," *Cinema Journal* 35, no. 2 (Winter 1996): 69.

7. Karin Blair, *Meaning in Star Trek* (Chambersburg, PA: Anima Books, 1977), 99–103. See also Karin Blair, "Sex and *Star Trek*," *Science Fiction Studies* 10 (November 1983).

8. April Selley, "I Have Been, and Ever Shall Be, Your Friend: *Star Trek, The Deerslayer* and the American Romance," *Journal of American Culture* 20, no. 1 (1986): 89–104.

9. Ibid., 89.

10. *Star Trek: Generations* (1994).

11. Hegarty, "Some Suspect of Ill," 55–64.

12. Emily Hastie, "A Fabricated Space: Assimilating the Individual on *Star Trek: The Next Generation*," in Taylor Harrison, et al. ed., *Enterprise Zones*, 115.

13. Ruth Benedict, *Zuni Mythology* (New York: Columbia University Press, 1935).

14. TOS's "Mirror, Mirror" and DS9's "Crossover," "Through the Looking Glass," "Shattered Mirror."

15. Consider, for example, the following: Vina in TOS's "The Cage," the Companion in TOS's "Metamorphosis," the salt vampire in TOS's "The Man Trap," "Mudd's Women" in the TOS episode of the same name, Lenore in TOS's "Conscience of the King," Ishara Yar in TNG's " Legacy," Minuet in TNG's "11001001," Rayna in TOS's "Requiem for Methuselah," Janice Lester in TOS's "Turnabout Intruder," the angels of death in TOS's "That Which Survives," Yuta in TNG's "The Vengeance Factor," T'pel in TNG's "Data's Day," and Marayna in "Alter Ego."

16. Ilsa Bick, "Boys in Space: *Star Trek*, Latency, and the Neverending Story," *Cinema Journal*, 35, no. 2 (1996): 43–60.

17. Ibid., 45, 48, 56.

18. Selley, "Your Friend," 100.

19. Elyce Rae Helford, " 'A Part of Myself No Man Should Ever See': Reading Captain Kirk's Multiple Masculinities," in Harrison et al., *Enterprise Zones*, 21.

20. Bick, "Boys in Space," 55.

21. Ibid., 17.

22. Ibid., 56

23. For an elaboration of these themes, see also Donna Reid-Jeffrey, "*Star Trek*: The Last Frontier in Modern American Myth," *Folklore and Mythology Studies*, 6 (1982): 34–41.

24. Jane Elizabeth Ellington and Joseph W. Critelli, "Analysis of a Modern Myth: The *Star Trek* Series," *Extrapolation* 24, no. 3 (1983): 241–250.

25. Elyce Helford, "Dating Data: Miscegenation in *Star Trek: The Next Generation*," *Extrapolation* 34, no. 3 (1993): 265–277.

26. Ibid.

27. Jon Wagner, ed., *Sex Roles in Contemporary American Communes* (Indiana University Press: Bloomington, 1982).

28. *Star Trek V: The Final Frontier*.

CHAPTER SEVEN

1. George Kateb, *Utopia and Its Enemies* (Glencoe, IL: Free Press, 1963), 9 (the word *person* was substituted for *man* in this passage to avoid distracting sexist usages).

2. Donald E. Pitzer, ed., *America's Communal Utopias* (Chapel Hill: University of North Carolina Press, 1997).

3. Eugene Zamiatin, *We* (1920; reprint New York: E. P. Dutton, 1952); Aldous Huxley, *Brave New World* (1932; reprint New York: Harper and Row, 1965); George Orwell, *Nineteen Eighty-Four* (New York: New American Library, 1949); Kurt Vonnegut, *Player Piano* (New York, Scribner, 1952); B. F. Skinner, *Walden Two* (New York, Macmillan, 1955); Aldous Huxley, *Island: A Novel* (New York: Harper, 1962).

4. Anti-utopian philosophies have been ably described (and to some degree answered) by George Kateb in *Utopia and Its Enemies* (Glencoe, IL: Free Press, 1963) and Chad Walsh in *From Utopia to Nightmare* (Westport, CT: Greenwood Press, 1962). We refer the reader to these works for a full treatment of the subject, but for our purposes we will synthesize the most cogent of these criticisms as we explore the utopian and dystopian visions in *Star Trek*.

5. James Fenimore Cooper, *The Pathfinder* (1840), *The Deerslayer* (1841). For a discussion of Cooper, Boone, Crockett, and the frontiersman myth, see Richard Slotkin, *Regeneration Through Violence: The Mythology of the American Frontier, 1600–1860* (Middletown, CT: Wesleyan University Press, 1973), Chaps. 12 and 13.

6. "The New England Reformers," in *Essays of Ralph Waldo Emerson* (Garden City: Famous Classics Library, 1941).

7. Rupert Wilkinson, *The Pursuit of American Character* (New York: Harper and Row, 1988).

8. Huxley, *Brave New World*, 183–184.

CHAPTER EIGHT

1. Mircea Eliade, *Shamanism: Archaic Techniques of Ecstasy* (New York: Pantheon Books, 1964).

2. Arthur O. Lovejoy, *The Great Chain of Being: A Study of the History of an Idea* (Cambridge, MA: Harvard University Press, 1936).

3. Philip Appleman, ed., *Darwin: A Norton Critical Edition* (New York: W. W. Norton, 1979), 85.

4. She is right to protest. The sudden introduction of humans 600,000 years ago would be hard to reconcile with the existence of the human species *Homo erectus* from long before until long after that date.

5. Rick Worland, "Captain Kirk, Cold Warrior," *Journal of Popular Film and Television* 16, no. 3, 1988, 109–117.

6. H. Bruce Franklin, "*Star Trek* in the Vietnam Era," *Science Fiction Studies*, 21 (March 1994): 24–33.

7. Worland, "Cold Warrior," 115.

8. Okuda, Okuda, and Mirek, *Star Trek Encyclopedia: A Reference Guide to the Future* (New York: Pocket Books, 1994), 128

9. These inferences are, anthropologically speaking, ludicrously inaccurate. The comically oversized "folsom point" that Spock observes would not, as he supposes, suggest premodern humanoids or crude, "inefficient" technology.

10. Quoted in Katrina Boyd, "Cyborgs in Utopia: The Problem of Radical Difference in *Star Trek The Next Generation*," in Harrison et al., *Enterprise Zones*, 101.

11. Okuda, Okuda, and Mirek, *Star Trek Encyclopedia*, 315.

12. For a treatment of TOS's Starfleet interventionism as an allegory of American foreign policy, see Mark P. Lagon, " 'We Owe It to Them to Interfere': *Star Trek* and U.S. Statecraft in the 1960s and the 1990s," *Extrapolation* 34, no. 3 (1993): 251–264.

CHAPTER NINE

1. Edward W. Said, *Orientalism* (New York: Vintage Books, 1979 [original 1978]), 203–204.

2. For an illuminating treatment of popular culture stereotypes regarding Arabs and Muslims, see Jack Shaheen, *The TV Arab* (Bowling Green, OH: Popular Press, 1984)

3. For example, in TNG (Levar Burton as Geordi La Forge, Michael Dorn as Worf, Whoopi Goldberg as Guinan), in DS9 (Avery Brooks as Captain Benjamin Sisko and Cirroc Lofton as Jake Sisko), and in VGR (Tim Russ as Tuvok).

4. David Golombia's article, "Black and White World: Race, Ideology and Utopia in Triton and *Star Trek*," *Cultural Critique*, no. 32 (1995–96): 75–95 argues that the plot's downplaying of Cheron's history of racial oppression (as revealed in the episode dialogue) trivializes racial conflict by glossing over the social forces that drive it.

5. "My Appointment with the *Enterprise*: An Appreciation," in *Star Trek: Four Generations of Stars, Stories and Strange New Worlds* (*TV Guide* Collector's Edition.) (Radnor: News America Publications, 1995), 124–125.

6. "George Takei," *Star Trek: Four Generations*, 57.

7. "Race in this sense is sometimes used interchangeably with "variety" or "subspecies" (although the latter labels are no longer applied to modern human populations). Some scientists object to the concept of race as applied to humans,

or even as applied to other species; see, for example, Stephen Jay Gould, "Why We Should Not Name Human Races: A Biological View," in *Ever Since Darwin: Reflections in Natural History* (New York: Norton, 1977), 231–236.

8. Studies like Richard Herrnstein and Charles Murray's *The Bell Curve* (New York: Free Press, 1994), for example, have been criticized for deriving biological conclusions from data organized on the basis of socially defined "race" groupings. For a thorough criticism of "scientific" racism, see Stephen Jay Gould's *Mismeasure of Man* (New York: Norton, 1981).

9. Okuda, Okuda, and Mirek, *Star Trek Encyclopedia*, 131.

10. Leah R. Vande Berg, "Liminality: Worf as Metonymic Signifier of Racial, Cultural, and National Differences," in Taylor Harrison et al. ed., *Enterprise Zones: Critical Positions on Star Trek* (Boulder, CO: Westview Press, 1996), 51–68.

11. Bill Bolsvert "Computer: End Program," *Grey City Journal*, 1, no. 28 (May 20, 1994): 1–5.

12. Stuart Hall, *Race: The Floating Signifier*, videocassette (Northampton, MA: Media Education Foundation, 1996).

13. Raymond Williams, *Keywords: A Vocabulary of Culture and Society*, rev. ed. (New York: Oxford University Press, 1983), 250.

14. Richard Dyer, "White," *Screen* 29, no. 4 (1989): 44–64; Ruth Frankenburg, *White Women, Race Matters: The Social Construction of Whiteness* (Minneapolis: University of Minnesota Press, 1993). Both are quoted in Rhonda Wilcox, "Dating Data: Miscegenation in *Star Trek: The Next Generation*," in Harrison et al., eds., *Enterprise Zones*, 73–74.

15. Golumbia, "Black and White World," makes a similar argument (see especially pp. 88–89).

16. Jeff Salamon, "Race Men and Space Men," *Village Voice* 38, no. 8 (February 23, 1993): 46–47; Golumbia, "Black and White World"; for further analysis, see also Vande Berg, "Liminality"; Wilcox, "Dating Data," in Harrison et al., *Enterprise Zones*.

17. Golumbia, "Black and White World," 87–88.

18. Katrina Boyd, "Cyborgs in Utopia: The Problem of Radical Difference in *Star Trek: The Next Generation*," in Harrison et al., eds., *Enterprise Zones*, 107. Boyd's essay emphasizes TNG over the other series.

19. Yvonne Fern, *Gene Roddenberry: The Last Conversation* (New York: Pocket Books, 1996), 87.

20. Edward Said, *Culture and Imperialism* (New York: Knopf, 1993), goes so far as to argue that the development of the European novel is inextricably linked to the European colonial experience. Concerning the influence of *Gulliver's Travels* on Roddenberry, see David Alexander, *Star Trek Creator:The Authorized Biography of Gene Roddenberry* (New York: Roc, 1994), 221.

21. Bolsvert, "Computer, End Program."

22. "The Significance of the Frontier in American History," paper presented at the World's Columbia Exposition in Chicago, July 12, 1893; see also Frederick Jackson Turner, *Frontier in American History* (New York: H. Holt, 1921).

23. For a penetrating analysis of America's frontier mythology, including references to space as an extension of the frontier, see the following works by Richard Slotkin: *Regeneration Through Violence: The Mythology of the American Frontier, 1600–1860* (Middletown, CT: Wesleyan University Press, 1973), *The Fatal Envi-*

ronment: The Myth of the Frontier in the Age of Industrialization, 1800–1890 (New York: Atheneum, 1985), and *Gunfighter Nation: The Myth of the Frontier in Twentieth Century America* (New York: Atheneum, 1992).

24. The idea of the garden as opposed to the inhospitable wilderness is treated at length in Leo Marx, *The Machine in the Garden: Technology and the Pastoral Ideal in America* (New York: Oxford University Press, 1964).

25. Mircea Eliade, *Sacred and Profane*, 29–32.

26. Ray Bradbury, *Martian Chronicles* (New York: Bantam, 1977).

27. Gregory M. Pfitzer, "The Only Good Alien Is a Dead Alien: Science Fiction and the Metaphysics of Indian Hating on the High Frontier," *Journal of American Culture* 18, no. 1 (Spring 1995), 51–67.

28. Robert Jewett and John Shelton Lawrence, *The American Monomyth* (New York: Anchor, 1977)

29. April Selley, "Your Friend."

30. The Traveler was previously seen in the TNG episodes "Where No One Has Gone Before" and "Remember Me."

CHAPTER TEN

1. Jack Solomon, *The Signs of Our Times: The Secret Meanings of Everyday Life* (New York: Perennial, 1988), 212–217.

2. See, for example, Steven Jay Gould, *Full House: The Spread of Excellence from Plato to Darwin* (Harmony Books: New York, 1996).

3. For further discussion of these episodes, see Chapter 4.

4. This aspect of the time travel paradox is discussed by Lawrence M. Krauss in *The Physics of Star Trek* (New York: Basic Books, 1995), Chap. 2.

5. Michael Okuda and Denise Okuda, *Star Trek Chronology: The History of the Future* (New York: Pocket Books, 1996).

6. Crusher, who in 2395 is Picard's ex-wife, is known at that time as Captain Picard.

CHAPTER ELEVEN

1. Ralph Waldo Emerson, *Nature* (1836).

2. See TOS's "Assignment Earth," "A Private Little War," "Return to Tomorrow." On the other hand, TOS's "Bread and Circuses," and "The Savage Curtain" suggest that a global war did occur in the twentieth or twenty-first century.

3. *Star Trek II: The Wrath of Khan.*

4. Alan Bloom, *The Closing of the American Mind: How Higher Education Has Failed Democracy and Impoverished the Souls of Today's Students* (New York: Touchstone Books, 1987).

5. For a well-reasoned critique of Bloom's arguments, see Lawrence W. Levine, *The Opening of the American Mind: Canons, Culture, and History* (Boston: Beacon Press, 1996).

6. Roland Barthes, *Mythologies* (New York: Hill and Wang, 1972), 101.

7. "Cyborgs in Utopia: The Problem of Radical Difference in *Star Trek*," in Taylor Harrison et al., *Enterprise Zones*, 95–114.

8. In Katrina Boyd, *Culture and Anarchy*, ed. J. Dover Wilson (Cambridge: Cambridge University Press, 1932).

9. For a different perspective on Boyd's equation of modernist liberal humanism with nineteenth-century utopianism, see Jon Wagner's introduction to Wagner, ed., *Sex Roles in Contemporary American Communes* (Bloomington: Indiana University Press, 1982).

10. See the following by Richard Rorty: *Contingency, Irony, Solidarity* (New York: Cambridge University Press, 1989) and *Objectivity, Relativism, and Truth* (New York: Cambridge University Press, 1991).

11. This point is eloquently documented in Levine, *American Mind*.

12. Mercia Eliade, *Sacred and Profane*, 23

13. Marilynne Robinson, "Hearing Silence: Western Myth Reconsidered," in Kurt Brown, ed., *The True Subject: Writers on Life and Craft* (Saint Paul: Graywolf Press, 1993), 136; for the full quote, see the epigram of Chap. 1.

14. David Alexander, "Gene Roddenberry: Writer, Producer, Philosopher, Humanist," *The Humanist* (March–April 1991): 30.

15. Marilynne Robinson, "Hearing Silence," 136.

16. The episode aired during February of 1998, in the month associated in the U.S. with "Black History." The only other Trek reference to the race of a "black" character that we know of occurred in TOS "The Ultimate Computer" when Dr. Richard Daystrom, who is played by an African-American actor, refers to Lieutenant Uhura as a "Negress."

CHAPTER TWELVE

1. These lines from Melville may have been altered for dramatic reasons. The Riverside Edition of Herman Melville's *Moby Dick* (Boston: Houghton Mifflin, 1956), 154 reads as follows: ". . . and then, as if his chest had been a cannon, he burst his hot heart's shell upon it."

2. This interplay is richly revealed in a discussion by Anne Collins Smith, "The Philosophy of *Star Trek*: Popular Culture as Hermeneutical Springboard," *Teaching Philosophy* 18, no. 4 (1995): 295–300.

3. The exploits of detective Dixon Hill are fictional fiction—a set of imaginary novels attributed to author Tracy Torme (a *Trek* writer) and probably modeled on the work of Dashiell Hammett.

4. Data's interest in Holmes began during the investigation of a murder in TNG's "Lonely Among Us."

5. The first two are TOS titles taken from *Macbeth*; the last, is a TNG title derived from *Hamlet*. Since these are only some of the examples that come to the attention of such casual readers of Shakespeare as ourselves, it is probable that a Shakespeare scholar would spot many others, and the same is probably true for the brief quotations also discussed in this context.

6. This is a burlesque of Shylock's plea for recognition of his humanity: "Hath not a Jew eyes? . . . If you prick us, do we not bleed?" (*The Merchant of Venice*, Act 3, Scene 1).

7. There is also an extratextual connection between *Trek* and Shakespeare, in that William Shatner (Kirk), Patrick Stewart (Picard) and Avery Brooks (Sisko) each had considerable Shakespearean acting experience prior to their casting in *Star Trek*.

8. *Extrapolation* 35 (Spring 1995). Articles include Stephen Buhler, "Who Calls Me Villain? Blank Verse and the Black Hat" (19); Mary Dutta, "Very Bad Poetry, Captain: Shakespeare in *Star Trek*" (38); Emily Hegarty, "Some Suspect of Ill: Shakespeare's Sonnets and the Perfect Mate" (56); Mark Houlahan, "Cosmic Hamlets? Contesting Shakespeare in Federation Space" (29–37); John Pendergast, "A Nation of Hamlets: Shakespeare and Cultural Politics" (10); and David Reinheimer, "Ontological and Ethical Allusion: Shakespeare in *The Next Generation*" (46). There is, unfortunately, considerable overlap among these articles in terms of coverage and substance . Some are quoted elsewhere in this book.

9. Hegarty, "Some Suspect of Ill," makes one of the more eloquent arguments along these lines.

10. Buhler, "Blank Verse and the Black Hat," 18–27.

11. Lawrence Levine, *Highbrow, Lowbrow: The Emergence of Cultural Hierarchy in America*. (Cambridge: Harvard University Press, 1988), shows that Shakespeare was immensely popular among urban and rural Americans of all social classes throughout the nineteenth century and was widely enjoyed in the form of full performances, short recitations, and burlesques. Hence, the idea that twentieth-century American *Trek* viewers can experience Shakespeare only as elitist, hegemonic oppression is by no means self-evident.

12. Sarah Projansky, "When the Body Speaks: Deanna Troi's Tenuous Authority and the Rationalization of Federation Superiority in *Star Trek: The Next Generation* Rape Narratives," in Harrison et al, *Enterprise Zones*, 34–36.

13. Jay Goulding, *Empire, Aliens and Conquest: A Critique of American Ideology in Star Trek and Other Science Fiction Adventures* (Toronto: Sisyphus Press, 1985). See also Chapter 5 for a further description of "The Cloudminders."

14. Golumbia, "Black and White World," 89.

15. Wilcox, "Dating Data," 73–74.

16. See the discussion of "A Private Little War" in chapter eight, pp. 154–55.

17. "Brent Spiner," *Star Trek: Four Generations* (*TV Guide* Collector's Edition), (Radner, PA,: NewsAmerica Publications, 1995), 59.

18. For what it is worth, nineteenth-century illustrations in *The Globe Illustrated Shakespeare* show Shakespeare's Puck and other such beings with pointed ears.

19. TNG's "Emergence" and "The Defector" (both featuring performances of Shakespeare) and "Devil's Due" (with a scene from Dickens's *A Christmas Carol*).

20. Krauss, *Physics of Star Trek*, Part II and especially Chap. 5.

21. Leo Marx *The Machine in the Garden: Technology and the Pastoral Ideal in America* (New York: Oxford University Press, 1964), Chap. I.

22. Kalton C. Lahue and Terry Brewer, *Kops and Custards: The Legend of Keystone Films* (Norman: University of Oklahoma Press, 1968), 114–115. According to the authors, Mack Sennett and most of his executive staff defected to Paramount overnight, leaving Keystone with little but its name and logo.

INDEX

About the Authors

JON WAGNER is Professor of Anthropology, Knox College, Galesburg, Illinois. He has published books and articles on Islam, utopian societies, gender, and contemporary myth.

JAN LUNDEEN teaches nursing in the Division of Allied Health at Carl Sandburg College. She has researched and written on the sociology of health care and gender in nursing education.